What You Don't Know
About Leadership,
but Probably Should

What You Don't Know About Leadership, but Probably Should

Applications to Daily Life

JEFFREY A. KOTTLER

OXFORD
UNIVERSITY PRESS

OXFORD
UNIVERSITY PRESS

Oxford University Press is a department of the University of Oxford. It furthers
the University's objective of excellence in research, scholarship, and education
by publishing worldwide. Oxford is a registered trade mark of Oxford University
Press in the UK and certain other countries.

Published in the United States of America by Oxford University Press
198 Madison Avenue, New York, NY 10016, United States of America.

© Oxford University Press 2018

CIP data is on file at the Library of Congress
ISBN 978–0–19–062082–0

1 3 5 7 9 8 6 4 2
Printed by Sheridan Books, Inc., United States of America

Contents

PART IV: *Applications to Daily Life*

Preface

WE LIVE IN A WORLD OF GROUPS. Almost every facet of daily existence—whether sitting in meetings, collaborating with co-workers, attending classes or programs, contributing to community or social events, participating in family gatherings, even enjoying coffee or meals with friends—takes place in group contexts. In addition, *everyone* finds themselves in leadership positions at one time or another, responsible for the welfare of others, not to mention being held accountable for successful outcomes whether those are defined in terms of goal attainment, entertainment value, or safety issues.

Leadership isn't just for traditional leaders anymore since teachers, parents, health professionals, police officers, even Girl Scouts, practice these skills on a regular basis. It is also curious, but nevertheless commonplace, that counselors, therapists, teachers, business leaders, executives, coaches, health professionals, and others in helping roles, who have been specifically trained in leadership, somehow fail to apply their knowledge and skills to settings in which they might matter most. The same professionals who guide others may not be able—or willing—to put that knowledge to work when they find themselves supervising peers, leading meetings, or even managing conflict at the dinner table. The reality is that many people experience required meetings and mandated group collaborations as tedious, repetitive, and often a waste of time that could be better spent doing other things that feel far more productive. Participants in meetings or groups are permitted to ramble and talk incessantly about issues that lead nowhere meaningful. Some people talk nonstop, repeating the same old stories, while others are never given a voice. Others check out completely or surreptitiously scan their mobile devices for messages.

Often leaders are so concerned with getting through their agenda that they don't attend to the needs of the people in the room to be heard, understood, and feel as if they are active members of the proceedings. At other times, conflicts, hostility, withdrawal, hidden agendas, and dysfunctional dynamics sabotage any attempt to keep things supportive and productive. At best, such issues and simmering conflicts are denied or ignored; at worst, they contribute to a toxic work or social environment in which people don't feel safe sharing their ideas for fear of ridicule or punishment.

It is more than a little ironic that although books and resources on leadership issues are among the most consistently popular sellers each year, they are obviously not particularly effective or else people would not continue buying more of them! This is consistent with the whole genre of self-help books that are allegedly designed to produce enduring change and yet only succeed in addicting readers to purchase more products that clearly have limited value— if the goal is to truly integrate ideas into daily life.

It's also interesting to consider that whereas many professions require some kind of credential, advanced degree, licensure, or certification to be considered minimally qualified, almost anyone can declare him- or herself a leader if he or she can convince a few others to follow. There's a line in the original movie *Parenthood* when a character comments on how you need a license to drive a car, or even catch a fish, but any jerk can be a parent. The same is certainly true with leaders as well, who may have ascended to a position of power without necessarily any relevant training or qualifications to actually do the job. In some cases, their signature qualifying trait was simply that they wanted the job more than everyone else for reasons that were designed to bolster their own self-serving interests.

Leadership is actually the single most studied aspect of all human behavior, even if most of the published books on the subject don't have much enduring effect. It has been estimated that somewhere between 30 to 70 percent (with an average of 50 percent) of corporate managers are described as incompetent in their roles, with any number of surveys reporting that three-quarters of employees say the worst part of their job is dealing with a terrible boss who is the single greatest source of their stress.[1] In addition, in spite of all the training programs, business schools, leadership institutes, development and mentoring programs, and coaching professionals, more than half of companies report a scarcity of qualified leaders to step into critical positions.[2]

According to a study conducted by the Center for Creative Leadership, most books on the subject are not very useful to professionals in the field.[3] In fact, most of those interviewed in the private and public sector, as well as small business owners, community activists, and educators, report that they don't find the most popular publications in the field to be particularly helpful at all. Instead, they prefer reading fiction or self-help books that tell stories about characters with whom they can identify, especially if they involve a struggle that might be connected to their own personal journey.

So, why does the world need another book on leadership given the more than 50,000 titles that are already on the market? First of all, the advice in many of the current options is usually rather logical and obvious, but rarely very realistic to put into immediate action. One example of this trend is an article titled, "10 Seconds to Take Your Leadership From Good to Great," which proclaims that it only takes a few moments to incorporate new strategies into daily life, just a second to "create a compelling vision" and another to "articulate your vision to others." I don't know about you, but I have always thought that it takes considerable reflective time to see the bigger picture, and really understand what might be going on, in any given situation.

It is also a bit of a mystery how so much training and resources in leadership are available, so many think tanks and institutes are devoted to the subject, so many mandated workshops and conferences on the subject take place, so much expertise is accessible, yet the reality is that the practice of these skills falls so miserably short of expectations. There is, unfortunately, widespread incongruence between what leaders and helping professionals supposedly know and are trained to do, versus how that expertise is translated into constructive action.

This book translates the latest research, theory, and skills into practical strategies that can be employed in *every* aspect of daily life, whether conducting a conference, leading a meeting, doing a presentation, or even hosting a social gathering. As the title suggests, it introduces ideas from an assortment of disciplines, including the social and biological sciences, organizational behavior, and human services, that have been re-interpreted and adapted to other settings in the worlds of business, education, healthcare, and everyday life. It integrates the latest research on group dynamics and process components of group behavior to fill the gaps that are often missing in effective and transformational practices of leadership. It also presents the wisdom and successful strategies of effective leaders from a wide variety of fields who talk not only about what works best, but also what they've learned from their most miserable failures.

Most of the existing books and resources available, especially those that have been most popular, either focus on prescriptive, practical advice about what to say or do during leadership challenges, or they present conceptual ideas related to how groups function and how they are best facilitated. Of course, both approaches are useful, especially when they are integrated into a style that feels organic and natural, rather than just following a template created by someone else.

This is a book about ideas related to leadership but also those rarely discussed in the context of broadening skills to a variety of arenas and our daily lives. We may cover some familiar territory, especially for those who are already well versed in the literature on leadership, or who have already undergone extensive training in the subject, but we will look at many of the concepts and applications through a different lens, one that helps to convert concepts to practical strategies that can be personalized and individualized to a greater extent.

The main theme of this book, which is notably different from so much of the literature on the subject, is that leadership begins, first and foremost, with taking charge of your own life. We lead others not just by purposeful planning, decision-making, and strategic actions at work, but by the ways we walk through life, modeling exactly those qualities and values that we consider so important for others. We not only have the opportunity to demonstrate the attitudes, beliefs, and behavior that we advocate and teach to others, but a mandate to be the kind of person we most wish others to become.

Acknowledgments

I'D LIKE TO once again thank my longtime editor and advocate Dana Bliss for his continued support and role as a muse for this project, as he has for so many others. Among all of our collaborations, this was the toughest one, largely because there is just so much already written and said about the subject of leadership that it was a challenge to truly settle on themes and content that were truly novel and all but ignored elsewhere. I'd like to acknowledge, as well, the guidance and assistance that I received from other Oxford University Press staff, including Andrew Dominello, Mary Funchion, Janet Foxman, and Patti Brecht.

I'm also grateful for the input and contributions of the following individuals serving in leadership positions within higher education, corporate and military settings, cybersecurity, politics, and charitable foundations: General (Retired) Thomas Kolditz, General (Retired) Robert Ivany, Officer Deon Joseph, Michael Skelly, Blake Mycoskie, Cary Kottler, Steve Parker, Nancy Dushkin, Jon Kottler, Jeremy Gaffney, and Sara Safari.

What You Don't Know About Leadership, but Probably Should

PART I

---

*The Nature of Group Behavior
at Work and Play*

I

Leadership at Work and Play

I CAN'T STOP watching the fingers drumming on the table. From where I sit, slouched in my chair, I have a perfect view of one horizontal slice of the people across from me. I watch their hands moving papers around, clenching, wiggling, dancing, searching for something to occupy themselves. Every so often, I see their hands slip down into their laps, where they believe they are secretly checking messages on their mobile devices. Everyone has checked out, is bored out of their mind, watching the clock whose hands seem frozen in place.

The person running the meeting seems oblivious to what is going on. Or if he notices that nobody is paying much attention, he seems unable or unwilling to alter course. And what he's doing is droning on and on about some issue that nobody cares much about. When he asks if anyone has any input, all of us studiously look at our hands—everyone except one person who seems to have something to say about almost everything. I know this for a fact because my strategy for managing my own frustration and disengagement has been to count the number of times she has spoken during the meeting. So far it's been 61 times and we've only been in the room for roughly 90 minutes, which means that a dialogue is ongoing between the leader and this sole woman, with the rest of us serving as mere spectators.

I've tried to insert a few comments on occasion, not because I have anything meaningful to offer on the subject, but rather because I'm just trying to keep myself awake. But since I'm interrupted by the overly talkative woman every time I speak, I decide to withdraw. I am pouting.

What's most curious to me is that everyone in the room—well, *almost* everyone—knows exactly what's going on, but doesn't say or do anything to change the dynamics of the interaction. The truly startling fact is that everyone in attendance is a psychologist who spends his or her time supervising and teaching others. In some cases, they even specialize in teaching group therapy, yet they (or I should more accurately say "we") insist on remaining oblivious, or at least mute, in the face of obvious group dysfunction. We all allow this unsatisfying pattern to continue week after week. Certainly, there is private grumbling and talk behind the scenes, but apparently not sufficient annoyance for anyone to actually *do* anything to change the basic interaction.

We've all sat in meetings like this, or been part of various group functions, in which it is clear to anyone who is paying attention that what's going on is not particularly productive and, in some cases, is downright toxic. This is especially interesting because there has been some fairly compelling evidence for a long time, replicated again and again in a variety of contexts and situations, that high-functioning teams and groups consistently demonstrate two signature qualities that lead to their exceptional productivity and member satisfaction.[1] First of all, their collective intelligence, which is usually consistently superior to the decisions of any single individual leader, results from optimal norms that develop in the group. These are the "rules" or conventions that guide what is considered appropriate behavior. One of the most important such rules is social sensitivity within the group, that is, the ability of its members to accurately read one another's subtle nonverbal cues to know what those people are thinking and feeling. This is key, because it means that group members are tuned into one another and operating cooperatively.

The second characteristic of high-functioning teams is relevant to the example mentioned above, that there is relatively equal participation and engagement by *all* members of the team. This isn't something that occurs occasionally but in every single meeting. Each person is encouraged to contribute, and efforts are made by the leaders, as well as everyone else, to make sure that all input is invited. Of course, such a phenomenon is somewhat rare in our lives, whether at work or play, since the familiar norm is that a few people always dominate and control the proceedings. It is also remarkable that many individuals who are in the best possible position to encourage and support others as a function of their training and jobs fail to apply these skills and experience to other situations with family and friends that matter the most.

One major premise of this book is that successful leadership is not only about performing effectively when on the job, but also about enjoying the benefits of applying this knowledge and skills in other areas of daily life. This means merging and integrating the major domains that include family, friends, work, community, and the spiritual self, yet doing so in a way that then enhances rather than compromises one another. This means a commitment to renewal, learning, physical and emotional well-being, as well as a sense of integrity, morality, and caring for others.

There is a lot of talk—*way* too much talk—about the idea of finding balance between work and the rest of your life. It is rather obvious and commonplace that leaders tend to work harder, spend more time, invest more energy, and experience greater stress than others within the organization. There is a sense of responsibility, as well as pressure, to perform at the highest level because so much is at stake. This responsibility may often result in spending excessive time focused on work priorities to the detriment (or even exclusion) of other aspects of daily life. This, of course, sets a tone for others within the organization, which may lead to optimal productivity in the short run, but always at a cost of collateral damage to health, relationships, and other aspects of daily life.

Loyalty and Responsibility to the Tribe

In spite of all the glorification of individualism and singular achievement, human beings evolved to function as part of a tribe. What we may lack in strength, speed, and claws, we make up for with our division of labor and cooperative responsibilities. We take care of one another as a community. We literally watch one another's backs. We have learned to hunt, gather food, seek shelter, build whole cities, and protect ourselves, through extraordinary and unprecedented interpersonal communication. We are among the most social animals on the planet, evolving cooperative strategies that may not rival those of ants or termites, but nevertheless form impressive alliances that allow us to control our environment and increase the probability of our survival. And all this occurs because of the groups we form and the ways those collectives work together toward a common goal.

In order for any group to function reasonably well, if not to best advantage, there must be some kind of delegated leadership. Ideally, this would operate in such a way that: (1) trust and respect are created to maximize safety and encourage participation; (2) all voices are heard so that participants feel a commitment to the decisions and outcomes; (3) proceedings operate efficiently with minimal distractions and unproductive digressions; (4) everyone present remains and feels engaged and a meaningful part of the discussion; (5) consensus is reached on issues that involve compromises without sacrificing effective courses of action; and (6) people leave the group believing that it was a helpful, if not an enjoyable, process. Actually, this description is not an ideal at all, but rather what we should consider to be absolutely mandatory in any group of which we are a part.

Alas, sadly, this is hardly the reality that we face in our daily lives. Most meetings often feel worthless, occupying the equivalent of two years of your life sitting in a room. For many top executives, 50 percent of their time is spent in such proceedings, two-thirds of which are described as a colossal waste of time.[2] Whatever decisions are made rarely represent a consensus, but instead are the result of a few people with the most power or the loudest, most persistent voices. And even those in leadership roles, with extensive training and experience, don't seem to apply what they know and understand to situations that clearly require some decisive intervention. They may allow certain people to ramble incessantly or take over the proceedings. Sometimes even worse, they allow others to feel invisible or become marginalized.

It has always been strange to me how a teacher, leader, or expert could stand before a room full of people who are obviously bored and yet continue with an agenda that is clearly not working. You look around the room and see people yawning, rolling their eyes, texting, doodling on pads, whispering to one another, even taking little power naps, and yet the speaker keeps going as if the audience is spellbound. Don't you ever wonder why you can see all this unfolding but the person in the front of the room, who has the best view of all, can't seem to figure out what's going on? Or more likely the case, the person is so locked into a structure that it feels impossible to change the plan, even in light of overwhelming evidence that such an approach is simply not working.

If there is a life skill that is more important than being able to read, decode, and lead groups, I'd like to know what that is. It is this knowledge, expertise, and interpersonal skill that makes it possible for us to get anything done. It is what makes a great leader, teacher, therapist, and supervisor, but also an extraordinary parent, sibling, partner, or friend. It is what creates the most enjoyment in life, feeling part of a group of like-minded people who function in harmony and joy.

So, if you were leading the meeting that I am required to attend, in which participants are disengaged and bored, in which only a few people dominate the conversation and everyone else has checked out, in which discussions continue *way* longer than they should and run over their scheduled time allotment, and after which follow-up rarely follows any decisions that are made, what would you do to change these patterns? This is a question you could apply to *any* group that you observe or participate in as a member. It is also the focus of this book, that is, how to apply the knowledge and skills of a superlative leader to make *any* group gathering more enjoyable, satisfying, productive, and high functioning.

"Leadership is an all-time thing"

Gordon Tredgold considered himself quite the authority on leadership.[3] He had been in charge of teams and departments for over 30 years, written dozens of articles on the subject, and achieved notoriety for launching one of the most popular blogs on the subject of management. His specialty was emphasizing how important it is for leaders to be good listeners and to be authentic and responsive in their relationships.

One day, Tredgold's wife shared the news that she had been reading his articles. He just couldn't help but break out in a prideful smile, appreciating the recognition, and then offered to explain or clarify any points that went over her head. If you think this condescending response might have been a bit annoying, you don't know even half of the problem.

His wife wondered aloud, "Could you explain why you don't practice any of this leadership shit at home?"

Tredgold was of, course, taken aback, not expecting this ambush. But then his wife pointed out that although he advocated the importance of active listening skills at work, he never seemed to apply those same valuable skills with her. "I can't remember the last time you commented positively on something I did. In fact, you barely even notice if I get a new haircut, let alone clean the house or do the washing."

Tredgold considered defending himself, or explaining that he was just too tired when he got home at night, or that he was stressed most of the time, but he realized how feeble and hypocritical those excuses would be. It was in this moment that he recognized the most important place of all to practice good leadership was with those he loved the most, not just those he was paid to help. His wife taught him an important lesson: "Leadership is not a sometime thing. It's an all-time thing."

This is what Stewart Friedman has referred to as "total leadership," striving for excellence in all domains of life, rather than believing that a commitment to work means sacrificing satisfaction in other areas that may also be significant.[4] In order to integrate the various aspects of life including work, home, family, community, and self-care, Friedman recommends conducting a series of experiments to determine what are truly your most important life priorities. This could include such actions as turning off (or leaving behind) your mobile device when you are out with friends or family; keeping track of how regular workouts at the gym affect your energy levels during the day; scheduling uninterrupted weekly "dates" with a spouse, partner, or family member to talk about intimate matters; or making time for leisure activities. In each case, the goal is to become a student of what is working most and least effectively in your life, both as a leader and a fully engaged human being.

What Is Leadership Anyway?

It is perhaps because the concept of leadership is discussed in such a multitude of contexts and settings that experts and scholars have so struggled to define what it means. On the simplest level, we could say that leaders lead. They help to organize groups in such a way that they accomplish desired tasks, and presumably do so more efficiently than if the members were left to their own devices. In fact, we know that chaos and conflict result in groups without some kind of benevolent and effective leadership.

Nevertheless, leadership, as a role and activity, is actually quite complex and multidimensional, especially as it relates to different situations. There are estimated to be almost 2,000 different definitions of leadership, each of which places particular emphasis on aspects of power, authority, skills, attitudes, virtues, models, roles, contexts, or environments.[5] That uncertainty leads to the following question: Who exactly *is* a leader? A corporate CEO, military general, president, or professional coach would certainly qualify. But what about a teacher? Or a parent? Or even an older sibling? There are so many settings in which leaders operate, whether within families, social organizations, or any time a group of three or more people find themselves together. *Someone* makes decisions or takes the lead to facilitate that process.

Leadership has been differentially described by professionals as *inspiring* others to take constructive action, *setting an example* that can be emulated by others, *providing solutions* to problems, *instructing* and *guiding* others in their development, *facilitating* a process that is conducive to growth, *creating* an environment that maximizes productivity, *building trust* among teams, among so many others. Note all the various verbs that are used, each of which emphasizes quite different approaches and values.

The distinction between what consists of leadership and what does not is not as obvious as one might think. "If a man runs down the street yelling that he's going to save the world, and someone follows him, then he's a charismatic leader," observes one author, but if on the other hand, nobody follows him, then he's regarded as a lunatic.[6] In other words, a leader's power and authority emanate not from a self-declaration, or even election or appointment, but rather from whether followers fall in line.

To consider the scope of what we intend to explore together, it has been observed by no less an authority than Warren Bennis—leadership scholar and adviser to presidents, who described his chosen field as both "hazy and confounding"—that "more has been written and less is known about leadership than about any other topic in the behavioral sciences."[7] When one peruses books on the subject of leadership, most of them fall into two broad categories: those that follow a "troubadour tradition" versus those that are more academic in tone.[8] Those that qualify for the first category, a far more popular group, tend to include promises of immediate application even if they are wildly unrealistic and impractical in the real world. They have provocative titles such as *Leadership Secrets of Attila the Hun* or *How to Seem Like a Better Person Without Actually Improving Yourself* (yes, these are real book titles). There are also memoirs of famous political figures and corporate CEOs who hope to set the record straight, or else seek retribution against those who have done them wrong. These books can be extremely entertaining even if their authors may have ulterior motives.

In spite of the emphasis in most business books on displaying confidence, authority, and control, researchers Robert Hogan and Robert Kaiser believe that most of these volumes are "empirical nonsense" without much evidence to support their claims. When they examined successful CEOs of Fortune 500 companies, there were two surprising findings regarding the leaders' characteristics. First, they were modest and humble, rather than arrogant and self-aggrandizing. And second, they were quite persistent in promoting their agenda that was believed to be for the greater good. In tribal communities, and our ancestral environment, "the head man is modest, self-effacing, competent, and committed to the collective good. And if he is not, he gets removed, sometimes quite violently."[9] In the good ol' days, if followers were not satisfied with the quality of leadership, or their needs were not being met, the king, chief, or elder might be exiled or assassinated.

Although academic research and literature are far more reliable than personal memoirs and advice volumes, with actual supporting evidence for the ideas presented, they often introduce a "collection of dependable empirical nuggets, decontextualized facts that do not add up to a persuasive account of leadership."[10] Research studies may examine specific components or features of leadership that appear to be most meaningful, yet they often miss the essence of the role that is not simply defined by someone who has managed to achieve power and authority. After all, those who make it to the top are no doubt very bright, ambitious, driven, hardworking, and politically savvy, but that doesn't mean they are actually the best qualified for the job.

Competing Theories That Don't Necessarily Play Well Together

One reason for the chronic confusion about the nature of leadership is that it is studied as part of so many different disciplines that are often not very well integrated. It may seem obvious that leadership would be a critical part of management or military training, or perhaps political science, but it is also investigated within psychology, sociology, economics, history, communications, education, evolutionary biology, zoology, primatology, and neuroscience. Even if professionals in various disciplines and contexts find it difficult to arrive at consensus on an optimal framework, or best practices, everyone would agree that leadership almost always involves some kind of influence and persuasion within a group.

There are schools of thought that believe leadership is really about certain personality traits related to charisma, wisdom, and passion, the so-called Great Man (or Woman) theory in which it is believed that certain virtues and characteristics empower leaders to make a difference. Then there are behavioral schools that examine specific styles of interaction, or relational approaches that focus on interpersonal skills that inspire trust, loyalty, and open communication. There are those who consider leadership a visionary process, or a biological phenomenon that naturally evolves. And still others view leadership as contextual, making it difficult to offer sweeping generalizations that might apply to a variety of situations or environments.

In spite of the varied opinions about the nature of leadership and its contextual nature, we know that it involves several key components.[11] First, it is clearly a *relationship* between someone in authority and those who agree to follow as a result of the leader's position. Second, it is concerned with accomplishing certain goals, whether it is teaching a subject, selling products or ideas, facilitating a collective process to make decisions, or reaching some outcome to increase profits, resources, or territory. Third, it involves not only some ultimate end but also the means by which to achieve these objectives. In other words, leaders are instilled with the power to create a culture and climate that are best suited to improve and support the well-being of followers.

As we will discuss in a later chapter on truly bad leadership, one can determine excellence from failure under certain conditions, the most common of which occurs when abuses of power or breaches of trust take place because the leader's own self-interest or personal needs supersede those of the organization or community. This can either occur through excessive self-promotion or simply a level of incompetence when the leader becomes overly concerned with meaningless details at the expense of the main goal, or stifles initiative because of micromanagement, unrealistic perfectionism, or self-serving goals. Serious damage is done when this escalates to the point where the leader is viewed as a controlling and insensitive bully who thrives on dominating others, oblivious or unconcerned with the consequences. Finally, problems occur when the leader decides to break established rules because he or she feels they don't apply to someone in such a lofty position.

We will look to combine several of these prevalent paradigms in order to gain a deeper and wider perspective on the nature of leadership, regardless of the setting at work or play. This means acknowledging not only certain traits that are indeed important, as are interpersonal style and decision-making skills, but also particular behaviors among leaders that are somewhat universal.

What Do Leaders Actually Do?

This question might seem redundant since I've already mentioned the obvious—that what leaders do is lead others. But whatever leaders are doing, or *think* they are doing, is often not working nearly as well as they believe to be the case considering how often employees complain that their bosses are so often a source of misery, rather than support.[12] This is such a problem that 90 percent of employees complain incessantly that their bosses don't provide them with the support, encouragement, and useful communication they need to do their jobs well.[13] And one study even found that the majority of employees are at greater risk of suffering a heart attack when their supervisors are perceived as incompetent, uncommunicative, or less than supportive.[14]

Digging much deeper, it is interesting to consider the specific tasks and roles that leaders adopt in order to complete their designated or chosen positions. Since leaders usually are imbued with some degree of authority or influence, they use this power to accomplish several tasks that are often part of group activities or assignments.

The initial task involves promoting a focused vision among followers that is based on consensual core values. This is usually followed with the more pragmatic realities of determining which options are most feasible and cost-effective; seeking agreement on these objectives is usually among the greatest

priorities. Once this plan is "sold" to followers, the next stage involves facilitating the action steps related to the goals (*What* should we do?), timing
(*When* should we do it?), strategies (*How* should we proceed?), and benchmarks (*At what point* should we change direction?).

Since there are almost always disputes, disagreements, differences of
opinion, and conflicts in any spirited discussion or plan, the leader's job also
involves negotiating and mediating these arguments in such a way that the
participants feel heard and respected, and yet are also willing to compromise
in order to seek consensus. The leader may additionally provide incentives and
rewards that more directly motivate and inspire others to complete their tasks
and work cooperatively. Finally, leaders are empowered to provide needed
support and resources to get the job done, as well as to ultimately evaluate the
outcomes and determine the consequences in what is perceived as a fair and
equitable way. And one final point, employees or followers most appreciate
clear and consistent communications regarding goals and ongoing progress,
including both *constructive* feedback and recognition of valued achievements.

What we know and understand for certain is that human beings are social
animals above all else. Our survival has always depended on cooperative and
collaborative behavior to secure food, shelter, and safety from predators, enemies, and natural disasters. Whereas this has led to more productive information sharing, division of labor, communal parenting, conflict resolution, and
successful hunting and gathering, large social networks depend on the organization of tasks to share the load. Thus, humans in every culture, throughout
every era, have needed leaders to guide and manage group behavior, whether
they have been elected, chosen, or inherited the position. In the animal kingdom, leaders emerge as alpha specimens that tend to be the biggest and strongest among the herd or group, those that have the optimal genetic material to
produce the most fit offspring to strengthen the group. Among all species of
living things, there is an incentive to aspire to such a position in order to gain
greater access to resources, higher status, and more desirable mates, as well
as the power to provide benefits to kin and cement alliances. There is, thus,
an internal struggle among leaders to reconcile their own priorities and best
interests with those for whom they are responsible.

No matter how strong the alliances, or how controlling and oppressive
the power exerted, though, followers within the group or tribe have their
own ways to rebel against leaders who are perceived as ineffective or unjust.
Assassination might be the most forceful, direct action that has occurred
throughout history (one-third of all U.S. presidents have been the victims
of such an attempt), but gossip, ridicule, and disseminating more accurate,

truthful reports on news outlets are also used to undermine power, as we have witnessed on the political stage. Recently, certain political figures have attempted to discredit media reports (so-called fake news) by spreading rumors and unsubstantiated rumors as a means to counteract perceived attempts to undermine them.

Leaders who find their positions in jeopardy also recognize potential threats of instability and so drum up imagined or real external threats as a way to stifle criticism. You may notice how often political candidates talk about impending doom, terrorist threats, immigrant violence, and exaggerate the plight of economic conditions, or the potential for attack by enemies as a way to neutralize threats to their power.

One reason for this ever-changing and fragile instability is that what is required of leaders to accomplish their jobs, the tools and tactics available, are always evolving. Consider the relative simplicity of Franklin D. Roosevelt's communications directly to followers through a single conduit, his fireside radio chats, to reassure and influence his constituency. During the 1960 presidential election, Nixon and Kennedy's debate was broadcast simultaneously on all three major television stations that existed at the time, again reaching almost everyone within range. Nowadays, a president, or any leader, must consider the hundreds of different television outlets, radio programs, blogs, newspapers, magazines, social media, plus public appearances, in order to get his or her messages across to an audience. In addition, a single lapse of judgment or impulsive action via social media can spark an international crisis, as we have seen repeatedly.

There is little doubt that a leader's job so often involves navigating complex interpersonal dynamics, coalitional alliances, and social behavior, figuring out who is a potential threat or ally, as well as who is most and least dependable. This is quite literally exhausting since nothing taxes the brain and neurological system more vigorously—which is why the size of the frontal cerebral cortex of primates is directly related to the corresponding size of typical social groups. So, if you sometimes feel exhausted or overwhelmed by all the pressure, chaos, and complexity within an organization, this is because of the high "cognitive load" that burns so much metabolic energy.[15]

A Unique Focus on Leadership and What It Means for Daily Life

One of the soundest principles of leadership is to avoid introducing a new product or service when the market is already saturated. This may not stop Starbucks from building outlets on every street corner in the world (there are over 250 within walking distance of someone living or working in Manhattan), but for the rest of us, it is senseless to try to sell a new idea when consumers are already overwhelmed with the choices available. As mentioned before, given that there are literally thousands of new books and programs on leadership offered each year, you might already be asking yourself what could possibly be different about *this* one?

So much of the literature, and so much of leader development, are focused on the bottom line, increasing profits, improving productivity, improving sales, or upward mobility within the organization. Yet work, however important, is only one facet of life, which includes so many others. Contentment and happiness are only partially related to job satisfaction—even wealth and health don't necessarily predict well-being or matter very much beyond minimal levels. Certainly, we feel a yearning to do something meaningful, to make a difference, to be successful in a vocation, but that alone may seem empty without supportive friends, family, and other interests. Just as companies or investors diversify their portfolios to minimize risk and increase the pathways to further growth, so, too, are most lives richer when we are able to integrate professional leadership pursuits with other aspects of life, including family, friendships, leisure activities, and community.

It is the hypocrisy that can be so bothersome when the same individuals who aspire to positions of authority, power, and influence, who are deputized to lead us to the promised land and take responsibility for our welfare, can't—or won't—apply to their own lives what they advocate for others. How do we take seriously a physician who is obese or a smoker? How do we respect a therapist or teacher or administrator or coach who preaches to others about the importance of integrity and hard work, yet doesn't apply those same principles in his or her own life? We are bombarded in the media with stories of corporate greed and deception, executive duplicity, political manipulation, hypocrisy at every level of government, undermining our faith and trust in institutions. We desperately need leaders who walk their talk, who don't just demand that others live by a code of conduct, but those who practice in their own daily lives what they expect of others.

Generals no longer ride into battle in front of their military troops; they sit at headquarters and bark orders from the rear. Many executives command salaries and benefits significantly greater than their employees, creating perceived increased distance between them. It is no wonder that leadership, as we've known it, is rapidly losing its luster. Never before have our political leaders been so poorly regarded, with trust at an all-time low. No matter who serves in the highest office, half the country becomes angry critics. Financial institutions, automotive companies, utilities, and other industries are increasingly viewed as unscrupulous entities. Political candidates spout all kinds of nonsense designed to provoke or entertain, or cater to the basest level, without concern for the consequences. We are so accustomed to the double-talk and deceit that it has become routine to say or do anything for attention or media coverage, then switch to another position to reach a different audience. It is no wonder that people have become mistrustful and cynical toward their leaders.

Putting aside for a moment how much more effective and accomplished you could perform at work if you practiced a form of total, integrated, and congruent leadership, what if this also allowed you to apply what you know and understand in every other aspect of everyday life?

Neglected Principles of Leadership

Given all the voluminous literature on the subject, I'll save you the trouble of wading through most of it and summarize the essence of what has been said most often, both within the academic domain as well as among practical, advice-driven sources. After reviewing many of the books, articles, and research on the subject, as well as having interviewed hundreds of accomplished leaders, I've discovered and distilled a few of the most basic points.

Like Everything Else in Life, Leadership Is About Relationships

Everyone says this. All the time. But they don't actually believe it. Even among psychotherapists, they agree that their relationship with clients is key. There is even lots of research to support the idea that most positive outcomes that occur from therapy result from the quality of the relationship, at least as it is perceived by the client.[16] The really interesting and amusing part of these studies is that there is such a disconnect between what therapists think matters most versus what clients report helped them most significantly. The correlation is close to zero. Whereas therapists consistently mention the brilliant techniques and strategies they applied, their clients instead talk a lot about feeling understood. In other words, therapists often believe they know what was helpful to their clients, but these assumptions may not be valid, at least as experienced by their "customers."[17]

In a similar vein, many leaders are obsessed with learning the latest techniques or strategies on the market, supposedly rendering everything they are already doing obsolete, or at least behind the times. Whereas new research and practice guidelines help us to develop more effective strategies for making decisions and implementing programs, they almost all succeed or fail based on the relational connections among team members. If you are trusted and respected, if people believe you have their best interests in mind, as well as the products and services provided, then they will literally work themselves to death. The Japanese, by the way, have a term for this, *Karachi*, to describe employees who literally expire from excessive passion and devotion to their jobs.[18]

Whether we are talking about relationships within the context of human behavior, or any species among primates, there are somewhat universal interpersonal patterns that have developed both by evolution and cultural considerations. Both humans and chimpanzees, for example, function in competitive environments in which resources, food, and mating opportunities are limited. In order to avoid constant battles, injuries, and intragroup fighting, dominance hierarchies naturally emerge in which high-ranking members are given increased access to opportunities and low-ranking members are consistently exposed to aggression and intimidation to keep them in line and accepting of their station in life.[19] Of course, we see this same template in organizations and communities around the world, regardless of whether we are talking about marginalized people, low-status employees, worker bees, slaves, serfs, or the poverty-stricken.

Alliances are formed among the underclass in order to bolster their power and influence. Chimpanzees form loyal relationships through their grooming behavior, spending hours each day, more than 20 percent of their waking time, picking fleas off one another (humans spend the same amount of time in a similar kind of "grooming" and bonding behavior called "gossiping" in which we trade intelligence and information about outliers within the group). Yet this is not really about looking good, or keeping one's fur in good condition, but represents a statement that someone is literally watching your back. It's interesting, however, in that a member's dominance ranking within the chimpanzee troop is what determines how much of the grooming time is actually devoted to taking care of his or her appearance, rather than being required to be the one doing all the work.[20] This is also a familiar theme within human groups in that it is fairly obvious that relative low-status followers or employees are often burdened with more than their fair share of work, or fewer privileges and opportunities to improve their position or opportunities. This is the way the world works in almost every domain, and it helps explain not only why alliances are formed but also why nepotism is so common, whether within corporations, political parties, governments, or drug cartels: We all collect favors for certain actions that are expected to be repaid. Those in power attempt to provide disproportionate resources and privileged opportunities for their own family members, friends, and allies.

For anyone who rises to a leadership position, and remains there for a period of time, it is likely a number of mutually reciprocal alliances have been formed. This is why there are "in-groups," as well as marginalized members, in every organization, and why favors are repaid to take care of debts and obligations. It is also the case that often those who aspire to positions of authority and responsibility do so not just because of the favors and privileges they can accrue for themselves, their kin and allies, but also because they feel a commitment to mentor and help others. Although such purely altruistic motives are sometimes found within other creatures, humans are somewhat unique in that many of us devote a considerable amount of time, energy, and resources to help those with whom we share no genetic material. This phenomenon, while not necessarily universal since there are many self-serving and selfish dictators, political figures, and CEOs in the world, is much more likely to occur during times when there are enough resources and food supplies available. It is easy to be generous when you've got plenty of stuff to share.

Creativity, Experimentation, and Reinvention

For those who work in arenas that maximize innovation and creativity, some of the "normal" rules of leadership are completely inappropriate, if not downright dysfunctional. The customary standard within most organizations or companies is that the leader sets the tone and makes the rules. There are established policies, specific contractual obligations, dress codes, carefully crafted boundaries for what is considered acceptable and professional behavior. Work spaces are often allocated based on seniority and status. There are even posted guidelines for what employees are permitted to do, and how they must do these things according to established standards. Disney Park employees are only permitted to point directions with two fingers or their whole hand. Amazon warehouse workers are not allowed to wear lipstick, chew gum, or drink anything other than clear water. A call center in Norway only allows a maximum of eight minutes for a bathroom break. Other companies prohibit facial hair, hats, water bottles, or food items. Then there are all the rules for appropriate conduct that have been mandated and strictly enforced, such as requiring safety glasses when using a stapler or prohibiting the rearrangement of any chair, desk, or table without calling a relocation specialist.

Leadership, however, is often about empowering followers, especially when the goal is to produce breakthroughs and creative excellence following rather unique rhythms and work styles. When Pixar decided to sell to Disney, its owners were less concerned with the valuation price than their demand that the stodgy, corporate parent respect and continue to allow their "cultural touchstones" to be honored.[21] Edwin Catmull, one of the founders of the innovative animation company, absolutely insisted that Pixar be permitted to maintain its playful and irreverent atmosphere given that the company was in the business of creativity. Pixar's office housed such traditions as a cereal bar, a "speakeasy" hidden in a secret closet, paper airplane contests, mail delivery via skateboards, and employees permitted to design their work spaces in the most whimsical and irreverent way possible, the exact opposite of the usual corporate culture.

Catmull outlined several other essential principles that were embedded in Pixar's group culture, ideas that would be considered heresy in the most traditional leadership manuals and corporate settings. These included actions like honoring noble failures that represented attempts at innovation, even if the idea did not pan out and utilized significant time and resources. The overriding philosophy was to make it safe for people to explore and share "crazy" ideas, as well as to challenge the status quo. As such, so-called crises within the company were often reframed as opportunities for growth and learning. Finally, management prioritized interpersonal and organizational processes as well as institutional goals. In other words, it wasn't just about the destination but also the journey.

Jeremy Gaffney is one of the leading innovators in the online video-gaming industry, having helped shepherd the development of some of the classic, most popular billion-dollar phenomena. He has launched startups, funding the projects out of his own pocket at times. Yet to do so meant he had to recruit some of the most brilliant minds in the industry—graphic designers, programmers, artists—all graduates from MIT or Cal Tech who would agree to work for future stock options and salaries less than $1,000 per month. Out of necessity, Jeremy had to learn to tolerate the eccentricities of his rather unusual collection of nerds, engineers, computer geeks, and gamers who would eventually develop the next *World of Warcraft*. He understood clearly that these geniuses would perform at their best only when allowed to work according to their own schedules and preferences. Although this might have resulted in some fairly unusual work habits, it also led to a very unique work environment.

"If you want to recruit geniuses," Jeremy remembered with a laugh, "and you can only pay them a token salary, *something* has to give—like hygiene, social skills, or even the ability to communicate with other humans."

Jeremy recalled, mostly fondly, the strange crew of employees working under his direction and all their rather unusual habits. One of his most brilliant graphic designers was absolutely terrified of other people, so he would hide under his desk whenever a stranger, usually a potential equity partner or investor, might visit the office. "The first thing they'd see is the guy looking at them with wild eyes who would then suddenly drop out of sight beneath the reception desk where he preferred to work. Then they'd see his head cautiously poke up and notice that he was breathing out of an oxygen mask to calm his nerves. He sounded like Darth Vader and that was the first impression people would have about our new company looking for money to support our projects."

Like Pixar and other creative enterprises, Gaffney recognized quite early in his career that this particular industry survives or flourishes based on the leader's ability to recruit and nurture the creative output of followers who don't necessarily even know how to play well with others. He remembers another programming wizard who preferred to work in a small closet under the stairs, justifying that he needed a space that was absolutely secluded and free from all distractions. Over time, he actually moved into this dungeon, whether to save money or because he felt comfortable there. The problem was that months went by without him bathing or taking a shower, so a rancid smell would waft through the office during the rare times he might open the closet door.

Finally, several of the other staff had enough, so one day they decided to take things into their own hands. "They dragged him out and the guy's yelling the whole time, calling us 'smell Nazis,' telling us he would never have worked with us in the first place if he'd been told there was a 'smell code.' They dragged him to someone's house, lathered him up with soap and shampoo while he was fully dressed, then stuck him in the shower, hosed him down, toweled him off, blow-dried him, all the time he's still screaming and calling us names. Then they dragged him back to the office and stuck him back under the closet for another month. And so this was our office environment, and honestly, it was a very weird place to hang out."

Gaffney explained his rather unusual tolerance and flexibility as absolutely critical in order to get the job done. He realized what was truly important was the quality of the product his workers were creating, and he wasn't willing to settle for anything less than crafting the best and most popular game on the market. This wasn't about a bottom line at all, but about pride in doing something extraordinary, perhaps something that had never been done before.

"I had to be willing to bend on things that were actually unimportant and not related to making something great. If that meant that somebody had rather unusual work habits or things they needed, it was no big deal to accommodate them." The big takeaway from this experience is one of those principles that is often neglected, if not ignored—that people do their best work when they are allowed to operate according to their own rhythms and style, assuming this is not terribly disruptive to everyone else on the scene.

Being a Model of Integrity

There's a lot of talk about the important leadership virtues of honesty, authenticity, and advocacy (especially by academics shielded from certain practical realities), a subject we will revisit later, but sometimes precious little action in this regard. Gaffney once again offered an important object lesson that was seminal in his own development during a formative time. Using the tech language of his discipline, he sees the main role of a leader as serving as an "avatar," the graphical representation of one's alter ego, an idealized self that cannot only exist in virtual reality but also in daily life. He remembers clearly working at one of his early start-ups when the CEO took everyone out for dinner one night. This was a guy whom he saw as a mentor and inspiration, until he observed the way he behaved outside of the office.

"The CEO would drink a lot at dinner and then start hitting on the waitresses, even though he was supposedly happily married. He thought he was being cool, showing us he was the alpha male, the big stud. But what he was really showing us was that his wife couldn't trust him. And if the person he loves most can't trust him, how the hell can the rest of us rely on him?"

Gaffney will never forget the lesson learned: that when you are leading others, they are always watching. "When you are working with others, you want them to have three attributes. You want them to be intelligent. You want them to be competent. But just as importantly, you want them to be honest and ethical." He laughed after rattling off the list, one finger at a time. "In real life, though," he admitted, "you usually have to settle for maybe two out of three. And maybe sometimes you have to settle for one out of three."

Ultimately, however, each of us has to live with ourselves. Gaffney would rather fail at a business than fail himself and his followers by compromising his integrity. "You have to be the avatar, the best of yourself, and even if the business fails, you still made yourself a better person. And that's really not that bad of a place to have ended up."

Altruism *and* Self-Interest

There has been considerable debate among scholars and researchers regarding whether the desire to lead is primarily driven by wanting to do good for others, or rather motivation based on padding one's own pockets, so to speak. I have a definitive answer on that one question: It is obviously both!

Leaders often enjoy special privileges and benefits that their followers both admire and resent, earning larger salaries, living in spacious homes, driving fancy cars, and having greater access to the rich and powerful. This provides huge advantages to their offspring, better positioning them for their own ascendance to positions of status and authority. The children of professional athletes, actors, or politicians are 100 times more likely to follow parental footsteps into these privileged professions than the general public without access to such resources and opportunities.[22] Such nepotism also allows leaders to offer payback to friends and followers to whom they owe a debt for their rise to power. For centuries, this has been the ruling policy to reward friends and punish perceived enemies.

Altruistic motives, though, are also part of the leadership package for most individuals who aspire to positions of responsibility and caring for others' welfare. If the only goal was the accumulation of wealth and power, a far more appropriate path would be a life of crime that provided much higher profits, deference, and power. Dominance may be the primary motive among primates and other animals, but humans have evolved other ways of achieving status through expressions of compassion and service. Thus, the best leaders among us have learned to rely on persuasive and influential tactics that emphasize collaboration and shared decision-making, rather than dominance and intimidation. This is a significant departure from the past when followers preferred their leaders in the form of a deity, monarch, or dictator. Nowadays, they usually want a respectful colleague.

Especially in America, we have this traditional vision of leaders as heroic, individualistic, self-reliant figures like Davy Crockett and Daniel Boone, who tamed the frontier through their fierce courage and determination, or visionary industrialists like J. P. Morgan or J. D. Rockefeller, or tech geniuses like Steve Jobs, Bill Gates, or Mark Zuckerberg. Yet now leadership is conceived more as a connective enterprise based on collaboration, empowerment of others, building alliances and coalitions, creating a sense of community.[23] The new order of the day, at least for cutting-edge leaders, is to be able to honor others' differences, as well as building a coalition of common interests. It is about creating a shared vision of responsibility and ownership that can only take place through a degree of transparency, integrity, and the willingness to empower others.

2

What Most People Don't Seem to Know and Understand About Leadership

IT IS REMARKABLE how oblivious many people in positions of authority are about some of the most important leadership principles and skills. One reason for this might be because there is so little consensus on even how successes can and should be assessed, or even what it truly takes to become an outstanding leader.[1]

Considering that more than 80 percent of U.S. workers are actually unsatisfied and disengaged in their jobs, many leaders are clearly out of touch with the needs of those who are in their care. One of the most common reasons for this disconnect between what followers really want, versus what leaders are actually doing, is that there have been so few ongoing, systematic efforts to gather meaningful information about the reactions and needs of others. Perhaps this is one of the reasons why only 1 in 10 innovations introduced by major companies ends up being successful,[2] signaling clearly that we are wrong far more often than right, at least when it comes to initiating change.

How Much We Think We Understand, How Little We Really Know

There's nothing more dangerous than leaders who think they know *exactly* what is happening at all times and what the single best course of action should be. Even more misguided is the belief by some that they actually understand all the intricacies of what is involved in leading others. One former executive and researcher on organizational behavior thought his knowledge of leadership was fairly complete during the days he was running a trade union. But once he began studying the field in greater depth, he reported that his understanding decreased in direct proportion to his increased knowledge and experience: "In effect, the more I read, the more I realized how ignorant I am."[3] Eventually, he surrendered to the reality that the subject, much less its practice in daily life, was far too complex and multifaceted to *ever* fully grasp all its nuances. This confession is hardly an exception, but rather the rule; when dealing with human beings, especially those in large organizational units, it is indeed virtually impossible to know and understand all their motives and behavior, much less their likely consequences. And this doesn't even take into consideration all the other aspects of leadership that involve accomplishing various tasks, increasing productivity, mastering finance, budgeting, forecasting, and predicting the future.

Michael Skelly has been involved in politics and launched several renewable energy companies that built massive infrastructure projects. He has found that one of his strengths as a leader is his willingness to admit what he doesn't know and understand. Whether he's talking to the media, or briefing employees in his companies, his goal has always been to just simply, honestly, and straightforwardly explain what he believes is the reality of the situation or task at hand. In his latest transmission line project, attempting to build one of the largest infrastructure projects in the history of the country, he has had to communicate with political operatives, landowners, governors, cabinet secretaries, senators, lawyers, and journalists, as well as his own employees, and one overriding philosophy has shaped his style. "There's no need to show how smart you are to others," he said to me with a shrug, "because it just confuses the audience. A lot of leaders, they think they have to show people how smart they are all the time. They think that gives them some kind of power because they think they know things that others don't." Skelly shook his head as he said this, "because when you are trying to persuade or convince people to do something, you've got to start where they are." That means, as much as anything else, being honest about what we don't know or understand.

Skelly decided to go to an Ivy League business school for an MBA even though he'd never worked in anyone else's business and never intended to do so, preferring to create his own organizations. It wasn't the classes he found nearly as interesting as the lessons he learned hanging out with some really bright people. "I realized I could hang with them and hold my own. So many of them were afraid to ask questions because they didn't want to reveal what they might not know or understand. They were afraid to be vulnerable. But I realized there was a lot of power in being willing to admit what I didn't understand. People think, okay, this dude had enough confidence to ask questions. I've just never been afraid to admit the things I don't know."

Comments like this aren't very surprising when you consider how little is truly understood, even after the barrage of books, manuals, speeches, studies, and training manuals that have been produced. Barbara Kellerman, an author of many of the popular books on the subject, as well as head of a leadership institute, admits "that we don't have much better an idea of how to grow good leaders, or of how to stop or at least slow bad leaders, than we did a hundred or even a thousand years ago."[4] That's a rather remarkable confession, isn't it?

It turns out there are so many accepted principles and standard operating procedures of leadership that are taken as gospel and yet have little actual standing in the real world, much less empirical support. There is a kind of "leadership industry" that has a vested interest in keeping the billions of dollars flowing for more workshops, training, coaching, seminars, and especially more published books. In his own book on leadership b.s. (bullshit), Jeffrey Pfeffer challenges some of the accepted "wisdom," such as the "virtues" paradigm that has been popular throughout history—the idea that all great leaders (and leadership writers) talk about the critical virtues of being selfless, trustworthy, and authentic.[5] "If anything," another critic comments, "they tend to be narcissistic, back-stabbing, self-promoting, and shape-shifting." He further notes that "leading is like starring in a lip-synched music video. The trick is to make it look convincing from the outside."[6]

Fairly cynical for sure! But this statement also hits home the notion that leadership just ain't what it used to be, no longer driven solely by power, authority, obedience, and loyalty. Rather than issuing orders from a lofty tower, organizations are now more decentralized and governed by far more collaborative, even democratic principles. Technology and pharmaceutical companies, hospitals, and academia are examples of organizations that favor "participatory leadership" in which employees are actively involved in decision-making. It is no coincidence that these are also places where people tend to be well educated and engaged in creative pursuits that virtually require a degree of initiative and self-sufficiency. It's also not surprising that the circumstance professors, doctors, scientists, and software engineers complain about the most is bosses meddling in their work.

In these volatile times, the conditions of disorientation and adaptation are frequently commonplace. The pace of change these days, with respect to the environment, technology, and the political arena, make obsolescence the norm rather than the exception, accounting for the life expectancy of major corporations being reduced in size to about a decade.[7] For centuries, the only technology that we needed to master was how to saddle a horse and throw a spear, or perhaps load a weapon. Within the span of a single lifetime, music has evolved from 78 RPM records, to 45s, then albums, 8-track tapes, cassettes, and now streaming online with songs floating in a "cloud." With regard to communication, in a single generation, sending telegrams has been replaced by airmail letters, then phone calls, faxes, emails, and instant messages. We can only imagine what is coming next. Virtual reality? Telepathy? Avatars?

This means that whatever we think we know and understand about leadership is always changing, making experience and existing knowledge somewhat limited as we anticipate new advances. It takes a high degree of flexibility and adaptability to anticipate whatever is coming next and make the necessary adjustments to address new challenges. Leaders are supposed to be the ones to corral the herd and guide them in roughly the same direction.

How and Why We Need Leaders

The birth of leadership as we now know it occurred 40,000 years ago, about the time that humans abandoned a purely hunter-gatherer existence and began the great migration to populate the rest of the world. Prior to that time, humans lived in small tribal groups of less than a few hundred members, spending their time in one region. Once on the move, there was a need for skilled and knowledgeable leaders, rather than operational managers of farms and hunting parties.

In this new more mobile, more dangerous environment in which humans thrived with advantages of greater technology and trading partners, cultural norms became more regulated and directed by leaders who achieved their positions via status, rank, dominance, or power. Dominance contests played out to compete for additional resources, opportunities for mating, and to demonstrate superior skills that might qualify for higher rank. We can witness these battles for power and control within any organization and also in the "training years" of most children in our contemporary world. Athletic and sports arenas earn young people certain advantages to gain access to greater status, popularity, and social currency. One can also witness how video and online gaming has become an alternative environment for children and adolescents (and adults) to demonstrate their prowess in vicarious forms of combat or problem-solving. They represent symbolic forms of dominance contests to establish hierarchies of status and power that may, or may not, result in leadership opportunities.

This form of emergent leadership is one way that leaders come to power.[8] It is the most fluid, informal, and unstable power base since you can instantly be replaced by someone else who achieves higher performance or ability. You may have noticed that in any leaderless group, the person who usually steps up to take charge is either someone who is driven by altruism and serving others, or else the person present who is most self-centered and narcissistic.[9] Both motives are considered highly adaptive at times, depending on the composition of the group. And even though it might appear that altruistic leaders are completely selfless, they also enjoy advantages by demonstrating acts of kindness. Such individuals appear to others to be more trustworthy, enjoy increased prestige, and improve their reputation, which brings additional benefits and goodwill. In that sense, an altruistic leader can be viewed as "showing off" like a peacock exhibiting its feathers, impressing others, attracting friends and potential mates, because of his or her image as a generous, kind, and caring person.[10] Who wouldn't want to be colleagues or friends with someone who appears so fair and giving to others?

In one study, women were shown videos of an attractive guy just hanging out, another guy volunteering to donate blood, a third guy donating money to a homeless person, and a fourth man retrieving a stolen bag, engaged in what is called "heroic altruism."[11] Guess which guy women were most attracted to?

When there are primarily cooperative individuals in the group, the competitive, self-centered leader can easily take over and enjoy success; when the group is populated by ambitious, driven members, then the altruistic leader will often be more effective. This also helps explain why work environments can sometimes feel so hostile and aggressive, why gossip and bullying are often present—there is perceived competition between rivals for the spoils of dominance. Although gossip often gets a bad rap for being petty, it is actually quite an important means to keep outliers in line, spreading information about those who are not doing their fair share of work, and enforcing organizational norms.[12]

Although my point is to emphasize why leaders are important to organize efforts and coordinate collective behavior, the best and most successful ones are not those who thrive on attention and accolades as a function of their own narcissism and need for attention, but rather those who know how to empower others. When basketball great Bill Walton was asked whom he considered the greatest players, his answer was surprising in that he didn't mention the likes of Kobe Bryant, LeBron James, or Michael Jordan. Instead, he explained, "I love selflessness and passing," meaning that he most admired Bill Russell, Magic Johnson, and Steve Nash because their priority was making teammates look good, rather than needing to be the players to keep the ball and score.[13]

In spite of all the attention directed toward leadership, those in positions of authority and power may not be nearly as important as they—and others—think they are. It turns out that leaders can indeed have a modest impact on organizational effectiveness, and can certainly exert a tremendous negative influence, especially when they maintain a selfish agenda. It is actually far more likely that employees or followers have a much more significant impact on results, regardless of who is in charge.[14]

That might be one reason why most leaders don't remain in their positions for very long before they are dethroned or quit. It is rare indeed that a CEO or coach keeps the same job for very long (less than 3 years in professional baseball, basketball, or football), and the only reason that politicians manage to do so is that they have discovered ways to stack the deck against any potential rival. Even so, consider how quickly a leader can fall from grace. Rick Perry couldn't remember the names of a government cabinet department and was toast (until invited to head the agency whose name he couldn't recall). Dan Quayle couldn't spell "potato" correctly and his career was over. Sarah Palin claimed she could see Russia from her Alaskan home and lost even more credibility. Howard Dean just screamed passionately in excitement and was thereafter viewed as an unstable figure. Trump's presidency was in immediate jeopardy because of his impulsive tweets. And then consider all those who were caught with their pants down, now relegated to history. Leaders survive, or vanish, at the whims of their constituency.

Hormones, Evolution, and Biology

One intriguing perspective in understanding leadership challenges is offered by evolutionary psychology to explain the reasons why the majority of leaders fail to meet their objectives. This model is based on the familiar idea that certain characteristics survive and behaviors persist because they once served significant survival mechanisms, at least in our ancestral environment.[15]

Traditionally, humans were organized in groups of 75–150 members, all of whom were related by kinship bonds. In such small units, there was little difference between public leadership and private behavior since everyone was known intimately. There was no concept of private space and relatively few secrets. There was also minimal difference in wealth, status, and rewards between leaders and their followers as a way to moderate power. Compare that, for example, to contemporary times in which CEOs routinely earn more than 100 times the compensation of other workers. Leaders are, thus, no longer perceived as "one of us" but as an "exalted other."

The environment in which we now operate is quite different from the one in which leadership roles originally evolved. Leaders of the ancient past were focused on promoting social cohesion and keeping followers satisfied—or they would be dethroned. Nowadays, leaders are more often accountable to their own superiors or boards than their workers. They are appointed by external authorities, rather than elected from within the group. And they often rule by dominance, coercion, and threats, rather than consensus and permission of their followers.

To make matters even more challenging, biological changes in the human organism have increased the pace of evolution 100 times to create genetic mutations within relatively short periods of time (a few thousand years).[16] Humans have developed thousands of new genetic alterations during the past few millennia that now provide immunities to infectious diseases or allow us to become lactose tolerant. The problem, however, is that many of our institutions, organizations, cultural norms, and environment remain locked into a kind of obsolescence that fails to recognize and respond to changes. It is theorized that is one reason why depression is becoming increasingly common among humans: "In effect, humans have dragged a body with a long hominid history into an overfed, malnourished, sedentary, sunlight-deficient, competitive, inequitable, and socially-isolating environment with dire consequences."[17]

Historically, leaders took on the mantle of responsibility based on their physical size, skills as a warrior or hunter, perhaps even propensity toward violence. Given all things equal, there is still a greater probability that individuals with certain genetic features, glandular makeup, physical characteristics, or neurological wiring will become leaders. People, especially men, who have high levels of testosterone, dopamine, serotonin, oxytocin, or frontal cortex "coherence" are more inclined toward aggressive behavior and thus more likely to battle for leadership positions.[18] In political contests, the more physically imposing candidate usually wins, just as in corporate environments, taller individuals often enjoy higher status and salaries, as well as greater leadership responsibilities.[19]

Hereditary leadership has been more common throughout human history in which kings, queens, chiefs, warlords, alpha males and females all slip into their positions because of parentage or genetic gifts. In the first instance, they inherit the job because of their "royal" birth, whereas in the second, their rise to power is determined by inherited characteristics that include size, strength, intelligence, or personal drive and ambition. After all, there are certain individuals who just absolutely *need* to be leaders to feel okay about themselves.

As we well know and understand, this does not necessarily result in the most qualified person taking on responsibility for everyone else's welfare.

One reason, besides the "glass ceiling," that so many more men than women end up in leadership positions is because they need the status position to gain access to other resources. Males, across the animal spectrum, usually end up at the extreme ends of the status continuum, whereas females are usually positioned in the middle. This means that when it comes time to manage communal parenting, tribal defenses, division of labor, collective farming, and other collaborative actions, men aren't necessarily more qualified for the job, but rather they are more desperate for the perks that come with privilege. Among many animal species, only the fittest are allowed to reproduce. That is one reason why in most group settings today, you will often find that men usually dominate, take control, and talk more than women: They need the attention.[20] It is also why throughout human history, women have developed a more "caretaking" style of leadership, whereas men have been fueled by testosterone to present a "take charge" attitude.[21]

Female leaders are held to a very different standard as well, since they are not "allowed" to operate in the same ways that men do. Thanks to evolution, women have developed a different set of abilities that permit them to equalize the playing field with men. They have thus become far more emotionally sensitive and expressive even though they are not permitted to "do anger" or "dominance" the ways that men can. If a male leader loses his temper or becomes irate or angry, he is just being an alpha guy, putting people in their place, but if a female leader displays anger, she is often called a "bitch." Differential standards are held in other domains in which women have only recently gained access. For instance, in the field of medicine, a woman doctor wrote an article in a flagship medical journal about "crying in the stairwells."[22] She was not allowed to show any weakness in front of her male colleagues (or the other women nurses) or she would be written off as unsuitable for the profession—because doctors don't cry. Yet there were times when she lost a patient whom she cared deeply about, so she hid in the hospital's stairwell to deal with her grief outside of others' view. Similar stories have been told by women leaders in other traditionally male-dominated fields such as engineering, litigation, and politics.

Finally, leaders are appointed by some legitimate authority or group such as a board of directors, supervisory hierarchy, or an ultimate authority like a CEO, president, or department head. In this case, the leader is usually held accountable to produce a result in keeping with established and negotiated criteria. If hereditary ascension to power results in incompetence (consider all the failed kings and dictators throughout history), then appointed leaders may be unresponsive to those they were hired to represent. In each of these cases, no matter how the leader came into his or her position, power becomes diluted and ineffective when, according to evolutionary psychologist Nigel Nicholson, "we pursue wealth and growth before peace and fulfillment."[23]

More recently, a "new world order" has changed the rules for political leadership and completely refashioned the qualifications, skills, and criteria for serving in public office. In the United States, Europe, and elsewhere, leaders have been elected and appointed, not based on their relevant experience to do the job, but rather their persuasive ability to connect with their followers. It is ironic that whereas overconfidence and narcissistic tendencies are quite effective in getting someone the job he or she so badly craves, these traits also mortally wound the leader to be able to perform competently. Such individuals ultimately fail because of their lack of self-awareness, defensiveness, refusal to learn from mistakes, and inflated, inaccurate assessments that are guided more by their biases and preferences than empirical data based in reality.[24]

"It's the way we do things around here"

Traditionally and historically, leaders served specialized roles, depending on whether there was a need to make tools, weapons, defensive strategies, or conflict resolutions. Tribal leaders were chosen based on not just their expertise in these areas but also their humility, integrity, fairness, and willingness to serve their followers.

When we compare the ways that we have lived for millennia to the current state of affairs, we can appreciate how far out of our evolutionary element we now reside. We live in communities that number in the thousands, if not the millions. We will likely never meet our leaders, much less ever feel they care about us as individuals or know of our personal problems and needs. We became more and more insulated from neighbors once structural changes were made in our dwellings and environment, such as those typical of suburban life—no sidewalks, air conditioning that keeps everyone inside, and even garages built as part of the home so you can drive right inside without having to encounter anyone along the way. Likewise, organizations and corporations house thousands of employees in their skyscrapers, making it impossible to ever get to know most of your colleagues. That's one reason why companies like Gore, Toyota, and Virgin Airlines decided to return to ancestral days and keep their work units rather small, reducing the size of their buildings to those that house tribal numbers of around 150 people. Everyone knows one another, and everyone *really* knows their leader. This creates a quite different organizational culture than can possibly exist in most corporate settings. Compare that, for example, with the Pentagon in Washington, D.C., that houses over 25,000 employees in 17 miles of corridors or the Apple headquarters that holds 15,000 employees operating in over 3 million square feet of space.

Just as tribes, villages, cities, states, nations, religions, and ethnic groups have cultures, so do organizations and companies. Culture is often conceived as a series of customs and rituals that bond people together according to their shared values and interests. Such cultural practices provide the norms or rules for what is considered appropriate and socially acceptable behavior. Although typically cultural norms are explored within the context of a national or ethnic group, many of the concepts apply equally appropriately to behavior in any setting. This includes such factors as the extent to which either individualistic or collectivistic values are considered most appropriate, whether one is expected to fall in line behind the leader's vision of a party line, or whether there is a great tolerance for creative interpretation of rules as suggested guidelines. Other cultural norms might be related to the extent to which people tolerate uncertainty, how they attain status, how they become marginalized, how power is distributed and controlled. Then there are all kinds of other cultural features related to language usage, dress and appearance, and certainly daily conduct.

As one example of these differences, General Tom Kolditz, now head of a leadership institute, personally corrected my misunderstanding of the adaptations he must now make mentoring university students instead of soldiers when he explained how different the norms are within various military units across the world, or even within the same service: "What I've seen in the American army is that you must lead by influence rather than by authority," he pointed out. "I've trained with other foreign armies in Bolivia, Russia, and Iraq and what soldiers typically do is stand around until some officer tells them what to do. But American soldiers and marines will take the initiative; they are now prepared to operate at a high level without anyone like me telling them what they need to do."

Jeff Bezos, CEO of Amazon, has taken some hits because of the cultural norms that developed within his company, norms that were turning people into competitive workaholics, modeled after his own driven habits. In a communication to his employees, he admitted the work culture that had evolved over time was not necessarily a good fit for everyone, which is why he initiated the rather novel policy of offering substantial bonuses to those who wanted to quit.

Bezos, like many good leaders, has learned to evolve and adapt. His decisions to acquire Zappos and Whole Foods weren't only about improving Amazon's profitability; they were also about adopting many of the cultural values of these successful satellites. Bezos commented on this new insight in a message to employees, "You can write down your corporate culture, but when you do so, you're discovering it, uncovering it—not creating it. It is created slowly over time by the people and by events—by the stories of past success and failure that become a deep part of company lore."[25] Bezos didn't appear to be simply defending the culture that evolved through his sheer force of will, but rather challenging his followers to take responsibility for how the culture would continue to evolve in the future.

Within organizations, culture can be quite explicit and structured, or else amorphous and seemingly undefined. Rather than representing the official party line that is included in the annual report, an organizational culture represents the more unspoken and implicit norms. Something like 80 percent of published corporate codes all say the same thing, mentioning they stand for innovation and integrity, but that hardly describes what really happens behind closed doors.[26]

Greg Smith, a former vice president of Goldman Sachs, wrote a notorious article in *The New York Times* indicting the toxic culture within the financial institution. Although the official cultural imperative was to emphasize teamwork, integrity, honesty, and humility, he confessed that such had hardly been his experience. "The culture was the secret sauce that made this place great and allowed us to earn our clients' trust," he wrote as he walked out the door in frustration, "I am sad to say that I look around today and see virtually no trace of the culture that made me love working for this firm for many years."[27]

If culture is indeed the "secret sauce" that Smith mentions, then it can be a poisonous concoction for workers in certain organizations and business climates. Dysfunctional or toxic cultures can lead to low productivity, poor morale, increased turnover and absenteeism, and employees who are in chronically bad moods, not to mention having serious health problems. Such conditions can result from a lack of transparency, rampant negative rumors ("Did you hear that they are going to sell us out?"), entrenched corruption, and ultimately, poor leadership. Examples of this phenomenon were observed in the Australian Olympic swim team that was supposed to win handfuls of gold medals at the 2012 Summer Games in London. But a culture of intimidation, bullying, illicit drug use, poor discipline, and their leaders' lack of moral authority doomed the team's performances. We have seen this scenario time and time again with other dramatically underperforming athletic teams.

Given the external threats and internal pressures within any tribal organization, it is inevitable that certain policies and practices will evolve over time and become standard operating procedures. When these lead to productivity and member satisfaction, as well as high-functioning collaboration, all is well. But when leaders ignore or mismanage the establishment and enforcement of optimal norms, toxic cultures evolve over time, leading to entrenched negative attitudes and poor morale.

Tribal Cultures Within Organizations

So far I've been discussing organizational culture as a singular phenomenon, as if everyone on board shares the same understanding. It is far more realistic to consider the number of smaller, tribal cultures that are formed whenever two or more individuals create a coalition or alliance. Within any company or organization, within any family or group, there are different rules and preferences for how things get done. There are cultural norms related to where an office is located (Southern California vs. southern Mississippi), how people are permitted to decorate their office spaces (Pixar and Zappos vs. Shell or Toyota), dress codes (Patagonia vs. Baker McKenzie Law Firm), and what is considered to be "appropriate" behavior with regard to communication and daily interaction.

Cultural norms within tribes or organizations even strongly influence how people respond to stress or crisis, depending on their particular stage in development.[28] In the earliest, most primitive stage of a tribe, everyone is just looking out for themselves, often at the expense of others. They have a pessimistic attitude, believing that basically life sucks and everyone is out to screw you. In the more advanced, later stages, assuming that development continues, tribal members function collaboratively rather than competitively.

Of course, a tone is set by those in charge, in terms of the behaviors they model to others, but group behavior becomes far more stable and entrenched when it is considered part of the dominant cultural values. This is certainly the case within organizational settings but even holds true in far more extreme conditions.[29] For example, when groups find themselves stationed in Antarctica or outer space for many months at a time, it has been found that some nationalities do better than others. Russians adapt better than Americans in such conditions, largely because they are more inclined to seek social support when they are struggling, a by-product of their culture.[30]

Certain leaders take pride in the cultures they have helped to foster within their organizations. Yvon Chouinard, the founder of Patagonia, a manufacturer of outdoor clothing and adventure-based equipment, considered the culture of his company to be as important as his service to consumers. He instituted policies that protected the environment, used many recycled materials, donated profits to charitable causes, even invited customers to resell their used, unwanted clothes even though it would cut into his bottom line. But just as important to him as influencing the public's values was creating a culture that would foster loyalty and satisfaction among his employees, even encourage them to create their own tribal cultures. The title of Chouinard's autobiography, *Let My People Go Surfing*, referred to the culture he wished to create that would allow workers to take time off from work to go surfing or skiing, or play outside when the conditions were optimal. Other companies like Google, Southwest Airlines, Facebook, or REI are well known for their permissive cultures that not only allow, but also encourage, an atmosphere of creativity in the ways that employees do their jobs. Zappos hires employees based on how they imagine prospective workers will fit into its culture. Like many other companies such as Nike or Twitter, there is an overriding belief that if employees are happy and having fun, then this attitude will be passed along to their customers. Nevertheless, it isn't just about having fun at work as cultures can emphasize other values, such as providing child care or concerns about the safety and health of their employees.

When I visited the offices of TOMS Shoes to talk with founder Blake Mycoskie, his vision of serving others, as well as making a profit, was obvious within the culture of his operation. Employees all had movable desks on wheels, so they could huddle together as needed. A barista set up shop in the middle of their converted warehouse, creating an informal meeting place to provide caffeinated treats. A slide had been constructed from the second floor as an alternative to stairs. Each aspect of the physical environment and space seemed to communicate that work can be fun and a highly social form of engagement.

When a colleague and I interviewed Mycoskie to inquire about the origins of his vision for his company's culture, he remembered feeling lost as a young man until he landed a place on CBS's hit television show *The Amazing Race*. He was able to travel the world as a result and vowed to return to the places he visited; his eyes had been opened to so many other cultural traditions, as well as the poverty and neglect of the people he encountered. He had always felt a passion for business but also wanted TOMS Shoes to be socially responsible and serve others. "When I was 19," he told us, "I dropped out of college to start my own business, and a mentor gave me a piece of advice I will never forget: The more you give, the more you live."[31] That has been the hallmark of his leadership style, a value that he has tried to instill among his followers, whether it is his employees or customers who understand that for every pair of shoes they buy, he gives away a free pair to someone around the world who is barefoot.

People thought he was crazy to propose such a ridiculous business plan for a company that was supposed to make a profit. "Here I was with all these shoes stuffed in my duffel bag," Mycoskie recalled laughing about the earliest days of his plan, "talking about a company that gives as much away as it sold. Looking back on it, it *was* pretty crazy, but excitement is contagious."[32] It is indeed!

Another example of such a unique business venture may be found at the Lucasfilm campus in Northern California that houses soundstages and a complex of buildings. George Lucas had built a pristine setting that encouraged deep, reflective thinking and was more like a university than a corporate setting. He had planned that the environment and spaces would lead to a culture that continued his studio's remarkable run of creativity. There were eating spaces supplied with unlimited trays of scones, muffins, and, of course, the requisite espresso machines. There was a library and deep, leather chairs that encouraged and supported research. Employees were encouraged to go on walks in this gorgeous setting. When I visited the Lucasfilm campus, the latest *Star Wars* film had just been released, and everyone's pride and excitement were palpable.

Another example of a leader who clearly understands the importance of tribal culture within his industry is Jeremy Gaffney, the online video gaming executive I introduced in the previous chapter. "Let's just say my business is populated by some pretty unusual people from all sorts of walks of life," he admitted with a laugh during one of our many conversations. He explained that in spite of what some might think, his is not at all like other high-tech companies: "It's even more of a very casual, laid-back atmosphere in many ways, where people are wearing board shorts and T-shirts, sometimes even barefoot. People are working hours that many industries would consider crazy—12 to 16 hour days. It's a combination of being totally laid-back and yet very hard core, which I think is rather unique."

Creative endeavors such as making movies or video games require a tremendous amount of concentration and focus from brilliant individuals who are sometimes rather eccentric. Gaffney doesn't so much see that he indulges the unusual habits of his employees as he simply respects that those with special talents need to operate in their own unique ways, so they are comfortable and hence most productive.

Although the cultures of tribes and organizations take on a life of their own, influenced as much by the members as any leader, it all begins with the initial vision and values of the person in charge. When the leader sets the tone for an organization by developing and maintaining a culture that emphasizes mutual respect and trust, this may be even more critical than any strategic plan.

The different kinds of cultures that often exist within high-tech start-up companies have been classified, for example, into a handful of different flavors.[33] The one that gets the most attention, *the superstar model*, is beloved by venture capitalists and equity partners because it produces the fastest results and return on investment. The problem is that the long-term success of such a culture with several alleged geniuses depends on employees who don't necessarily work very collaboratively or cooperatively with others. It's nice to have a few on board—because who *wouldn't* want the best and brightest? However, the price paid for such individuals is that initial great ideas may end up flaming out without the greater collective effort committed to a mutual goal.

Among the other cultures identified—such as the *engineering model* composed of worker-bees who toil away in their cubicles, or the *bureaucratic model* that captures traditional corporate culture—none is nearly as productive as what the researchers refer to as a *culture of commitment* in which employees work together toward a common goal and in which each person feels as if he or she has a valuable role to play. By the way, that doesn't mean they *do* actually play an active part, but rather that they are encouraged to *feel* this way because of a culture that reduces conflict and rivalry and emphasizes shared participation.

Companies like L.L.Bean, Zappos, or Pixar have such low turnover (less than 3 percent) and high employee morale, in large part, because a culture of shared participation is a major focus of the organization. Others like Massachusetts Mutual Insurance or Amazon have employees who remain with the company for an average of only 9 months because of the high levels of stress they experience on a daily basis.

The best organizations spend a lot of time and resources studying not only the needs and preferences of their employees, but also those of the customers they serve, allowing them to make swift and strategic shifts as needed. Within that context, organizations also have a huge advantage to respond to changes if a culture has developed that not only permits, but also encourages, people to continually offer honest and pointed feedback, input, and criticism regarding what appears to be working best and what really isn't working at all.

It's What You Don't Know That Counts the Most—If You Admit It

"Boys, if you ever pray, pray for me now," Harry Truman declared to reporters at a press conference upon being elevated to our nation's highest office. "I don't know whether you fellows ever had a bale of hay fall on you, but when they told me yesterday what happened, I felt like the moon, the stars, and all the planets had fallen on me." Truman wasn't far wrong in his prediction about the job since he later likened it to "riding a tiger," because he felt that at any moment he would be swallowed up. He often felt overwhelmed by the demands of the presidency, and no one was more relieved than he when his full term ended and he was able to go back home to Missouri and lead a quiet, simple life.

One of the most difficult challenges of being a leader are the unrealistic expectations that people have in terms of infallibility and omnipotence. While it is true that leaders know and understand certain things that followers might not grasp, it is also the case that leaders don't know and understand nearly as much as others think they do. If we are truly honest, we'd have to admit that a lot of the time we are pretending to be more aware of what is going on than we actually are. Yet people expect us to always be decisive, in control, and most of all, completely aware of every contingency. It would be terrifying for our followers if they really understood how frequently we are operating in the dark, or sometimes have no idea at all what is going on.

My experience of leading a group, *any* group—whether it is a board of directors meeting, staff meeting, classroom, social event, or psychotherapy group—is that most of the time I don't understand what is happening in the room. Oh, I'm clear about what I have in mind, what I'm thinking, and where I'm headed, but there are so many interactions unfolding at any one point that I feel overwhelmed by the flood of information I see, hear, feel, and sense. During any particular moment, my mind races with thoughts and questions about what is transpiring and what it means. When those two people at the end of the conference table gave each other a certain look, was that a signal of recognition, or rather disappointment? Why has the guy next to them scooted back his chair? Is he disengaging? And why are the silences so long after I ask a rather simple question? Do people disagree with where we are going, or are they just afraid to speak up?

In other words, on the outside, we usually appear poised, confident, wise, and knowledgeable; on the inside, there is often something quite different happening. We frequently feel doubts and uncertainty, even if we can't admit it as often as we would like. We rarely have enough of the information that we need. And let's be clear: You can never, *ever* really understand another person's true experience, much less those of a whole group of people, no matter how hard you try. Most of the time, you don't even understand what *you* are thinking and feeling, or what you really want most—and you've been living with yourself your whole life.

The circumstance of being in a position of not-really-knowing, or not-really-understanding, is one that leaders must accept as part of the job. It is actually one of the most fun and exhilarating parts of what we must contend with since it means we are constantly improvising. I hear leaders complain about this all the time, that if only they were given more data, more resources, more time, more money, more opportunities, more *something*, they could really do their jobs the way they want and deserve to. Alas, so much of the confusion is not so much related to limited information as it is connected to harboring unrealistic expectations, misreading situations, and being blind to one's own mistakes and limitations, a subject we will discuss in another chapter.

Just as I hear leaders commiserate—a lot—about if only their followers were more cooperative, more skilled, better trained, more patient, more something-or-other, so, too, do teachers constantly gripe about how their students are not up to par. Builders complain constantly about the unreliability of their tradespeople. Likewise, physicians complain frequently about their patients being noncompliant and uncooperative, refusing to follow their instructions and prescriptions. They view this behavior as lazy, obstructive, or even defiant. Yet the reality is often far different from what doctors think is going on. Given that the average patient only has about 18 seconds to describe symptoms before he or she is interrupted, and 90 percent of patients are never allowed to finish their description, one can imagine that both parties experience plenty of frustration in the examining room. The physician is just trying to obtain enough information to get a handle on the diagnosis and decide on a treatment, without a lot of extraneous information; he or she has patients waiting in other examining rooms. The patient becomes frustrated when he or she is constantly interrupted and not permitted to fully describe his or her condition. More than half of patients leave the examination not understanding what their doctor has said and what is expected of them. In other words, they are supposedly resistant and noncompliant because they are stubborn or stupid when, in fact, they are just confused. And the worst part is that many doctors don't understand this.

If you connect this example to leadership situations, you will see that there is often a similar dynamic at play. Leaders expect, if not demand, that their followers act in a particular way, and when they don't, we make all kinds of assumptions that may not be valid. Almost all interpersonal conflicts or misunderstandings are an interactive effect, meaning that both (or all) parties play a role contributing to the ongoing struggle. Everyone is triggered by someone or something else. And whether you are cognizant of it or not, you consistently annoy or frustrate others in ways that you are not yet aware of and don't fully understand.

It is as if we all walk through life with our zippers open or spinach in our teeth. Almost everyone else can see our embarrassing lapses, but nobody says anything about it—or more likely, people in the past have *tried* to tell you, but you either weren't listening or couldn't hear what they were telling you. But I promise that you consistently do certain things that are off-putting to others, that compromise your effectiveness, and these are things about which you are only partially aware.

Today (and I do really mean this just happened a few hours ago), someone said upon encountering me in the hallway at work, "Oh, sorry I couldn't attend your briefing. I had to finish that report that was due."

Now, the guy should have just kept his head down and walked on, or better yet, avoided me completely, but he just couldn't help himself. In the past, I have tried repeatedly to give him feedback suggesting that he comes across as so ambitious and driven that it gets in the way of his working cooperatively with others. He is extraordinarily competent and smart, but he only seems to care about his own advancement rather than our collective mission.

I knew it was futile to say something to him over his comment because in the past he seemed so resistant to hearing feedback on his behavior—but I just couldn't help myself as his excuse seemed so feeble and ridiculous. "Let me get this straight. You didn't come to the briefing because you had to do this report? Today? At 1 p.m.? You couldn't have done it yesterday? Or this morning? Or later this afternoon?"

Now, what he should have done is apologize, or admit he made a mistake. Actually, he made three mistakes. The first was making a decision to skip the meeting and the second was to lie about why. And the third was that after he was clearly caught in the act, he tried to defend his actions, only making things worse. But the most interesting aspect of this interaction, and similar ones that we encounter every day, is that he was genuinely oblivious to what he had done and how it might be interpreted. I'm fairly certain that later on he would have talked to others about our conversation and would have very much felt like a victim and that I was being unreasonable in my expectations of him. That's how the interaction might have felt to him, so, on one level, such an assessment of it is valid. But on the other hand, I've heard over and over from people who work with him how frustrated they feel by his behavior, preferring not to work with him at all. This last point is important because the theme explored in this chapter is how we determine what aspect of difficulties "belongs" to us and what "belongs" to others. In other words, how much of this uncomfortable interaction was related to his behavior and blind spots, and how much was related to my own?

I know that we have to pretend to know more than we really do. That is to be expected. But sometimes leaders start to believe in their own omnipotence, missing their blind spots. In the words of Socrates, "True wisdom is in knowing you know nothing."

What You Know, What You Think You Know, What You Don't Know at All

There are things you know for sure—about yourself, about others, about the ways in which the world works. Let's say, for instance, that you have a good idea of a few skills that you have mastered exceptionally well. Over time, your confidence has soared because of the consistently good outcomes that result from them, as well as the positive feedback you receive from others (and you are also certain these reactions are genuine and honest).

Then there are the things you *think* you know. And this is a fairly frightening area because it is based on assumptions and hypotheses that are not necessarily valid. The biggest danger is that the same misguided overconfidence that leads someone to act in decisive, supposedly well-informed ways can end up in disaster because of consistent misinterpretations of others' behavior, or the larger culture within an organization or economic climate. Such a scenario happens a lot these days because so much communication now takes place through sketchy, incomplete messages, rather than face-to-face interactions that provide more reliable and complete data on others' reactions and true feelings. Tweets, texts, emails, and voicemails provide only fragments of information, unaccompanied by the more complete thoughts and feelings associated with them.

Finally, there are your blind spots, the things you don't know that you don't know. These are particularly destructive because they are based on assumptions and beliefs that are both inaccurate and biased, confirming what you already think is true. These can often result from particular signature strengths that disguise or hide other factors that might be even more important.[34] Imagine, for example, an executive who presents herself as the kind of leader who empowers others. But in fact, she is perceived by followers as being overcontrolling and micromanaging every decision, refusing to turn over responsibilities, and meddling in areas that she has already delegated to others. The worst part, however, isn't just that her organization suffers as a result of these aspects of herself about which she is oblivious, but that she has no idea people feel this way about her and her management style.

Among the most important attributes of any great leader is self-awareness, especially recognition of your limitations and weaknesses, knowledge about your impact on others, understanding of your underlying motives, and learning from mistakes and failures.[35] Of particular interest is the fact that most training programs for leaders emphasize extensive accumulation of information, technology, management policy, finance, economics, and so on, but relatively little focused on increasing a leader's commitment to self-assessment.

The higher one moves up the ladder, the more challenging it is to receive reliable and accurate feedback on your own behavior. People lie—a lot. They suck up to you, tell you what you want to hear, focus more on winning your affection and approval than providing any valuable intelligence. That's one reason why it is so important to have clear perceptions of your own behavior and its impact. There are, thus, several questions that are useful to ask yourself periodically in order to assess how you and your actions are interpreted and received by others.[36]

1. How clearly do followers understand and agree with your vision for your work together?
2. To what extent are you spending your time efficiently focused on what you believe matters most?
3. How often are you providing others with the direction and feedback they need in order to feel supported and guided toward desirable goals?
4. How well are you delegating tasks to others and empowering them to make their own decisions?
5. How can you alter the structure of communication with subordinates, colleagues, clients/customers, and others to receive more valuable input from them?

6. What are the most stressful triggers that are compromising your ability to operate in more fully functioning ways?
7. To what degree are you being true to your own values and personal style?

These are just a few of the questions we should all be asking ourselves in front of the mirror to become more intimately familiar with our own forms of ignorance and self-deception. It's important to realize, however, that while asking such questions of oneself may be a good first step, it must also be accompanied by critical inquiry into how you are perceived and experienced by others.

Blind Spots and Self-Delusions

Later we will discuss how particular leadership traits, even those that result from dysfunctional personality dimensions, can lead to success or failure depending on how behavior is moderated and expressed in several areas that matter the most.[37] There are times when leaders use their power to push or force higher levels of performance, and other times when they attempt to empower others by creating optimal conditions for collaboration. There are other circumstances when leaders operate strategically by setting priorities and facilitating innovation. Finally, there are operational tasks that involve completing specific goals in order to meet deadlines. Some of these relate less to *what* leaders do than to *how* they function in terms of interpersonal style. And style matters a lot!

So, the issue is not whether you, or any leader, is flawed, but rather the degree to which (1) you are aware of what gets in your way; (2) have access to reliable, accurate, and honest feedback from others as to how you are perceived and experienced; (3) have demonstrated a commitment and willingness to alter your behavior in light of input you hear from others, as well as attention to performance indicators that go beyond the bottom line.

Everyone has blind spots, obstacles that take us by surprise because we didn't see them coming in the rearview mirror. We recognize patterns only when they seem familiar in some way; we tend to categorize data into existing schemas or discard those that don't seem to fit. Our attachment to certain ideas, cognitive biases, perceptual distortions, confirm what we think we already know and understand. This leads to errors in judgment and a marked reluctance to admit mistakes, mostly because it may not be evident that considerable distortion is occurring.[38]

I once worked with a group of leaders in Hong Kong and organized them in a circle to discuss some of the challenges they face most frequently in their jobs. It was tough going, and for reasons I didn't yet understand, the Chinese participants were rather reticent and shy. Only a few people were willing to speak aloud, and I had generated a few hypotheses about that before settling on their self-consciousness in speaking English. I had already figured out that the hierarchical structure of Hong Kong culture only permitted the eldest in the room to speak, while the younger leaders were supposed to always defer to them. This was especially problematic because I had already observed that some of the younger leaders were actually the most experienced in confronting a greater variety of issues we were there to discuss. But since hardly anyone, except a few of the older people present, would say much at all, the whole program was falling flat.

Then I had an idea. "Why don't you talk to one another in Chinese?" I instructed them. "Since some of you are hesitant to express your ideas in English, maybe you'd feel more comfortable doing so in your own language?"

With that permission, they were off and running. I was truly amazed at how heated their debate became. Everyone in the room was speaking up with passion and enthusiasm, interacting with one another in ways I didn't think were possible. Even more remarkable, there was relatively equitable sharing by everyone present, with nobody dominating or controlling the discussion. Considering this was a collection of experienced leaders, I was quite impressed.

I was enthralled not only by how wonderfully the leaders were discussing the leadership issue on the table, but I was mighty impressed with myself as well. "Look at me," I thought, "I'm teaching in Chinese! I'm leading a discussion, an incredibly engaged one at that, in a language in which I don't speak a single word! Am I something, or what?"

I waited impatiently for the discussion to slow down a bit because we had gone over the time limit before a scheduled break. And these people were serious about their breaks, having preordered all kinds of delicacies and snacks to consume. I kept waiting for a moment to interrupt, but the discussion kept going on and on with continued interest. Again, I patted myself on the back for figuring out this brilliant way to enliven the program.

Finally, I jumped in to announce that we needed to temporarily halt the discussion to take a break. It seemed, reluctantly, they disengaged and headed over to the table where food and tea were waiting. I sauntered over, my chest puffed out, quite proud of this breakthrough I had orchestrated. Am I an amazing leader of leaders, or what?

"So," I mentioned casually to a few of the people standing around the table, "that was some interesting conversation you all were having."

They just looked at me and nodded while nibbling on their snacks.

"I'm curious, though, exactly what you were talking about? My Chinese is a little rusty."

I received an expected but polite laugh, but nothing else was forthcoming. So I decided to be more direct. "Could you summarize for me the themes that you were discussing, so we can follow up with them after the break?"

"Nothing much really," one of them said.

"Nothing much? Are you kidding? That was the most interesting and dynamic discussion you've ever had with one another!"

"We were just talking about where we should go to dinner tonight after the program is over?"

"The whole time? For twenty minutes that's *all* you were talking about?"

The guy just shrugged. "Well, there was some disagreement between us as to the best place to go."

Cognitive Errors and Biases

Clearly, we all have blind spots and perceptual distortions that lead us to see things in a particular way, often wildly inaccurately even if they confirm our preferred vision of the way the world operates. These kinds of cognitive biases lead to two sorts of leadership errors that have been programmed into our systems by evolution.[39] The first is seeing a large stick in the road and believing it to be a snake, thus overreacting to only imagined danger. The second kind of cognitive error is far more serious and involves mistaking a real snake for just a stick and failing to take defensive actions. It turns out that my cognitive error during the meeting in Hong Kong, called "self-evaluative bias," was just wishful thinking, like wanting desperately to see a stick when it was really only a line in the sidewalk. But circumstances could have become far worse if I had not checked out the accuracy of my assumption and thus been led to make similar mistakes in the future.

Self-evaluative biases inevitably lead to false confidence and inaccurate assessments of one's own competence.[40] Whereas historically that would usually get leaders in trouble quickly because they could not defeat their enemies or locate food sources, nowadays a leader's overconfidence can flourish for some time without being challenged by underlings. The more serious problem is that such leaders often do not learn from previous mistakes because they consider themselves infallible. This may be fine as far as image management and public perceptions are concerned, but it can also lead to some consistently poor decision-making over time. One common example of this situation is what happens when an overconfident leader receives feedback that a new idea or program is failing miserably. Rather than cutting losses and moving on to more fertile territory, the leader invests even *more* commitment, resources, and money in the project, determined to save it at all costs.

It has been found that leaders tend to make mistakes in several areas, beginning with the ways they collect and make sense of information, as well as the ways these data are used.[41] One's biases, limited resources, or interpretations of information may lead one to make invalid assumptions or misconstrue the meanings of what has been provided. This is known as "confirmation bias" and acts to distort the flow of interpretation since the priority is to simply validate what you think you already know and understand, ignoring any input or data that conflicts with your preferred beliefs. In other cases, the information collected is skewed and hardly representative of what might really be happening. In still other instances, there is a flood of data that can be overwhelming and just as useless because it is so difficult to determine what is most salient or to make the necessary connections. For example, it has been estimated that 15 percent of all medical diagnoses are wrong because doctors fall into cognitive traps, seeking to confirm the simplest explanation for presenting symptoms without looking any further.[42]

There are, of course, different levels and degrees of obliviousness. First of all, there is a lack of awareness about current conditions or capabilities, leading to miscalculations that can be relatively minor and insignificant, or else potentially catastrophic. A military leader who dispatches his troops into battle, or a sales manager who sends her staff into the field, without awareness of the immediate conditions, competition, and environment, will usually be disappointed with the results. The second most common form of selective blindness is a kind of denial whereby the leader is either unable or unwilling to recognize certain realities that will definitely have an impact on one's plans. Edward Smith, captain of the *Titanic*, consistently denied that the ship was at risk heading across the North Atlantic. His alleged last words to the crew as their fate was sealed instructed them to keep a stiff upper lip, so to speak: "Be British boys, be British." But even that report is just as unreliable as Smith's own assessment of potential dangers since there are various other eyewitness accounts that he was last seen in the wheelhouse, the radio room, rescuing a child, releasing his crew from their responsibilities ("Every man for himself"), or that he committed suicide by jumping into the icy water.

If one is unaware of an impending threat, or makes an inaccurate or faulty assessment of a situation, then this type of blindness can be even more destructive—representing a failure to respond when decisive action is needed. Thomas Gage, another Brit who earned notoriety for his failure to act, was the commanding British general during the early part of the American Revolution. His timidity to attack American strongholds became a serious problem that eventually led to the collapse of their attempt to stop the colonial rebellion.

Are You Really Sure You Want to Know the Truth?

The simplest and most direct way to find out what your own blind spots might be would be to ask those who know you best. That is the rationale behind the "360-degree assessment" often recommended by business consultants and executive coaches. The idea is to interview a broad swath of individuals who have interacted or worked with you in a variety of contexts and situations, including colleagues, subordinates, customers, supervisors, and anyone else who might have useful opinions.

This process can be undertaken in a far more informal, and perhaps meaningful way, by soliciting honest input from almost everyone in your life who might have an opinion. Since this is a book about leadership in everyday life, it makes sense that those who are perhaps most "qualified" to offer an opinion are those who really know you best, such as friends, family members, and those with whom you socialize. Granted, anyone who is asked for input is also acting in his or her own best interest, offering opinions that represent personal preferences and experiences, and such feedback may not necessarily be desirable or helpful to you. Nevertheless, most people appreciate being asked in the first place; if you contextualize the feedback and resist the temptation to respond defensively, you can learn a lot. The assumption is that other people around you know all kinds of interesting things about you that you don't recognize yourself. These can be really big shortcomings that have always gotten in your way or limited your optimal effectiveness, or little things that are annoying to others even if they aren't serious problems.

The unvarnished truth does sometimes wound because we just don't see ourselves the same way that others do. We are indeed blind or deaf when it comes to certain consistent statements or actions of ours that are off-putting to others. And when the shoe is on the other foot, so to speak, when we are in a position to tell others how we really see them, it is quite difficult to offer the feedback in such a way that it will be heard without the other person feeling attacked or criticized.

The other day, I noticed that someone I supervise usually raises his voice at the end of his sentences, as in, "I tried to get his attention so we could agree *on a solution?*" In other words, whenever he makes direct statements, they sound like questions, diminishing their value. So I thought to point this out to him—that his speech cadence makes him sound hesitant a lot of the time. When he raises his voice, he seems unsure of himself even though I know that this is not what he means to communicate. I was quite excited about delivering this observation because I thought it could make a huge difference in terms of how he comes across to others.

Unfortunately, either the timing or delivery was not as strategically chosen as I imagined. Whereas I thought the colleague would be very grateful for my potentially life-changing advice, I could see that, instead, he turned his head away and seemed to feel hurt by what I'd said. He did not appear to be at all appreciative of what I'd just offered him. I could easily have told myself that this was his problem, not mine; that if he can't deal with input from a supervisor, then maybe he doesn't belong on my team. But if I'm more honest, I have to accept a certain responsibility for not handling this interaction as well as I might have. The point is that people have to be ready and open to hear honest feedback about their blind spots because such input is potentially (and usually) destabilizing and uncomfortable. Essentially, you find out that you are not really viewed by others the same way you see yourself.

Illusions and Clarity

Illusions about oneself, or others, are not always a bad thing. But there is an "optimal margin of illusion," a sweet spot, that make optimism and hope and confidence possible. Sometimes clear-headed realism is both discouraging and disheartening; we need illusions of the possibility to do things that have never been tried before. Henry Ford is one example of a visionary whose initial world-shattering success was eventually completely destroyed by increased isolation, distortion, and illusions that were not grounded in any semblance of economic reality. Ford was the first to build a reliable and affordable automobile that could be mass produced and by the 1920s had managed to control more than half of the industry. Yet as the public clamored for more variety and options in their vehicles, Ford insisted he would only manufacture his simple, black model. Every year, he watched his market share decline but refused to alter his business plan, even with all his advisers begging him to do so. Because he was so stubborn, and blind to his failings, Ford was eventually fired from his own company (a familiar scenario that Steve Jobs would reenact in the next generation). Spectacular successes sometimes lead to insidious blind spots precisely because the visionary believes that he or she can do no wrong.

We can't possibly be exceptional at everything we do in leadership roles. It takes a special professional indeed to become a master of both management responsibilities as well as strategic actions, since each role relies on very different skill sets. One focuses on handling the present, putting out fires, responding to crises, getting things done, organizing others' behavior, measuring results, motivating people to keep the momentum going. Strategic initiatives, on the other hand, are mostly about the future and rely far more on creative, visionary thinking. Someone who excels in this second mode of operation may become lost in the operational details of running an organization or event.

The important thing is to know clearly, honestly, and accurately what your signature strengths are, as well as your weaknesses, and compensate accordingly. In an ideal world, a leader would be good at both sets of managerial and visionary skills; in the practical world, we have the opportunity to compensate for blind spots and weaknesses by empowering others who can literally watch our backs, so we don't become blindsided. This will happen, however, only if we are clear about what we don't do well.

What Makes a Great Leader?

Of course, there is no one style of leadership that is appropriate for every culture and context, but there are a few personal qualities valued in leaders across eras and locations. Certainly included would be passion, the fuel that powers persuasive influence in any setting. If you don't care passionately about your role as leader and the mission entrusted to you, it's hard to motivate anyone else.

Then there's the "vision thing," meaning a clear idea about the best direction a group should head. It also helps—a lot—if you know how to get there and can convince others to follow (back to passion). Thus during times of need, when a group of people are oppressed, it takes a determined leader like Moses, Marx, Gandhi, Mandela, Friedan, or Martin Luther King to lead them to freedom, not through battle but via inspirational spoken words.

The leaders of times past—transformational figures of industry like Andrew Carnegie, Walt Disney, or Steve Jobs; political figures such as César Chávez or Abraham Lincoln; military generals like Napoleon, Alexander,

Eisenhower, or Chief Joseph—are now somewhat rare in our fractured, decentralized, often dysfunctional governments and organizations. More than ever before, CEOs are discredited for their unscrupulous behavior leaving consumers and employees disenfranchised. There has been war between, or within, our government institutions, whether the executive branch, Supreme Court, Senate, or House of Representatives, for as long as we can remember. Whoever is elected president, from either major political party, faces disapproval from half the populace. It would seem that great leaders are no longer cast in the mold of inspirational figures, but rather as facilitators of organizational behavior. In the case of well-known leaders of technology enterprises such as Google, Facebook, Apple, Amazon, and Tesla, the CEO's name may be well known, but he or she is not necessarily admired. The likes of Susan Wojcickli (YouTube), Jeff Bezos (Amazon), Sheryl Sandberg (Facebook), Larry Page (Alphabet), Tim Cook (Apple), or Richard Branson (Virgin) are not necessarily viewed as inspiring figures as much as they are seen as skilled visionaries and managers.

What's the difference, you might ask? Our times.

People no longer jump to attention or follow unquestioning orders without knowing why. Even military structures have become more democratic, discovering that Special Forces personnel, for instance, tend to be more successful in their operations when given the freedom and latitude to improvise and minimize authority of rank and seniority. The power of social movements like the civil rights movement's March on Washington, the Arab Spring, Occupy Wall Street, the Dreamers, and Black Lives Matter have leveled the playing field more than ever, with their followers able to influence or even neutralize the decisions of those who hold power.

Whatever one learned about leadership even a decade ago is now outdated, if not obsolete. And whatever we think we know and understand will eventually be superseded by new discoveries that advance our knowledge. Readers of a certain age will surely remember the "truths" of our childhood that have long since been disputed: that going in the water after eating will lead to stomach cramps and certain death, or that drinking water during exercise will compromise your performance. Likewise, the leadership truths of yesteryear are just as outdated. Whereas once upon a time leadership was about commanding, directing, punishing, dominating others—all to ensure obedience and compliance to a central authority—nowadays leaders are far more likely to facilitate, suggest, motivate, and inspire. This is what has led one expert to insist that it is precisely this "decoupling of power" that has made it possible for almost anyone to become (or at least think of oneself as) a leader in many other aspects of daily life.[43] This may indeed be an exaggeration, but it is certainly the case that what you know about leadership is not what always matters most, but rather the position and opportunity you yourself find to make a difference in others' lives.

3

Facilitating Connections and Meaningful Interactions

"OKAY, SO NEXT ITEM on the agenda relates to the new administrative policy related to travel reimbursement. You will no longer file expense reports on the 409 forms but are now required to first receive authorization before making any reservations. It has come to our attention. . . ."

I'm sure this information is important, but if you were to scan the room of people listening, you would notice that most seem to be nodding off. A few are surreptitiously checking messages on the devices they think are hidden on their laps. Many in the room are simply bored; others are just doing what everyone else usually does in such meetings—occupy chairs while drifting off somewhere else.

It is more than a little interesting that the mere *presence* of a phone or mobile device sitting visibly on a table, even if it is turned off, can change the dynamics of interaction in a room.[1] People are more likely to keep the discussion light, avoid topics of controversy or significance, minimize empathic connections between one another, and unconsciously prepare for frequent interruptions. "Even a silent phone disconnects us," observed Sherry Turkle in her studies of how intimate and meaningful conversations have been hijacked during our digital age.[2]

Given that the average adult now checks his or her phone an average of every six minutes and that teenagers send more than 100 texts per day and actually *sleep* with their phones, this has become the new normal in daily interactions. Close to a majority of young people are inclined to answer their phones or respond to messages in movies, or even during exercise or sex. Many college students, while sitting in class pretending to take notes, are simultaneously following several kinds of media at the same time (texts, email, online shopping, sports scores and news, social media etc.). Obviously, in this age of multitasking, efficiency and swift responding have been prioritized over the quality and intimacy of personal interactions.

This is one reason why conversations in general, and meaningful face-to-face meetings, are becoming increasingly rare, even though they can be so crucial for advancing new ideas, solving intractable problems, and planning for the future. In addition, the experience of being in a room with people, with no other agenda except to engage with one another about ideas, reactions, thoughts, and feelings, has been cast as a colossal waste of time. People have now become accustomed to constant streams of information from multiple sources, leading to increased stimulation but also high levels of distractibility, lack of focus, impulsive actions, compromised cognitive processing, ignoring environmental information, and lost productivity. It takes something like six minutes to metabolize and recover from an incoming text, email, or message, and then resume the prior task that occupied one's attention. In addition, people are not nearly as productive as they think they are handling multiple tasks while simultaneously engaging with their mobile devices.[3]

For leaders involved in high-level or important negotiations, multitasking or attention to mobile devices seriously undermines desired outcomes in that their partners perceive them to be less trustworthy and competent to follow through on agreements.[4] As important as it might seem to check messages during a meeting, discussion, or business lunch, others in attendance perceive the leader as less professional, capable, and trusting than if he or she remained fully present during the meeting. This may seem surprising considering how ubiquitous such behavior is in almost every setting imaginable, but nevertheless most people recognize that split attention is not necessarily conducive to attaining the best possible outcomes for the task at hand.

Juggling Multiple Streams of Continual Information (and Interruptions)

If you look at the reasons why people are so attached to their mobile devices, to the point that they consult them every few minutes regardless of what else is happening, it does signify a degree of self-importance. After all, consider how vital you must be that people are sending you inquiries that require such instant, immediate attention. Yet short of being a neurosurgeon on call, an expectant parent with impending childbirth, or waiting any second for a deal to close, I can't think of any reason why *anyone* needs to review and respond instantly to emails or texts or answer phone calls just because they are signaling attention.

Some leaders, with major daily responsibilities, are choosing to leave their phones at home when they are out for dinner or socializing with friends or family. This represents a priority that there is nothing that anyone could possibly contact them for that requires an immediate response and that would be considered more important than the people they are already with. Others have instituted a new policy of not reading or responding to any messages after 7 p.m., which they've figured out is far better for their sleep patterns. There are only three possibilities for an incoming message that arrives after hours: (1) It is bad news in the sense that someone wants something from you that means more work or effort, or provides some disappointing report; (2) it is some spam or unwanted message that will slightly annoy you before you delete it or send it to junk mail; or (3) it is encouraging news that might feel good but, again, won't help you to relax and sleep well—instead, you will likely end up thinking about the message instead of whatever is really more important at home. After all, what are you really going to do that can't wait until the next day?

Since this is a book as much about leadership in everyday life as in the business world, I would be remiss if I didn't mention how crucial this issue is in the lives of our friends, neighbors, coworkers, and family. How often have you witnessed (or done this yourself) a family, or several close friends, sitting in a restaurant yet everybody is actually not talking to each other but to someone else who isn't even there? Recently, I was at an elegant restaurant and noticed one table at which all three children were watching videos on their phones while absentmindedly forking in a few bites of food. Both parents were also otherwise engaged with their devices, texting or emailing others with their fingers furiously dancing across the screens. I watched their expensive meals congealing on their plates, no longer a priority any more than their engagement with one another. Alas, this has become the new norm, rather than the exception. People no longer expect to have anyone else's undivided attention.

I was recently walking across campus, waiting to cross the street, when I couldn't help but overhear the conversation between two young people, a guy and a young woman, standing in front of me. I was riveted by the talk because the woman was telling the guy that her mother was dying of cancer and I could see him nodding and listening. It wasn't until the light changed that I could see that the whole time he had been texting on his phone *to someone else* while she was pouring out her heart to him. But the truly amazing thing about this interaction is that it didn't seem to bother her at all! There is a new word to describe this now commonplace kind of interaction, "phubbing," which means the ability to text at the same time you are maintaining eye contact with the person who is speaking to you.

There are many other reasons, besides conveying self-importance, why people remain so tethered to their mobile devices. Sure, they don't want to miss anything. In the case of junior high school kids, many of them report checking their phones up to 300 times per day as a form of "self-defense." They are terrified that someone will post something shameful about them on social media and they want to be available to immediately counteract the attack or gossip. Many people, in fact, feel quite lonely and isolated and so collect "friends" on social media to bolster the belief they are popular and appreciated. There is also the advantage that you can better control interactions through texts that represent very strategic and limited communications: "Sorry, can't make the meeting. Maybe next time." End of story.

People are often feeling more and more avoidant of the unknown or spontaneous exchanges they can't control. And personal identity is the most sacred possession of all, meaning that social media allows one to project whatever desired image one wants to convey: We can be whomever we wish to be as we advertise that particular image on social media. Our mobile devices have not only become the primary means by which we express ourselves, but they also stave off boredom or uncomfortable feelings. Unfortunately, one of the repercussions of this preferred means of engagement is that our levels of empathy toward others are eroding and people lose their ability to accurately read and decode others' nonverbal emotional cues. Take away people's phones for a week, and their caring and sensitivity toward others bounce back.[5]

Becoming More Fully Present

Leaders must set the stage and model for others their optimal standards of performance. This means that if you want others to be fully present when you are talking about something important, then it is crucial that you demonstrate what you want from others. That's why some leaders who value deep engagement and meaningful face-to-face conversations institute norms for appropriate behavior. People may be asked to put their phones in a basket on the table, or to attend the meeting "naked" (without any devices or laptops), and instead to use notepads if they need to write reminders for follow-up actions.

Some CEOs have recognized the renewed benefits of organizing the kinds of meetings that actually lead to free-flowing conversations without other distractions. This is consistent with much of the research that people are often more productive when they are able to talk to one another directly on a regular basis. This is not only the case with respect to formal meetings, but also with regard to the kind of informal networking that goes on during coffee breaks.[6]

Meaningful work, for most people, usually involves some kind of collaboration, the sort that provides encouragement, support, and critical, honest feedback. There are, of course, many tasks that are best completed in solitude, especially those that involve reflective thought and concentrated effort, but one of the most important tasks of a management team is to look deeply at issues and talk about viable options that might work best, as well as to process past efforts in order to learn from prior mistakes. Of course, there is also the reality that human beings simply enjoy hanging out together and work is often the "excuse" to do just that. The purpose of work undoubtedly is to get things done, to earn an income, to be productive, but it is also about social engagement and enjoying comradery. More than ever, many people crave intimacy, especially because conversations have become so abbreviated, time-limited, and coded into brief messages that are now reduced further into emojis or smiley faces.

Working in Pajamas

It is certainly reasonable to ask, as a counterpoint, who needs an office anymore, much less weekly meetings in the same location? Telecommuting is becoming more and more popular, supposedly adding to productivity by saving drive time. One-quarter of Americans say they spend some time working from home and that figure is growing every year, although with mixed results that may lead to reduced quality and productivity depending on the job.[7]

Indeed, there are a number of challenges associated with working at home, many of which can compromise quality of life and family relationships.[8] Telecommuters report being, and are perceived to be, more isolated (they also are less likely to receive promotions than workers who are in the office). They lose out on all the informal communication, gossip, and interaction that take place while people are hanging out before and after tasks and meetings. Their sense of loyalty and commitment to the company may also be reduced because of less investment.

It is clear that changing times and more flexible work environments require leaders to change the ways they operate to maximize productivity and morale. Since there are fewer collegial interactions, sources of informal information, and strong relational connections, the leader plays a more important role in providing constant input and support, as well as assessing outcomes. When employees are asked what they want most in such circumstances, they mention infrastructure support from the organization and frequent and reliable communication from their supervisor embedded in an open and trusting relationship.[9]

Some companies are scaling back on options for telecommuting, finding that it decreases innovation and creativity with employees working alone instead of talking to people. The CEO of a consulting company had noticed that his experiment with telecommuting wasn't working out very well, at least with respect to the vision he had for his organization and the quality of work that he had hoped for. The employees, of course, loved the flexibility of being able to work from home in their pajamas, saving time, commuting costs, and inconvenience, but productivity was suffering. Even though this is clearly the direction in which many companies and organizations are moving, allowing more employees to enjoy the flexibility of working from their phones or laptops, the leader wanted to change the culture and trajectory of his company despite the inevitable resistance that would likely result. Several years ago, management mandated that everyone would return to their corporate office and participate in face-to-face meetings that focused on actual conversations and discussions, rather than just getting through agendas of action items. They soon found that their growth increased five times over what it had been previously.[10]

Within universities, there is a clear movement to offer more and more classes online, which students claim to love. Unfortunately, that isn't necessarily because they are learning more, but because it is a more convenient and less expensive option. I remember a time when students would actually talk to one another during breaks, or go out for coffee to discuss matters from class, or work side by side in study groups. Likewise, the old "water cooler" conversations in offices helped to bond coworkers as they discussed the television shows from the previous night. Now that people don't usually watch the same shows at the same time because of streaming video and recording devices, and colleagues rarely stand around talking by the water cooler or copy machine, there is significantly less intimate interaction except in the form of brief emails or truncated video conferences. And let's be clear: Just because people are participating in tele or video conferences doesn't mean they are, in fact, fully present. At least in a conference room, you have to pretend to pay attention; during distance-based meetings, people are always multitasking, reading and sending messages simultaneously, looking through recipes for dinner, writing notes, or signaling others who might be around. I've had students admit to me that they don't actually watch the online lectures they are required to attend, but just log into the site and occasionally press a button to indicate they are tracking progress. One student disclosed to me that she has her children watch the lectures for her while she is making dinner or doing household chores. They then call her over to the computer whenever she needs to respond to a prompt.

With all that said, it is clear that telecommuting or distance-based work settings will continue to rise considering that 80 percent of workers would like to try it if given the opportunity.[11] And there are very good reasons for this beyond the convenience. It does save money, for both the organizations and its employees. Companies save a fortune in real estate costs and operating expenses. Employees save transportation costs, estimated to be several thousand dollars per year.

Very few leaders have been specifically prepared and trained for their roles in a virtual universe in which those under their responsibility are located all over the country or world. Managers need to significantly adapt their programs and style, not to mention their schedules, to fit the particular needs of geographically diverse followers. There are several areas that require considerable flexibility and reflection, beginning with the leader's own attitudes (and perhaps biases) toward this structure. If telecommuters feel as if they are out of the loop, or treated like second-class employees (or even classified as contractors), they may not feel inspired to do their best work and remain loyal to the organizational mission.

We talk a lot about the importance of diversity related to gender and cultural differences, but what happens when team members live in different cities, states, or even countries? Differences in time zones, climate, geography, local norms and rituals, and ethnic and religious backgrounds make effective interaction even more challenging. Among all the assets of a virtual manager, one of the most important involves building collaboration, support, and engagement within a team, a task that is already difficult when everyone is in the same location and a hundred times more so when people are spread across the globe.

Leaders have to focus their efforts on building feelings of inclusion since not everyone gets together over lunch or drinks after work. This means spending time together, via phone, video, or in person, to connect with one another beyond the agenda and business at hand. Taking just a few minutes to check in with each employee with some meaningful message or comment helps build intimacy, trust, and relational connections.

Meetings, Meetings, Still More Meetings

You likely spend more time in meetings than anything else you do in your job. There are daily meetings, weekly meetings, monthly meetings, annual meetings, impromptu meetings, committee meetings, subcommittee meetings, special project meetings, informational meetings, legislative meetings, executive meetings—many of which are necessary and useful, some others just a waste of time. And it's only going to get worse. Fifty years ago, managers typically spent an incredible 69 percent of their day attending or leading meetings. Thirty years ago, that number increased to 72 percent.[12] In more recent surveys, roughly half of all executives and managers predicted the frequency of meetings is likely to increase still further. This leads to questions about the exact functions meetings serve since they appear to be the main activity that takes place during a workday. The sad part, of course, is that the vast majority of people describe them mostly as an interruption to the "real" work that needs to be completed. You would probably also not find it very surprising to learn there is a direct correlation between how much time people spend in multiple meetings that interrupt their work and how much they dislike their jobs.[13] In surveys, the number one most commonly mentioned scourge of productivity is required attendance at meetings.[14]

It begs the question: What are meetings really for? Back in 1976, the *Harvard Business Review* published an article about how to run meetings after reflecting on the functions they actually serve.[15] They are intended as "tribal gatherings" to meet needs for social attachment and organizational loyalty, but they are also the means by which issues are stalled and decisions are postponed, and they become institutional "memorials to dead problems." Yet, at least by intention, meetings are primarily designed to: (1) build the collective identity of a team, (2) update information and intelligence, (3) coordinate collective actions, (4) unify allegiance to a decision, and (5) display positions of status and hierarchy of power. In addition, a meeting is sometimes the only time and place where a leader is actually seen doing his or her job.

Jon is the sales manager for a service provider in the real estate industry. He recently attended the regularly scheduled monthly staff meeting of one of his best clients. He immediately recognized the familiar way the meeting started, as if everyone read the same instruction manual entitled "Meetings for Dummies." They went around the table and shared their successes from the previous weeks, bringing everyone up to date. But Jon also noticed a huge difference in the way that everyone responded, as if they really listened and cared about what others were saying. As he stated to me, "I was in awe of how engaged everyone was and how openly they were talking to one another, not only just about their victories but also their uncertainties and mistakes. This invited supportive input from others."

Jon noticed that throughout the meeting, people were playful, joking around, actually laughing at times. They asked one another questions and commented on one another's personal lives as if they really knew one another in an intimate way. "I started to feel a bit emotional during the meeting, kind of sad, because this was so different from what I was used to in my own office."

"In our meetings," Jon explained, "nobody talks except the principals who rule with fear and intimidation. Nobody ever volunteers anything unless they are directly asked. All we hear are so many catchphrases, slogans, and acronyms that somebody read in a book somewhere and don't mean anything. The one true, accurate saying that is never mentioned out loud but we talk about among ourselves when we are alone is, 'Beatings will continue until morale improves.'"

Jon has been told repeatedly that any time he has a question or a suggestion, "There are already systems in place. Just follow them." Unfortunately, whomever Jon seeks out for an explanation of these systems greets him with a shrug. This creates an underground "pre-meeting" before each scheduled one so that everyone can figure out the playbook and plan how they will support one another when someone is jumped on during the meeting itself.

Jon is clearly miserable, just as he says almost everyone else in the company is, completely discouraged by management priorities. "Instead of occasional praise for the 99 tasks that are done well, we are berated for the one task that doesn't meet their expectations. This creates an atmosphere in which nobody has time—or makes time—to help anybody else as we all live in fear of not getting all of our own stuff done." Jon feels like he is constantly in the cross hairs of the CEO but knows he is not alone. During his private meetings with the boss, he hears nothing but the most disparaging remarks about everyone else, so he assumes the same criticisms are leveled against him when he isn't in the room.

There are some things that will never change within this company, but one shift that would make a dramatic difference to collective morale would be if meetings were scheduled and run in such a way that the participants truly felt like part of a team that was working together on the same objectives. Rather than a competitive, punitive atmosphere, they long for a far more supportive climate that encourages their initiative instead of stifling it. Unfortunately, this particular scenario is more common than should reasonably be expected, especially with all the resources available that are designed to make meetings more productive—and fun.

Some Neglected Secrets of Leading a Meeting (That Most People May Know but Seldom Follow)

As mentioned, you will likely spend half your working life sitting in meetings, whether on the phone, via virtual media, or stuck in a conference room. Given the number of vertical layers, interface structures, technological changes, coordination bodies, and decision-making processes, it is no wonder that the actual number of meetings required has increased 7 percent each year; in some organizations or companies, the frequency of such scheduled gatherings has skyrocketed by 350 percent.[16] We are meeting more—and enjoying it a lot less.

It isn't just the annoying number of meetings we must attend that is so disheartening—it's also the effects of such interactions that impact the larger organizational arena. At best, they can be boring, tedious, and a simple waste of time; at worst, a toxic dump of complaints, negativity, and discouragement. People may be either fortified and energized, or discouraged and emotionally exhausted after a meeting has ended. There's little doubt that these feelings continue to fester for hours or days afterward. "Personally," one manager disclosed, "I so dread showing up in that room that I literally get a stomach-ache. I have to make sure I don't drink any coffee that morning, just to keep myself calm, but then I just feel so dragged out, I find it hard to stay awake at times. And that's a good thing—because when some of these people go after one another, I just want to hide under the table. I know I'm probably overreacting—they tell me I'm just thin-skinned—but I get the jitters the rest of the day. Sometimes I can't even sleep at night I'm so upset about the ways that some people act in there."

Indeed, certain counterproductive attitudes, as well as most effective and productive behavior, are manifest in group sessions, just as they are first developed in such meetings. In fact, the *quality* of meetings has been found to be significantly related to overall job satisfaction and well-being, both at work and in daily life.[17]

There are clearly certain behaviors that occur in meetings that have been consistently found to have a negative impact on outcome, especially when participants feel unfairly criticized, disrespected, ignored, or shamed (see Box 3-1); more importantly, such actions can have a profound effect on

BOX 3-1

Functional and Dysfunctional Behaviors in Meetings

Functional Behaviors	Dysfunctional Behaviors
Courteousness	Shaming, criticizing
Problem-solving	Complaining
Inviting collaboration	Stone-walling and interrupting
Exploring mistakes	Making excuses and being defensive
Transparency and authenticity	Manipulating and back-biting
Suggesting constructive action	Rambling and digressing
Clarifying group process	Operating on a self-serving agenda
Attentiveness and hovering focus	Distracting
Speaking incisively and selectively	Withdrawing and disengaging

productivity and feelings about work in general, which, in turn, affects other aspects of life.[18] In any group setting, whether at work or in daily life, these sorts of behaviors either lead to greater collaboration or discouragement. In some cases, there is compelling evidence that permitting "bad" or dysfunctional behavior in meetings contributes to feelings of emotional exhaustion and burnout that bleed into other areas.[19] In addition, anything positive and useful accomplished in a meeting can be overshadowed by the negative energy in the room.

Some Secrets to Leading Far Better Meetings

There are all kinds of tasks for which leaders are formally prepared. They are required to attend courses in finance, decision-making, inventory control, management theory, strategic vision, data analysis, supplemented by other training in specific organizational policies and procedures. But hardly any attention is devoted to the secrets of running meetings in such a way that participants feel satisfied with the *experience*, regardless of the actual goals, agenda, and content. I'm talking about the kind of meeting that is not just efficient and goal directed, but also one in which every voice is heard and respected; when people walk out the door, they feel engaged in the process.

There are a number of practical matters that should be considered, and often implemented, by anyone who wishes to structure meetings in such a way that time is optimized, productivity is increased, and participants are most fully involved with one another. Some of these points may be derived not only from the leadership and organizational behavior literature, but also from all the research related to how people grow, learn, and change as a result of group experiences.

"What are we here for?"

One of the universal rules for holding meetings in successful companies like Google and Apple is to make certain that there is a definite, compelling purpose for taking people away from the important work they are already doing. One firm has a policy to avoid meetings altogether, conducting communications solely via email and messaging, but when a meeting is unavoidable, it upholds the following three rules: (1) Keep it short. Really, *really* short. (2) Have a clear agenda. (3) Invite as few people as possible.[20]

Meetings can be most useful if they do deal with important issues that can't be effectively debated and discussed via messaging and if they lead to closer affiliations and collaborations among team members. The problem is that two-thirds of meetings have no planned agenda, and half of participants consider them a complete waste of time.

On the other hand, there are times when spending relatively unstructured, unscripted time together allows the most creative ideas to come to fruition. The truth is that everyone is so busy and overscheduled all the time, there is little opportunity to talk about issues, exchange thoughts, and share perspectives. That is why sometimes it is a welcome change of pace to have an occasional meeting without an agenda, when participants can draw a breath and interact in a meaningful way, not just about *what* they are doing or accomplishing, but exploring the underlying processes and dynamics related to *how* they work together as a team.

"Do we *really* need to be here?"

Keep in mind that the average amount of time that a human being can sit passively in a room and actually listen attentively is about 25 minutes. After that, daydreams and fantasies intrude; participants start thinking about all the other places they'd rather be, all the things they need to get done, what they want to eat for dinner, how they are going to tell off someone who has angered them, what the person across the room would be like in bed. This holds true as much for lectures as it does for meetings, so that means when any session goes on much longer than a half hour, it is more for the leader's entertainment than because anyone is still listening eagerly.

What does this mean exactly? Whenever practical, participants should be actively engaged instead of sitting mutely in their chairs. It's a good idea to plan breaks occasionally, even if they combine refreshments with assigned tasks. "Okay," one leader instructs participants, "let's take a break for fifteen minutes but during that time I want you to leave your phones in the room and instead team up with someone here you don't know that well and continue the discussion we just began. Come back here with your coffee and at least two observations regarding what you think matters most."

Note the features of this seemingly innocuous announcement: (1) A specific time period was announced; (2) participants are prohibited from using their mobile devices so they remain engaged (very difficult to enforce); (3) they will build a relationship with a team member they don't know well; (4) they are prescribed a task they would do anyway (continue the discussion), but directed to focus on something positive instead of complaints or annoyances; and (5) they are held accountable to return with an outcome. So although it would appear participants are taking a break, they are just continuing the conversation in a different context and setting.

One other thought. Just because staff meetings might be regularly scheduled doesn't mean they can't be abbreviated or even cancelled altogether. Yes, it's good to have regular bonding time to check in with one another, listen and make reports, initiate plans for the next time period, but it is also a waste of time to meet when there is no compelling reason to do so. This is especially the case when in some organizations employees are forced to attend meetings every day, diverting them from all the other overwhelming tasks they need to complete. That may be one reason why 75 percent of participants admit that they do other work while sitting in meetings, and 40 percent disclose they are sometimes so bored, they fall asleep.[21]

Who Should Be Included?

Only those individuals who have the need and can provide significant input ought to be invited. On its meeting agendas, Apple, for example, includes a DRI (Directly Responsible Individual) next to each item. This is the person who will discuss or report on the assigned task, minimizing any confusion about who is in charge of that project or activity.

One advantage of including fewer individuals in a meeting is that it's likely that more will be accomplished and everyone will be more actively involved in the proceedings. When the hourly rate for each participant in a meeting is multiplied together, especially when senior executives are attending, meetings can become ridiculously costly in terms of everyone's time, exceeding tens of thousands of dollars per hour. It's been said that meetings are a great idea—if you don't want to get anything else done.

One counterpoint to this argument was offered to me by an executive who talked about the transparency meetings promoted among employees within his company. Although there are a lot of ups and downs within the trajectory of the firm's progress because of constant changes in legislation and shifting political winds, management still wants everyone to know exactly what's going on at all times. One way they do this is by opening up their weekly Monday morning management meetings to any and all employees who wish to attend. This includes not only those directly part of decision-making teams but also the engineers, legal staff, project developers, even the office assistants and receptionist. It makes for a crowded room, but in this case, the managers believe that such a process better facilitates loyalty and shared commitment to their goals.

What Makes for an Amazing Meeting?

Okay, "amazing" is a little too optimistic, but how about an *interesting* meeting? Looking at groups from the perspective of a leader who is trained as a psychologist, I am particularly attuned to the more subtle, disguised undercurrents of human interaction. I'm also frequently surprised by how often others fail to recognize and respond to phenomena and behavior that appear obvious to me—to understand what group participants are really saying or feeling. I scan the room systematically and frequently, trying to get a sense of what is going on, how each person is responding, what each speaker means by what he or she is communicating, or not communicating.

All human conversations include both content (the surface meaning of the words), as well as an underlying process (deeper, implied meanings, interactive dynamics, unexpressed feelings). For example, someone speaks up in a meeting and states the following content, with the process features in italics:

"It's not that I don't agree with you (*I really disagree with you*), it's just that I think there might be some other options we could consider (*I don't like what you are offering, resent you are in charge, and think that I could do a better job*). When you suggested that we take a few minutes to reflect on alternative courses of action, I think that makes sense (*Actually, I think you are just stalling*). I really respect what you are trying to do with us (*I don't respect you, or what you are doing*). It's just that I wonder if it might be better for us to revisit what we've already been doing (*Since I developed this policy*).

In this instance, duplicity and double-talk occurred because the speaker did not say what he or she really believed. In most cases, however, group members may not realize what is happening in the room in terms of underlying processes and dynamics between and within the members. Leaders who attend to process, as well as the content of discussions, are able to hone in on not just surface communications but also their underlying, deeper meanings. I have seen board meetings led not only by the director who serves an administrative role, but also a "process observer" whose sole job is to name what he or she sees ongoing in the room. Some of the observer's comments might include statements like the following, which are rather simple examples:

> "I notice that so far only four people have been doing most of the talking and others are very quiet, almost invisible."
> "I hear many people agreeing with the decision but there have been very few who have brought up potential hazards of proceeding in this direction."
> "I see several people looking at their watches and seeming impatient right now."
> "After Brooke commented that she didn't feel comfortable sharing her thoughts about this matter, several of you looked at one another and smiled. I'm not sure what that means."

Of course, if the goal is to keep the dialogue solely focused on a content level, just getting through agenda items as fast as possible, zeroing in on process features would prove time-consuming. Our discussion, however, is about what makes a meeting *interesting*. And surely you'd agree that human interactions are far more stimulating when people are challenged to say what they really think and feel instead of just reciting what is expected and desired by whomever is in power. As long as a rule is enforced that interactions between members must remain respectful, such exchanges will not only lead to better outcomes but also more spirited and engaged discussions.

"Thanks for the input, but who else has something to say?"

Some people (including, or *especially*, the leader) talk *way* too much. Other members, who perhaps might have the most valuable contributions, don't talk at all. It's important to balance participation, to invite as many voices as possible, to make everyone feel heard. This means that it is important to cut off rambling, block digressions, refocus discussion, scan and cue members who look like they have something to say. The easy part is to recognize that the dialogue has drifted off topic, or that someone is talking too much; the hard part is intervening in such a way that others don't feel publicly censured or shamed. One recent example occurred in a group in which I was coaching the leader. I noticed that a member was secretly checking his phone for messages while someone else was speaking about something quite personal and emotional. The leader looked at the guy with the phone and said in a somewhat scolding voice, "Would you please put that away?" The intervention was definitely called for, but it stopped the person speaking dead in her tracks. The guy with the phone turned bright red, scooted back his chair, and pouted the rest of the meeting. When we debriefed the incident afterwards, we talked about other ways of blocking that behavior in such a way that it would not result in public humiliation, such as just gently whispering to the person to put away the phone or even speaking to him after the meeting ended. Of course, if the goal was to send a loud and dramatic message to everyone in the room that such behavior would not be tolerated, then a verbal censure does work, even if it has the side effects of sparking resentment and perhaps even retribution.

When studies have been conducted about what leads to maximum productivity and member satisfaction in meetings, the results are fairly consistent: It is mostly about feeling safe to express one's opinion without fear of humiliation and criticism. When everyone in the room feels like they have a voice that is valued, when interruptions are minimized, when the leader clearly demonstrates deep listening skills that are modeled for everyone else, a culture of collaboration flourishes.[22]

What Are the Rules for How We Should Act?

In recent years, there has been increasing research focused on "debugging" human interactions among teams and in meetings, just as has been done by engineers to improve software performance. Google has been a leader in this area, investing a lot of resources into its People Operations Division that is saddled with the responsibility of helping to improve employee satisfaction and performance, not just at work but in their daily lives. Laszlo Bock, the head of this operation, summarized what has been learned from all these investigations of diverse working groups of engineers, sales and marketing staff, software personnel, and every other group within Alphabet, Google's parent organization.[23] It turns out that there were some surprising results that fly in the face of many assumptions among leaders.

The assumption has always been that you need superstars to produce the best work, but it was discovered that fairly average performers would, in fact, rise to the occasion as long as certain norms had been established in meetings, as well as in daily interactions. "You can take a team of average performers," Bock explained, "and if you teach them to interact the right way, they'll do things no superstar could ever accomplish."

So, what is the "right" way?

It turns out that the two overarching themes, mentioned previously, are related to mutual and collective respect and sensitivity among staff, and making sure that everyone's voice is heard, acknowledged, and honored. What's particularly interesting is that it doesn't seem to matter whether the opinions or input were eventually acted on, just as long as members felt that others understood what they were offering. Other norms that were found to be useful, not just in meetings but within teams, are summarized in Box 3-2.

"Please, please, can we end early?"

Always start and end on time in order to reinforce dependable boundaries. Better yet, bring things to a close as soon as business is completed and everyone (who matters) has had their say. People feel as if you value their time and have given them a gift when you let them out early.

"Could you please put that away?"

I know I keep bringing this up, but I suppose that's because hardly anyone actually listens to this research-based advice. If the goal is truly to keep everyone engaged with one another, then it is a good idea to limit phones and mobile devices, or ban them altogether. Use pads and pens if people need to take notes. If the purpose of a meeting is to discuss matters in depth and make decisions, it is best for everyone present to be fully engaged with one another. The only participants who need a device open might be the leader or someone providing specific reports (which are best distributed ahead of time).

BOX 3-2

Norms That Lead to Optimal Outcomes

- Members feel that their voices are heard, acknowledged, and respected.
- People have clearly defined roles, but they are permitted to venture beyond those positions to offer other perspectives.
- Those in attendance (including the leader) avoid interrupting others (except to block incessant rambling or inappropriate digressions).
- The leader (and others) frequently summarize and reflect back what has been heard and understood, both to acknowledge contributions as well as to "reframe" ideas in more palatable or useful form.
- When someone is evidently upset, confused, frustrated, or otherwise emotionally aroused, that person can sometimes be invited to talk about his or her concerns.
- Humor, playfulness, and irreverence are not mere distractions to getting through an agenda—they are essential for creating bonds between and among members.
- Participants should be encouraged to demonstrate sensitivity and caring toward others in the room or within the team.
- Conflicts, disagreements, and competitive behavior should be acknowledged and discussed openly within the group, rather than behind the scenes.
- It should be safe for participants to take risks, make mistakes, and admit what they don't know or understand—without being shamed, ridiculed, or criticized. This starts with the leader modeling such a norm, as well as all others listed here.

It is the scourge of instructors and presenters in this day and age that when audience devices are open, people rarely take notes on anything that is being said. If you should happen to sit in the last row of any lecture at a major university or conference center, such that you can observe everyone's computer or mobile device screen, you will see all kinds of things going on, none of which directly relates to what is supposed to be happening in the room. People occupy themselves reading and sending messages, posting on social media, shopping, watching videos, reading news, following live sports events, and yes, even viewing porn, all the while occasionally looking up to make sure everyone else is doing pretty much the same things.

As I've already mentioned, more than ever new research is demonstrating how easily we are distracted by multitasking and continual interruptions from messages, calls, emails—and meetings.[24] With some workers fielding hundreds of messages per day, and each message costing them several minutes to refocus, we can readily see that performance and quality suffer as a result. Not only are we losing the ability to concentrate on important tasks, our capacity for empathy is being further eroded, not just among our staff, but within our own families. Ironically, while it might seem as if multitasking would relate to greater efficiency, accomplishing more things more quickly, the opposite is frequently the case.[25] This is true whether applied to students doing homework while simultaneously texting, watching television, listening to music, or carrying on conversations, or an executive who is talking on the phone while checking messages and/or reviewing a report.

"Oh, no, is this another slide show?"

I recently sat through a board meeting for which the president prepared a series of detailed, beautifully rendered slides. He distributed them to us ahead of time, so we'd have time to review the information pertaining to budget projections, expense summaries, and strategic plans for the next year. He then spent the whole meeting, every single minute, going through the slides one line at a time. After each slide, he would then ask us if we had any questions.

Complete silence. Everyone was just shuffling papers, doodling on a notepad, not even pretending to hide the fact that we were all reading and sending messages on the devices on our laps.

"Okay, then," he'd say, and continue on to the next slide.

When the board meeting came to an eventual, interminable end 90 minutes later, the president summarized, "Okay, then, outstanding meeting! We accomplished a lot today and I'm very grateful for your help and input."

Yes, he actually said that. Even more incredibly, I'm fairly sure he believed that was the case, that it was an absolutely fabulous meeting because he managed to get through his agenda. There was very little, if any, discussion about anything—and perhaps that was his goal—a filibuster, so he wouldn't have to deal with any issues he couldn't anticipate or control.

But this is not leadership; it is simply managing a situation in such a way as to prevent any meaningful input or conversation. He may have been pleased that he had accomplished his goal, but I know the board members were frustrated by the experience, leading to unrest behind the scenes that would likely take him by surprise some day.

It is for this reason that quite a number of companies and organizations have actually banned slide presentations from meetings, describing them as the "straitjackets to discussion."[26] The Department of Defense, Amazon, and LinkedIn are just a few examples of organizations that have realized that once the lights dim and the slides begin, everyone just checks out. The slides are usually excessive, poorly designed, and often don't offer anything that couldn't have been presented in a summary handout. As we will discuss in a later chapter, one rule of thumb to determine if a slide is actually necessary is to make sure it doesn't contain more than a handful of words that are designed as a talking point, rather than a source of information.

> "What have you done? What are you going to do?
> How and when will you report on the results?"

There is nothing more useless than a meeting in which it is all talk and little, if any, follow-through. In fact, this is one of the most frequent complaints about meetings: They don't necessarily lead to any decision or action plan. Members should leave the meeting with a clear sense of exactly what they are expected to do, when they are supposed to do it, and how they will report what was accomplished, as well as what was not completed or achieved. It is this latter part of feedback that is just as crucial—not to scold, shame, or punish the individual, but rather to learn more about what adjustments should and could be made in the future.

Although our discussion thus far has focused on the secrets to organizing and leading effective meetings, once the proceedings are underway, there are several instances in which an intervention is necessary in order to move things along or accomplish one of the objectives that has been identified. There are some useful guidelines derived from the group psychotherapy literature and practices that can be adapted and applied to almost any setting.[27]

When to Intervene in Meetings—or Any Group

When is it necessary, or at least advisable, to intervene in a meeting or anywhere else, whether on the job or even at a social gathering? Since our goal is to examine leadership within not only a work setting but also other aspects of daily life, there are specific instances when some kind of response is needed, such as when someone talks too much, or engages in other inappropriate behavior.

When I was initially learning group leadership skills, I was so nervous about running my first group that I made a list, a "cheat sheet" of sorts, to help remind me when I needed to do or say something. I wasn't yet certain exactly *what* to do if someone rambled a lot, was disrespectful, or displayed disruptive behavior, but I wanted to catalogue those times when I'd have to do something. I taped on my refrigerator door a list of those times when I wanted to signal to myself that something might be ongoing in the group that would require me to either stop or encourage that action. Over time, I could kind of hear a bell ringing in my head, screaming at me, "Do something! You gotta do something right now!"

Even after all these years of leadership practice, I am still somewhat confused and overwhelmed by all the choices related to precisely what action I should take in any given situation, but I'm fairly certain that *some* intervention is required. The good news, which we will discuss later, is that if you have developed solid relationships with the participants, they will usually forgive awkwardness, mistakes, miscalculations, so if you don't get it right the first (or second) time, you can eventually hone in on the best option.

Rather than studying notes, or the slides I prepared, I watch everyone in the room very, *very* carefully, noting nonverbal behavior and level of engagement. I am constantly scanning the room, collecting data, watching how each person is reacting (or not reacting) to whatever is going on. If I notice someone secretly checking a phone, and that is against our agreed upon rules, then I need to do something—although I'd prefer not to be the one to point that out because I have too much power. When I interrupt someone or point something out, all too often it feels to subordinates as a scolding or censure, which carries undesirable side effects. So instead, one of my favorite strategies is to look around the room and notice who else seems bothered by the action. Then I cue that person.

> "Kyle, I notice you are looking over at Morgan while we were talking. What's going on?"
>
> "Nothing." Shakes his head and averts his eyes, which is the usual response of denial.
>
> "Oh," I say innocently, "I just noticed that you seemed bothered by something when you looked over at him."
>
> "Well, I just noticed that Morgan was. . . ."
>
> Pointing toward Morgan, "Talk to him directly."
>
> "Well, Morgan, I noticed that you were checking your phone and we had agreed we wouldn't do that."

Morgan gets the feedback but hears it from someone within the group who is enforcing normative rules. That is almost always preferred over a censure from the leader.

So, the following paragraphs offer a list of times when it is usually necessary, or at least helpful, for the leader to intervene in some way. This is hardly a definitive catalogue, but rather represents examples of somewhat common instances that require some leader response. Given that every group and context are unique, this list could be amended by deleting those that don't seem appropriate and adding others that might be more useful. Many of these may seem obvious, or even familiar, but this is one of those areas in which leaders don't actually apply what they may think they already understand.

Initiate Check-In and Maintain Focus

One way to ensure that each group member has a voice is to include a brief check-in prior to launching into the business at hand. I consider this such a critical step to include in any group, regardless of setting and context. It takes so little time, whether in a work meeting or at a social event, to just give everyone a chance to say a little something about where their heads (or hearts) are before you commence a more in-depth discussion. This not only helps everyone feel involved but also functions as an initial assessment of everyone's state of mind, not to mention readiness to jump into the proceedings.

Sometimes the worst thing that any group leader can do is to make assumptions about what might be going on without testing those beliefs. Things change. A lot. Especially in people's lives. What seemed important when planning a meeting may no longer be an issue by the time it begins. In addition, it makes little sense to stick with an agenda if there is some major issue circulating within the room that renders everything else significantly less important.

Depending on the number of people present, it may take just a few minutes to go around the room and ask each person to share something meaningful, personal, or interesting. This can involve business-related activities: "Let's have each of you talk briefly about one thing you accomplished since last time." It can also be far more personal: "What is one thing that you are struggling with in your life right now?" or "What is one thing you are feeling especially proud of today?" The mood can be lightened before hard work begins by asking people to disclose the funniest thing they've encountered lately, or the silliest thing they've done recently, or it can also be designed to build greater cohesion and intimacy by asking people to share something important about themselves that nobody else knows.

The goal of such a beginning activity is to give each person a chance to connect with others. It need not require a lot of time and should be seen as an "investment" that results in more accurate data about where others stand in that moment and how they are feeling. It also tends to loosen everyone up, increasing the likelihood that there will be more active participation once business begins.

Review Agenda and Goals

This is standard operating procedure. Unfortunately, reviewing the agenda is often done solely by the leader without input from members. When agendas for a meeting are distributed ahead of time, participants can be asked to suggest other issues that should be considered, as well as to identify those listed that may not be much of a priority.

The main questions we should be asking ourselves, and the participants, prior to beginning any meeting are: What do we want to accomplish before we finish today? What discussions, decisions, resolutions, issues, and outcomes do we want resolved before the meeting is over? Keep in mind that most agendas are far too ambitious and cover too much ground, and too many issues, to be adequately covered in the allotted time; it is far better to narrow discussion to the few items that are most urgent.

Enforce Rules of Respect and Caring Attitudes

I've been in meetings when people scream at one another, when they call one another names, when they accuse each other of being clueless, stupid, or incompetent. I've been in meetings when people roll their eyes in disgust or contempt. I've been in meetings when people have been ridiculed or humiliated or just ignored completely. I've been in meetings when people whisper and snicker to one another while someone is speaking. I've been in meetings when the tension is agonizing.

Granted, there are some individuals who are very difficult to interact with, whose behavior is provocative or hurtful toward others. There are people in meetings who are rude and insensitive. There are certain personalities that are domineering and incredibly self-centered. All true. Nevertheless, one reason leadership is so challenging is because someone has to be in charge of making sure that the environment is safe, that people's rights are protected, that casualties are minimized. This can only happen when there are agreed-upon norms of civil and appropriate behavior and these boundaries are enforced consistently.

Any time someone in the room behaves in ways that communicate insensitivity, incivility, or aggression, it calls for an intervention. I realize that this, in itself, is not exactly normative in many work settings in which employees are actually encouraged to challenge one another. It is not, however, the act of confrontation that is the issue, but rather how it is done. Disagreements, debates, heated discussions are all inevitable, even necessary, but it is imperative that the environment for such interactions remains supportive and respectful or else people shut down.

When the leader must intervene in almost any of these situations, the most difficult challenge is how to do so in a way to block inappropriate behavior, but without leading to resentments and retribution. I wish I had some easy advice about the best course to follow, but frankly, this is an area in which I don't exactly shine. Because of my age and position of power, all it takes is a blank look directed toward someone to send that person off into a fit of shame. As careful, sensitive, and diplomatic as I try to be when cutting someone off or redirecting his or her behavior, I still witness this individual's withdrawal and feeling of hurt. It would be easy to write this off as his or her problem because the person is so oversensitive and personalizes everything, but I prefer to deal with lingering negative feelings in a private conversation. I'm also not shy about apologizing if I was perceived as too strident or critical—even when I don't believe that was the case.

Cut Off Distractions or Digressions

This is worth mentioning a second time because leaders are often so neglectful when managing the flow of interaction. If you are scanning the room, reading nonverbal behavior, tracking the distribution of input, then there is plenty of incoming data from which to draw out those who have been silent and to block excessive speakers. This is also one of those leadership skills that translates quite well to application in the everyday world since some people talk *way* too much, repeat themselves endlessly, and tell the same stories over and over. People do this for a variety of different reasons that could represent dominance ("I'm more important than you"), narcissism ("I'm so interesting that I love to hear myself talk—and you love it too"), or simply forgetfulness ("Did I tell you this before? Maybe you'd like to hear it again?"). In any case, it is the leader's job to balance participation whenever a group of people are together so that every person feels valued.

When it's time to redirect discussion, or intervene when someone is repeating him- or herself or disproportionately controlling the conversation, it takes all one's tactful skills to do so in such a way that the person will not feel shamed. It's easy to just say to someone, "I think we've heard enough from you right now," or "Let's hear from someone else since you've been talking for quite a while," which will effectively shut the person up, but at the expense of perhaps feeling censured. There is also the danger in any group setting that when one person is cut off, others will vicariously identify with the "victim." In other words, even when people are really annoyed with someone who is acting out in all kinds of ways, if the leader should "wound" this person for the greater good of the group, participants may still feel that individual's pain or humiliation.

One favored method for cutting off rambling or digressions involves reflecting the content of what is being said, strategically inserted during the filibuster.

> ". . . .and then, as I was telling you, I just think that we are moving too slowly to take advantage of this situation. It presents this wonderful opportunity that we must capitalize on. It reminds me of that time that I was. . . ."

> "So, Caitlyn, we appreciate that reminder about how important it is to limit our caution and hesitation so we are best positioned to move quickly. Who else has some ideas about that? Trent, I notice you looked like you had something you wanted to say."

In this brief intervention, the leader accomplished several things at the same time. The person who was rambling was clearly forced to stop. Hopefully, this was done in such a way that she felt like her main message was received and heard, as demonstrated by the summary statement. Others in the room were invited to join in, helping to distribute the input more equitably.

Model Appropriate Ways of Being

This is one of the main themes of the book, that we should be the kind of person we wish others to be, not just by what we say but how we treat others. This is especially the case with respect to how we function in meetings since it is often the main and only venue in which we are public figures. Followers watch us carefully for all kinds of reasons—to discover how we really feel about them, to predict and anticipate our behavior, to win our approval, to seek guidance about what actions they should take. They scrutinize us for any sign of our innermost reactions. A smile, a frown, a puzzled expression all indicate our personal reactions.

I'm not suggesting that we necessarily have to guard against being transparent and authentic, although a certain degree of caution and self-control is appropriate. It is important, however, that we demonstrate compassion, caring, and respect in our interactions with others, especially in group settings. Even though the public image of many prominent CEOs and leaders is of individuals who are domineering, autocratic, frightening in their countenance and aggressive behavior, this is not ideal for most of the rest of us who depend on loyalty and support to get our jobs done. If you've already got a billion dollars, own your company outright, and only care about productivity rather than employee morale and satisfaction, then you can be and do anything you want. However, for those of us who do sincerely want followers to enjoy their work, who hold certain values that we believe are good for others, that objective begins with our own behavior. If we want people to feel comfortable admitting what they don't know and understand, then we have to be prepared to do the same thing. If we want people to be open and honest, then we have to show others that path. If we want people to aim for the highest goals but also be forgiving when they fall short, recalibrating to more attainable objectives, then we have to do the same thing.

Stop Complaining

I once worked as a junior high school counselor and learned very quickly that the last place I ever wanted to hang out was the teachers' lounge. All everyone seemed to do there was whine about being overworked and underpaid—the usual. They were unhappy about their lack of resources, the quality of students, administrative policies, and especially available staff parking. It was discouraging, especially for someone just starting his career with bursting enthusiasm.

I've had a rule ever since then to circumvent, as much as possible, any attempt by anyone to complain about something we can't do anything about. Growing up in the Midwest, I could never figure out why people spent so much time complaining about how cold the winter was since that's just what the weather is like there at that time of year, and there's nothing we can do to change it. Likewise, when discussion devolves into complaints about budget cutbacks, business climate, economic conditions, political gridlock, government regulations, on and on and on, I immediately jump in to reframe the issue in a configuration that increases the likelihood that we can have an impact on the result.

When someone in a meeting says, "We can't do that," I immediately react inside my head with, "Why not?" or "Who says?" And then I start considering a number of ways we could circumvent the limitation, or adapt the rule, or challenge why some option is really off the table. The result of such reflection is that rather than argue with someone about a limited vision, instead I agree—with a twist. "You're right of course, we aren't supposed to do that." Then I pause. "But what if we *could* do that? I wonder what that would entail? And I'm just curious about what that would mean?"

Regardless whether such a query leads to a reversal of the perceived prohibition, I prefer to change the nature of the discussion from a complaint about the way things are to a vision of the way things could be. That, by the way, is the formula for any inspiring speech (think Martin Luther King's "I Have a Dream" speech, Abraham Lincoln's Gettysburg Address, and Steve Jobs' introduction of the iPod).[28]

Reflect Feelings and Content

The most commonly employed intervention of a psychotherapist is a deceptively simple skill that demonstrates you not only heard clearly what someone said, but also understood its meaning. You prove to whomever was speaking that what they were saying was acknowledged and its deeper meanings reflected back. This accomplishes several different tasks at the same time. First of all, it validates someone's experience—which always feels affirming. It also helps the person to express deeper feelings that would not necessarily be evident at a superficial level. It shows everyone in the room that you care deeply about what they are offering, as well as making linkages between others' statements and identifying salient themes. Given that such a relatively basic response can do so much, that's why therapists rely on this intervention more than half the time. It looks and sounds something like the following conversation in a meeting, reflecting both the content of what is said as well as the underlying feelings.

"I know some of you might disagree with this, but it might be good, you know, if we invited some of the other units to collaborate on this project so we don't get stuck with all the responsibility."

"You have some concerns about whether we can handle this on our own." *(Reflection of content)*

"Well, yes. Don't you?"

"It seems a bit scary that this could all fall apart on our watch and then you would be the one stuck cleaning up the mess." *(Reflection of underlying feeling)* "Monica, this is related to an earlier point that you raised about how we even determine whether the project succeeds or not." *(Drawing a connection and identifying a theme)*

"I do agree with what you're saying. We could be the ones stuck holding the ball at the end of the game."

"You are also feeling apprehensive about what we are planning but I also sensed earlier that you were excited about the possibilities." *(Reflection of feeling and summary of content)*

If this looks and sounds familiar, it's because this is called "active listening," the technique by which a variety of different helping professionals (including parents, teachers, coaches, leaders, counselors) engage others in deeper conversations about issues. This is, in many respects, an almost magical way to respond to people, to anyone in any situation, that shows them clearly that you are listening with all your being. And it's fairly rare these days, with all the distractions and intrusions from mobile devices and technology, that anyone ever feels like they have someone's undivided, completely focused attention. When you can reflect back to others what you heard them say, and do so at a level that uncovers unexpressed, or more subtle, feelings, you earn their loyalty and appreciation.

Among all the skills, techniques, and interventions mentioned in this book, this is the one that has the most universal appeal in *every* aspect of your life, in every situation you might find yourself in. A family member is telling you about something that happened during the day and you make a choice, a conscious, deliberate effort, to put everything else aside and attend fully and completely to the conversation, reflecting back to the person not only what you hear but also what you sense and feel from him or her. Like anything else in life, it takes practice to integrate this habit into daily interactions, remembering to (1) listen carefully and deeply to what someone is saying; (2) pause to ask yourself what the person is really communicating, both on the surface and at a deeper level; (3) reflect back what you heard and understand to communicate this deep listening and acknowledgment.

Shift from Discussion to Action

Talking is good—within certain limits. There is a point when it is time to move forward to action: specific, definable, accountable action. After discussing a plan of action that includes incremental steps, measurement outcomes, and clear desired objectives, meetings flounder if there are not realistic ways to transform the vision into a reality.

Just as every meeting can begin with a brief check-in, each session can end with a check-out that might address questions such as the following:

- "How are you feeling about what we've done today?"
- "What are you going to do between now and our next scheduled meeting?"
- "What concerns do you have that were not yet mentioned but that you think would be important to put on the agenda for next time?"
- "What are you taking with you from the meeting that seems most interesting or useful?"

It's the second question, in particular, that hones in on accountable actions and makes certain that talk really does lead to action, justifying the actual productive value of the meetings. And yet, this emphasis on action must be balanced with respect for the underlying process ongoing in the room. There are all kinds of subtle and disguised dynamics going on, the so-called *meta-communication* that reveals what people are *really* thinking and feeling, rather than what they are actually saying—or *not* saying.

Summarize or Draw Closure

This chapter comes to an end, just like a meeting, and you are left wondering what this all means, what you can take with you and hold on to. There are so many books like this that you've encountered before that seemed to offer something valuable, even transformative, but now you can't quite remember what that might be. Likewise, meetings end. People return to their offices, cubicles, cars, homes, or lives, and wonder what happened and what to do with it. There is usually far more going on in the room, or in the videoconference, than meets the eye. There were all kinds of interesting dynamics operating; people signaling one another; strange, inexplicable tension; confusing interactions; things you didn't quite grasp or understand.

It is important that people leave a meeting (or a chapter) with a sense of what was presented that might be most significant. In the case of our conversation with one another during the last dozen or more pages, there is just one enduring message that I'd like you to remember, to internalize and make part of your style. It isn't necessarily related to any of the skills or interventions that were highlighted, but rather has to do with one overarching theme: Work groups or team meetings are organic processes—they are ever-changing. Most of the action that is really taking place occurs behind the scenes and inside people's heads and hearts when they are no longer in a public forum. How we respond to others, how we lead them, depends on factors that go way beyond our own agenda and preferences. In order to be maximally responsive to others, we have to develop a sense of exactly where they are in the first place, in addition to where we would like them to go next.

It is also important to point out that meetings, in themselves, are not just the dreaded scourge of most executives; it's their excessive frequency that appears to matter most, as well as how they are managed.[29] When meetings are (1) scheduled only when absolutely necessary, (2) limited to those who have a direct role in the proceedings, (3) organized in such a way that all participants have a chance to speak, (4) led in such a way that there are spirited discussions, and (5) directed to some definable decisions or actions by their conclusion, employees not only tolerate such gatherings but actually look forward to them because of the opportunities for interaction.

Like most things in business, and in life, it isn't what we do that matters, but how well we do it. The most frustrating and disappointing conclusions from all the research on meeting effectiveness is that most people are aware of sound practices that maximize productivity and engagement, but don't actually apply what they know.

PART II

How Leaders Try—and Usually Fail—to Make a Difference

4

Personal Qualities of Leaders

A FEW SIMPLE THINGS THAT MAKE
ALL THE DIFFERENCE

LEADERS COME IN all kinds of flavors, shapes, and sizes. Some are outgoing and overtly charismatic, others low key and reflective. There have been leaders in the mold of Abraham Lincoln, somewhat withdrawn and glum, and others like Lyndon Johnson, who was famously gregarious and playful. Johnson enjoyed playing hide-and-seek with his Secret Service agents, challenging them to find him. Then there was Calvin "Silent Cal" Coolidge, who was a man of such few words that guests at White House dinner parties would place bets on who could make him talk.

The differences among great leaders are reflected in not only their personalities but also their assigned roles embedded within particular environmental and cultural contexts.[1] There are charismatic leaders we hear so much about, for instance, the Dalai Lama, Nelson Mandela, Franklin Roosevelt, Oprah Winfrey, and Mother Teresa, who operate more as spiritual figures than in executive roles. There are ideological leaders driven by a strong, inflexible agenda, such as Fidel Castro, Steve Jobs, or filmmaker Michael Moore. Then there are pragmatic leaders, such as Warren Buffett, Bill Gates, and Harry Truman, who tailored their strategies to align with whatever approach circumstances dictated. Each style can be identified by the ways in which these leaders communicated their visions to followers, whether focused on the future (charismatic), personal values (ideological), or measurable outcomes (pragmatic).

Even though the particular qualities embedded in their personalities may differ significantly, one consistent theme is that the best leaders have developed a personal style that capitalizes on their own strengths, priorities, and abilities while minimizing their liabilities. They learned some relatively simple lessons early in their careers and invested the time and effort to transform them into signature characteristics of their leadership style.

Lyndon Johnson was supremely skilled in being able to read what others wanted most and then used that ability to dominate, cajole, and persuade them to do his bidding. Other presidential leaders made the best of their strengths while trying to curtail their weaknesses. Ronald Reagan struggled with Alzheimer's disease and significant memory problems during his final years in office, and compensated for these deficits by sticking to prepared scripts as much as possible. Likewise, Franklin Roosevelt never allowed himself to be photographed in a wheelchair, fearing that people would lose confidence in him if they saw their president in a physically diminished state. He even pretended to walk to podiums, swinging his hips back and forth, as two aides at his side would carry him by his elbows.

Before we delve into leaders' differences, though, it's also important to recognize how the images of most traditional leaders, whether in politics or business, have been "filtered" and are relatively homogeneous, with the leaders almost being interchangeable in terms of their background and experience. Most presidential candidates, for instance, have been far more alike than different. They attended the same Ivy League schools, usually served as governors or senators, tended to hold moderate beliefs, and were endorsed by party elites.[2] This convention has certainly changed most recently, which is a clear sign that the populace has tired of the same familiar templates.

Moments of Greatness

All leadership moments are hardly created equal. Most of the time, we are operating on autopilot, doing the things that seem to come naturally even though they represent skills and experience honed over time and tested under fire. Nevertheless, we become comfortable, if not complacent, in the management of daily responsibilities. Then there comes a time when we must step up in ways we never have before—a new challenge or a novel or recurring crisis. This is what Robert Quinn refers to as "moments of greatness," those opportunities when we must rise to the occasion.[3]

Many years ago, Mihaly Csikszentmihalyi introduced the concept of "flow" to refer to the state of transcendence when we function at optimal levels.[4] World-class athletes or performers achieve this altered state of consciousness when they are able to totally immerse themselves in the moment in a kind of effortless way. He first became aware of this phenomenon while listening to rock climbers, chess players, surgeons, or recreational athletes describe their transcendent experiences that seemed to become magical moments of achievement. Everything seems to be "flowing" along at peak performance, yet without conscious effort. Once you stop to consider questions like "Gee, maybe I should do this next?" or "What would happen if I tried to do this?," some interesting rational insights may indeed ensue, but this is not "flow" in the sense that you are reaching a moment of greatness.

Csikszentmihalyi reported one example of flow in which a surgeon had been engaged in a complex procedure when an earthquake rocked the city. The operating room started to shake, with objects falling to the floor, and even the ceiling partially collapsing. The surgical staff fled the room in terror. But the surgeon had been so engrossed in the operation, so focused on what he was doing, that he didn't notice what had happened at all. It was only after he completed the surgery that he looked around and wondered what had happened.

Whether we are talking about leadership, or another high-level performance-based ability, sometimes there are these special, transcendent moments when we actually lose ourselves in an activity. This can most easily happen when you become immersed in a film or a book or a conversation, but also takes place during ordinary moments when you completely focus on what you are doing without conscious thought. Things are just humming along at remarkable speed and you're producing extraordinary results. And once you stop to think about what is happening, the flow abruptly stops. It is a process that requires you, to a certain extent, to just let go and trust the way you are responding. This is the moment when we may achieve true moments of greatness, whether involved in leading others or anything else that we do.

The conditions under which these extraordinary moments occur are more likely to take place during times of transition or a novel challenge when any customary and usual strategies would not be appropriate or useful. You are forced to abandon what you think you already know and move from a more externally based framework in which you listen to advisers, colleagues, and books like this, and instead transition to a more internally based system that relies on your own intuition. Somehow, instinctively, you seem to know what to do even if you can't quite explain it.

One excellent example of this surrender to flow is the improvisation that accompanies playing jazz. "Jazz is smooth and cool," relates actor and musician Nat Wolff, who as a young boy watched his father performing. "Jazz is rage. Jazz flows like water. Jazz never seems to begin or end. Jazz isn't methodical, but jazz isn't messy either. Jazz is a conversation, a give and take. Jazz is the connection and communication between musicians. Jazz is abandon."

For those of us who worship at the altar of order, structure, and predictability, this might seem at odds with the impulsiveness, spontaneity, and unscripted improvisation that results in great jazz, but I speak of those rare moments of greatness when the gods, fate, or the marketplace opens up the skies in a huge storm, with no immediate safe shelter in sight. This is a time when we become less focused on ourselves and more focused on those we serve. And it is a time when we witness a new part of ourselves in action, or discover something quite simple that makes all the difference in our performance.

Flamboyant Leadership and the Force of Personality

There is a clear consensus that certain personality traits in a leader are more important than others, although considerable debate has occurred regarding which ones matter the most. Although everyone more or less agrees that social and emotional intelligence are highly desirable, even those attributes are up for debate when you consider that some extraordinary military, political, or corporate leaders have been incredibly narcissistic, autocratic, and domineering, at times totally oblivious to the needs of others.

During various times throughout history, leadership has been conceived as a function of particular, and quite different, personal traits. Lao-tzu believed that those who hold others' welfare in their hands should be, above all else, selfless, honest, and fair in their actions. Homer depicted the leaders in the *Iliad* and *Odyssey* as heroic, courageous, fearless characters who were willing to risk their own lives in order to serve a greater good. Plato instead emphasized that leaders should make wisdom and reasoning the centerpiece of their behavior. Aristotle, in turn, focused on virtue, while Machiavelli offered a counterargument that wielding power was most important, and had no qualms if this involved manipulation and absolute control. And so in every culture, during any era, whether among the Babylonians, Egyptians, or Vikings, there were some rather clear visions of what qualities were essential in leaders.[5]

This search for optimal traits was actually the prevailing model for centuries. It was assumed that certain kinds of personalities were better suited for leadership than others. Of course, it makes sense that someone who is timid, shy, fearful, and hesitant, or perhaps insensitive and overbearing, would not be well received by followers or inspiring to them. After considerable debate, not only among ancient philosophers but also contemporary scholars, it would appear as if there are indeed three main attributes that distinguish great leaders from poor ones.[6]

1. *Self-confidence.* It certainly makes sense that others are more inclined to follow leaders who believe in themselves and their vision. They are calm under pressure, skilled at controlling their emotions, and exude a sense of self-efficacy.
2. *Proactive spirit.* They are often described as optimistic, hopeful, and enthusiastic. They are viewed as flexible and pragmatic in order to get things done. They are conscientious and dependable in following through on commitments, characterized as men and women of action.
3. *Relational capacity.* They inspire loyalty in their followers, who feel a commitment to not only a cause but also the leaders themselves. Although there are notable exceptions, more often than not such leaders are experienced as agreeable, sensitive, and empathic—at least among those who manage to hold on to their positions of power for some time through means other than dominance and control.

Nevertheless, leadership is an interactive phenomenon that depends on not just a leader's personality traits but also the characteristics of his or her followers and other contextual considerations. It is also interesting how the so-called Big Five Traits are sometimes a mixed blessing.[7] *Being agreeable* is often appreciated, for instance, because people prefer leaders who arc altruistic, caring, respectful, sensitive, and supportive, but such individuals may also be conflict avoidant or reluctant to make tough decisions because they value harmony over challenging the status quo. *Emotional stability* is also highly valued in leaders but may restrain one's passion and persuasive ability to influence others. *Extraversion* is often prized because of its association with being energetic, enthusiastic, and inspirational, but this trait may compromise self-reflection and lead more often to interpersonal conflict because of perceived aggression. In other words, it isn't so much which qualities you have that are important as much as how you adapt and use them to match what is most needed in any situation or environment. What works well as an officer in the Marines would not necessarily be appropriate or useful working at Google or Toyota.

Although it is certainly true that charismatic, flamboyant leaders get a lot of press, and appointing such an individual to a position of prominence might temporarily increase a company's stock value and public image, it is actually somewhat of a myth that personality traits are necessarily the driving force of greatness. It turns out that while we might love the powerful simplicity of attributing the success of someone like Steve Jobs to his charisma, it is far more likely that it was his "thoughtful involvement in every step of an unusually expansive leadership process" that was significant.[8] He became involved in collecting voluminous intelligence about his competition and rivals, recruited and assembled teams of the best and brightest, meticulously planned and implemented innovative product development and distribution. In other words, it was *in spite of his personality,* rather than because of it, that he and his companies were successful.

Researchers have settled on a consensus regarding which personal qualities tend to get leaders in trouble the most, and the findings are not all that surprising. Those who are overly excitable, moody, intense, and emotionally volatile drive others crazy. Leaders who value boldness and risk-taking above all else may do so because of unrealistic self-confidence and grandiosity, accompanied by an unwillingness to recognize mistakes. Leaders who are unusually diligent, precise, inflexible, and perfectionists create all kinds of problems for others who don't operate exactly the same way. Whereas extreme manifestations of any one characteristic might create difficulties for a leader and the task at hand, a middle road is usually far more desirable.[9]

An excessively visionary leader may hold strong beliefs about the goals of the organization that can compromise valuable input from others and insulate him or her against needed criticism. But at the other end of the continuum, a lack of vision would signal an absence of imagination and initiative. Similarly, being too bold can get one in trouble quickly, but so can being extremely timid and risk avoidant. There are thus optimal levels of each trait along a continuum.[10] Many of these differences are evident when examining the distinctive leadership styles of prominent political figures.

Leadership Style Among U.S. Presidents: A Study of Extremes

In many ways, it is surprising how different leaders can operate according to their own personal styles. When we consider those who have served in the highest office in the land, we see just how varied those styles have been, depending on early upbringing, life experiences, personality traits, interpersonal skills, core values, family and social support, and a host of other variables.

Even if there are certain commonalities in the personalities of U.S. presidents, in terms of self-confidence and a sense of driving ambition, huge differences have also existed.[11] Ironically, two presidents who couldn't have appeared to be more different—Lyndon Johnson and Richard Nixon—were a lot alike, at least with regard to their dominant personalities. There were strong introverts like John Adams, Woodrow Wilson, and Calvin Coolidge, as well as those philosophically inclined such as Thomas Jefferson and Jimmy Carter. There have been "performers" on stage like Ronald Reagan, Warren Harding, and Donald Trump. And there were the gregarious, bigger-than-life personalities such as Teddy Roosevelt and his cousin Franklin Roosevelt. Many of the presidents can be grouped according to those personality traits that were most dominant in their leadership style. For example, whereas Gerald Ford, Ronald Reagan, Ike Eisenhower, George Bush (1 and 2), and Barack Obama were considered quite emotionally stable, there were neurotic personalities as exemplified by Richard Nixon, Lyndon Johnson, John Quincy Adams, and Donald Trump. Some presidents were inclined to be introspective (Coolidge, Hoover, Wilson) or philosophical (Jefferson, Lincoln, Carter), whereas others were considered extroverts (T. Roosevelt, Clinton, Nixon) or highly pragmatic (Jackson, Truman, Grant). Some were characterized as highly agreeable (Harding, Lincoln, Carter, G. W. Bush, Obama) and others as very stubborn and inflexible (Nixon, Johnson, F. Roosevelt, Trump). It therefore appears that no single personality profile is *necessarily* optimal.

Even among the extreme differences, there are still certain predictors of who is likely to be most successful in the job. Not surprisingly, it takes a certain intelligence to hold the highest office, and indeed, most of those elected tend to be in intellectual terms very smart and curious (some more so than others). Also obvious is that such individuals would have to be extremely driven and ambitious to tolerate all the annoyances and sacrifices required to run for office, the favors traded, and deals that are made. As such, they tend to be extremely competent in organizing their staff, or at least know enough to recruit skilled partners during this process. They are also generally emotionally stable, having learned along the way to avoid brooding too much or holding grudges; they let go of things that they can't control and move on to others that are within their power to influence or change.

The lessons learned from a study of the presidency is that great leaders learn to compensate for their weaknesses and build on their strengths. Some of the greatest presidents, for example, were not great communicators or public speakers at first. When Franklin Roosevelt delivered some of his early speeches, audiences were distracted by the slow pace of his delivery. When

John Kennedy first entered Congress, his public speaking was quite weak. Ronald Reagan didn't find his stride as an impromptu orator until his acting career abruptly ended and, to earn a living, he had to rebrand himself as a public speaker. On the other hand, George H. W. Bush was very aware he was not the most charismatic speaker, so he figured out ways to use the press briefing room to present key policies and instructed his speechwriters to keep the prose simple and clear.[12]

Among all the attributes of successful presidents, chief among them was their emotional resilience, their ability to recover from setbacks and disappointments. They were either relatively free from psychological problems and seemingly unperturbed by the stressful demands of the job (Eisenhower, Ford, Bush 2, Obama), or else they developed ways to compartmentalize their negative feelings and emotional difficulties in such a way that it did not much affect their job performance (FDR, Truman, Kennedy, Reagan). Then there were others who were subject to wild mood swings (LBJ, Trump), extreme rigidity (Carter), impulsivity (Clinton, Trump), memory impairment (Reagan), or depression (Lincoln, Nixon), and yet still found ways to function reasonably effectively in spite of their personal challenges (with some exceptions). Thus, great leaders can be flawed and imperfect, even emotionally vulnerable and oversensitive, as long as they are well aware of these limitations and have developed coping strategies to compensate for them.

Leadership Has Evolved

The conception of what constitutes a good leader has significantly evolved over time, not just as measured by centuries but even decades.[13] Prior to the 1980s, the operative concepts concerned the wise and judicious use of power and dominance, stereotypical values of masculinity. During the 1990s, there was far more emphasis on the bottom line, what leaders could do to cut expenses, increase productivity and profit, increase customer satisfaction, all outcome driven. At the turn of the 21st century, the emphasis shifted toward issues related to creativity, innovation, agility, and also personal integrity. This was influenced by some of the disastrous mistakes of leaders who engaged in fraudulent or dishonest practices, as well as the technology industries that required a very different kind of stewardship than traditional corporate structures. Since the early 2000s, there has been a recalibration once again, keeping integrity at the forefront along with a sense of fairness coupled with toughness, although this, too, is evolving in more recent years. In summary, just like everything else in life, things change—and unless leaders are prepared to evolve to meet the rapid shifts in what their jobs require, they will be left behind.

So many industries that were popular not too long ago are now obsolete after long runs of prosperity. Just think about all the once commonplace items that have been shoved aside over the last decade: fax machines, printed catalogues, photographic film, maps, pay phones, VCRs, DVDs, CDs. What's next? Newspapers? Paper? Laptop computers? A printed book like the one you may be holding in your hand? How does one adapt to such frequent changes in technology, consumer demands, and cultural shifts?

One answer to questions like this is to treat our assumptions and knowledge as time-limited. Whereas once upon a time, we could expect that our tools and everyday knowledge would remain consistent and dependable throughout a lifetime, nowadays every few years whatever we have come to rely on is replaced with some new gadget, software update, or theory that renders previous functioning obsolete.

Likewise, the kind of personality that would have worked well for a presidential (or corporate) leader a century or two ago is no longer optimal in today's climate. One presidential scholar mentions several examples of how things have changed since the early days of the republic when presidents weren't required to make public speeches since all the action took place in back rooms.[14] You'd expect, for example, that George Washington must have had charisma in spades considering he successfully led our troops during the Revolution. In fact, Washington was rather timid and shy, neither particularly charming nor outgoing. Indeed, all the earliest presidents—Adams, Jefferson, Monroe, and Madison—were well below average in the charisma department. It wasn't until Andrew Jackson, and especially FDR, that passion and charisma became crucial attributes. Many of our latter-day public officials like Kennedy, Johnson, Reagan, Clinton, Obama, and Trump were all about charisma, which is associated with greater success in issuing executive orders. Nowadays, it sometimes appears that charisma and exuberant charm seem to be more important than other abilities, like relevant qualifications and domain expertise that would be crucial for the job. It is also the case that our earliest presidents, who were focused on making deals behind the scenes, would never be elected today.

Given the ever-changing nature of the environment, marketplace, culture, technology, organizational demands, even the climate, what is required for accomplished leaders to succeed is constantly a moving target. Yet there are still a few things that remain much the same—in particular, a certain clarity about the ways in which overconfidence and arrogance can lead to disasters.

The Dangers of Hubris

Throughout the history of human mythology, legends, literature, and seminal events, there is no attribute that has contributed more often to catastrophe than when a hero or heroine displays hubris. This is the classic tragic flaw so prevalent in Greek mythology, such as when Oedipus defies the gods' prophecies and pays the price. Likewise, military leaders with excessive hubris such as Napoleon and Hitler both made the same mistake of invading Russia, ignoring the advice of commanders, thereby dooming their armies as a result of overconfidence. In 1812, Napoleon commanded an army of a half million troops, the largest such mobilization in history, and yet these numbers were not nearly enough to compensate for his unbridled arrogance. Only 5 percent of his army survived the invasion of Russia, one of the worst military disasters in history led by the world's greatest military genius who took himself way too seriously.

Leaders in any field who get carried away by their single-minded goal or mission, and refuse to look clearly at the impact of their behavior, end up in a lot of trouble. We also see this among many celebrities whose fame and pride clouded their ability and willingness to honestly assess the consequences of their behavior. A number of well-known actors, professional athletes, and politicians have watched helplessly as their careers tanked, completely unaware (or unconcerned) that they came across as self-involved jerks.

The hubris syndrome kicks in when a leader, first of all, has enjoyed some previous success, perhaps in a quite different arena. This results in a sense of pride and overconfidence in the leader's own abilities and intuition, as well as underestimating uncertainties and other variables. There is also a common misattribution of the reasons why past successes have been achieved, with the leader believing that they are solely the result of his or her own actions, rather than the contributions of external or random variables. Under such circumstances, leaders are seduced into thinking there are relatively simple explanations for, and solutions to, very complex problems.

Once a hubristic leader makes a decision, or initiates an action, based on misguided intuition that is both unreliable and invalid, while discounting input from multiple sources of information, a cascade of problems often follows. Such leaders become grooved into obsolete, limited thinking that forecloses more creative or innovative options; they stick with what is familiar and comfortable since it worked in the past (or they believe this is the case).

In the next stage of the hubris syndrome, the president, CEO, or coach begins to believe in his or her own omnipotence and infallibility, perpetuated

by romantic images in the media that promote a mystique of heroic invinci-
bility.[15] Naturally, this also leads to significantly distorted, exaggerated, and
wildly inaccurate assessments of what is realistic or possible. Once such an
inflated sense of self is in place, it is frequently followed by discounting the
opinions of, and input from, others who may be in a better (or different) position to perceive reality. The most disturbing aspect of this destructive pattern
is that the hubristic leader will not only surround him- or herself with advisers who agree with and support the current path, but when contradictory or
alternative opinions are suggested, they are immediately disqualified.

It's almost always interesting—and revealing—to look at gender differences in the ways that leaders operate in the world, especially given the somewhat specialized gifts that men and women enjoy. These are not simply the
result of cultural indoctrination and socialized roles that shape different styles
of interaction and leadership, but are also the result of biological processes.
Given the relatively small number of women (less than 1 percent) who attain
positions of great power, such as a general officer in the military, a CEO of a
Fortune 500 company, or a U.S. senator, it is useful to speculate what might
shift if more women were awarded such responsibilities—or if more male
leaders were to adopt a more androgynous style that capitalized on the relative strengths of both genders.

Evolution has programmed men, and especially males in leadership positions at the pinnacle of power, with abnormally high levels of testosterone,
the hormone most associated with aggression, dominance, and unbridled
hubris. It has been demonstrated that violent criminals are fueled with unusually high levels flooding through their systems. But what is less well known is
that male leaders, who also score high in this dimension, are prone to greater
impulsivity, misguided or dangerous risk taking, delusional optimism in the
face of contradictory evidence, and are less likely to alter direction in light
of significant feedback that signals a serious error in judgment. They tend
toward a degree of arrogance, overconfidence, and narcissism that blinds
them to recognizing their mistakes, much less ever correcting them. They see
themselves as infallible, unwilling to acknowledge that they are anything less
than omnipotent.[16]

Six months into Donald Trump's term of office, after securing the lowest
approval rating in modern history for a new U.S. president, after miscalculat-
ing repeatedly in his selection of staff, policy decisions, and impulsive social
media proclamations and threats, he announced: "With the exception of the
late, great Abraham Lincoln, I can be more presidential than any president
that's ever held this office."

Regardless of one's political affiliation, or assessment of the 45th U.S. president, it must be acknowledged that it is very difficult to learn from one's mistakes, or change direction from an ineffective leadership style, without an honest and accurate reading of what is working best and what is not working at all. Leaders demonstrating excessive hubris are also at a distinct disadvantage when they rely only on the stereotypical qualities of their gender. Thus, female leaders are expected to be communal, nurturing, and sensitive, while male leaders are supposed to be aggressive, domineering, and strong in the sense of being overpowering. In the words of one political columnist, Trump's greatest liability is being "trapped in a caricature of masculinity that corrodes his judgment."[17]

Access to Accurate and Reliable Information

Knowledge is everything. Knowledge about who is doing what to whom. Knowledge about what people are saying when you are not around. Knowledge about what people like most—and what they don't like at all. Knowledge about who are the best sources of accurate and reliable information. Knowledge about whom you can trust and who has your back. And knowledge about who has a knife, ready to stab you in the back.

Frequently, a leader's job is to try and predict the future. How much inventory do you need? Should you hire more staff or let some employees go? What will your competitors do next? What's the next hot commodity? If you take some particular action, what will its ultimate result be? What is the more reliable economic forecast? Are interest rates on their way up or down? What is going to be the price of oil? We survive or fail based on our ability to make decisions based on probabilities and uncertainties—and these are based on the assumptions that we hold, which may or may not be valid depending on the information at our disposal.

Having knowledge is also quite different from knowing how to use it most effectively. This depends, in part, on how well you can make sense of the data, interpret their most salient features, and decode underlying patterns that reveal significant information. One of the most interesting challenges for a leader these days is how to make sense of the overwhelming flood of data that flows in every day, every hour, and every minute. There are reports, statistics, economic forecasts, production figures, publications, social media, gossip, rumors, innuendos, overheard conversations, plus the usual barrage of personal emails, texts, tweets, and phone calls. There are primary sources, which may or may not be accurate and reliable, as well as secondary and tertiary conduits. There is "truth" and also "fake news." Then, once we collect all this information, how do we know what is most significant and useful?

During emergency or crisis situations, whether on the battlefield or in the office, the most frequent problem is not a dearth of information, but rather too much incoming data, with great uncertainty about what is most relevant and potentially helpful. In such situations, there is a natural tendency to freeze and foreclose on additional evidence for the sake of (over)simplifying the situation.[18] The mind literally closes off potential options that might be considered, and one has a tendency to just grab the nearest, easiest, or most obvious path in order to cease the agony of "second-guessing ourselves into a state of paralysis."[19]

In a study about the underlying thought processes of leaders, it was discovered, perhaps not surprisingly, that U.S. presidents accessed their information in very different ways.[20] Whereas George W. Bush claimed that he never read newspapers since he had others to inform him about current events, and Donald Trump relies primarily on "friendly" news outlets, Barack Obama worked hard to remain in constant communication with a variety of friends, advisers, and confidantes in order to gain multiple sources of information that he could then triangulate and digest. Franklin Roosevelt went a step further and rarely trusted traditional channels of intelligence, instead creating his own network of reliable sources.

In other words, exceptional leaders have access to multiple sources of information that provide an up-to-the-minute read on the pulse of a group or organization, as well as to particular group members who are known to have influence. Those who rely mostly on a chief of staff (like George W. Bush or Eisenhower), rather than informal and diverse channels, receive sanitized and limited data that may skew perceptions in a direction that is less than optimal.

Thus, for a leader, the first part of building an effective information network is gaining lots of valuable intelligence about what is really going on, and the second part involves deciding what to *do* with that information. Sometimes the most difficult decision is to choose *not* to respond to provocation; other times, avoiding such decisive action only emboldens your adversaries to continue stirring up trouble. Lyndon Johnson is an example of a leader who was perhaps the most accomplished of all at accessing, digesting, and employing all kinds of information that helped him to negotiate and control the mechanisms of the Senate when he served as both minority and majority leader. He not only had access to the Senate calendar, which determined what issues were up for debate, but he also knew exactly how everyone would vote on particular agenda items, often before they were sure themselves. He didn't just collect and sift through information, he was actually in a position to create whatever intelligence he believed would be most crucial in deciding whether legislation passed or not.

The willingness, and the ability, to sift through an avalanche of information, data, opinions, rumors, and intelligence reports are contingent on another relatively simple thing that controls everything else we do—the ways in which we manage limited time. The most consistent experience of leaders is that there are far too many tasks to accomplish and work to complete within whatever time is available.

Managing and Reclaiming Time

What would you guess is the average number of hours that a professional executive in the United States works each week?

Since you no doubt assume this is a trick question, or at least one with a counter-intuitive answer, perhaps you'd estimate beyond the typical 40-hour work week and estimate about 50 hours. Or maybe go *way* out on a limb and say 60 hours. You'd still be wrong.

In one survey of 500 leaders, it was found that more than 60 percent of them worked an estimated 72 hours each week![21] This included typical 13-hour weekdays and five hours each day of the weekend. If you do the math, this means the leaders had less than three hours each day to accomplish anything else, including exercise, eat, shower, complete chores, shop, spend time with family and friends, indulge in favorite pastimes. Of course, a lot of work takes place beyond the office: at home and on the go while talking, texting, emailing, and conferencing on the phone. Also of interest was that most of these same individuals didn't complain about the long hours because they (apparently) so enjoy what they do for a living.

Whether it is true or not, many among us regard long, grueling hours as a requirement of our job. And perhaps it is accurate that those who are most successful are not only lucky but also flat out work harder than others. For several years, the research on professional mastery widely circulated in popular media and books has attested to the so-called 10,000-hour rule, the idea that extraordinary professionals practice reflectively and systematically the things they are not good at. This is just as true for world-class athletes or musicians as it is for leaders. Indeed, a number of well-known CEOs are famous for their work ethic and brutal hours.[22] Vittorio Colao, head of Vodafone, wakes up every morning at six, exercises for 40 minutes, then begins a workday that doesn't end until 11 at night. And for those whose businesses span across the globe, their hours are even more excessive because of the time differences in the various countries where they operate. When he is in the United States, Sergio Marchionne, CEO of Fiat/Chrysler, rises every morning at 3:30 a.m. in order to deal with issues in his company's European market. Many other prominent executives routinely start their days before the sun rises and don't finish until the rest of the world in their time zone has gone to sleep. The important question is whether such an approach is really necessary.

In the context of organizations, time has different dimensions. There are deadlines imposed by some external source, whether a boss, regulatory agency, or board of directors, time constraints that tend to carry dire consequences if ignored. Then there are the requirements within the system, again making demands that certain tasks be completed within clear parameters. Once again, penalties are usually incurred if these obligations are not met since peers would lose trust and work would not be finished as expected by others who depend on this result. Finally, there is the one domain where we actually have control over time, and that is our own self-imposed expectations related to what we could—and should—be doing. We may not be able to alter deadlines imposed by others, but we have control over the priorities we value most and the discretionary time that remains otherwise unscheduled.

Executives, managers, and other leaders complain a lot that they don't have time to do the things they insist are most important. But that, of course, is not strictly true. In spite of what others demand, what we believe are the requirements of a job, we still decide for ourselves what is most deserving of our attention. Patrick is managing partner of a boutique law firm that specializes in intellectual property. He makes a seven-figure salary and has been working 60 to 80 hours per week for the past several decades. He leaves the house before 6 a.m. each morning to avoid the worst of rush hour traffic and returns home most nights around 9 or 10 p.m., long after his children are in bed. He remembers being told during his first year at the firm that if he didn't come to work on Saturday as well, then he shouldn't bother to return on Sunday, communicating clearly what was expected.

The thing is that Patrick really enjoys his work, even though he complains constantly about the hours he puts in, the demands of his responsibilities, plus all his kids' soccer games and gymnastics tournaments that he has missed. He describes himself as a dedicated father and husband, and is proud of the financial support he has been able to provide to his family: their gorgeous home in the suburbs and fleet of luxury vehicles. But the one experience Patrick has never had—or at least told himself he didn't have time for—is hanging out with his family and friends. "It's not that I want to go into the office today," he would tell his wife and children, "but I have to do it. People depend on me." And he truly believed this. We all do when we make statements like this.

The reality is that many of us do have the discretion and freedom to spend our time doing whatever we want, as long as we are willing to accept the consequences of such decisions. Patrick had been told early in his career that if wasn't prepared to devote an inordinate amount of time to his job, he'd never make partner. It didn't feel as if he had a choice. But, of course, he did.

I remember one day, not too long ago, when I was absolutely overwhelmed with work to do. I had papers to read, articles to review, meetings to prepare for, travel reservations to make, manuscripts to complete, and dozens of unread messages to respond to. And, yes, I also had to get ready for the next morning's packed schedule, figure out what to wear and what I'd need to bring with me. And, oh, I was two episodes behind on one of my favorite television shows and the recording device would soon erase them out of spite if I didn't take care of that unfinished business.

There was a spectacular storm outside, lightning across the sky, and thunder so powerful I could feel vibrations in my feet. My 2-year-old granddaughter was terrified of the thunder and so grabbed onto my legs and wouldn't let go as I headed toward my study. So much to do and so little time. I heard a ping on my phone, signaling that yet another message had just arrived like an avalanche bearing down on me.

I had just written several paragraphs on how distracted we become once engaged with our phones, how our priorities are out of whack with respect to the attention we give to those we care most about. I had also just built a strong case for why it is so important for those of us in leadership positions to practice in our personal lives what we say is so important to our followers. So as my granddaughter was pulling tearfully on my leg, I looked longingly at my phone vibrating inside my pocket. Then I nodded to myself in a secret promise, realizing so clearly what was most important to me.

I picked up my granddaughter in my arms and we went outside to the covered patio. Aliya stretched out on my lap as we watched the lightning sparkle like fireworks. Every time it thundered, we'd both scream and yell and clap our hands. We screamed for more. We did a thunder dance. And I can't recall a more meaningful and important half hour that I've ever spent in my life. To heck with the work and all those incoming messages that are not nearly as critical as I sometimes make them seem.

Being Dependable and Conscientiousness

Throughout this chapter, we've explored the personal traits and simple skills that distinguish exemplary leaders. Clearly, one such ability is the willingness to establish and enforce clear boundaries that both maximize productivity, but also a healthy lifestyle in which work is balanced with other interests, time for family and friends, as well as pursuing leisure interests. Unfortunately, this is not only difficult to do given all the outside pressures, it is also something for which most of us are unprepared and may result from painful lessons and prior mistakes that ended in conflict, losing one's job, divorce, or health problems.

It would be hard to overestimate the importance of leaders being conscientious and dependable throughout their daily lives, both at work and elsewhere. People who demonstrate careful diligence early in childhood tended to do better at school, enjoy better friendships, and stay out of trouble. As adults they have better friendships, longer marriages, and even greater longevity in their jobs. Leaders who are especially conscientious in their behavior earn higher salaries, have better impulse control, and are more successful to attaining articulated goals.[23]

People who are exceptionally conscientious might be more inclined to follow rules and less likely to break the mold but also enjoy far greater health benefits and actually live longer. They engage in fewer impulsive, risky behaviors like smoking, excessive drinking, illicit drug use, or driving recklessly. They take their health more seriously and thus maintain better diets and consistent exercise regimens. And they make much wiser and considered choices about creating the kind of work and social environment that nourishes them.[24]

With all the attention devoted to supposedly essential leadership skills, including such activities as developing a vision and goals, delegating responsibilities, managing personnel, allocating resources, negotiating contracts, running meetings, and everything else under the sun, the one domain most neglected is the way in which we organize and conduct our own personal lives in responsible ways. Unless we are able to take care of ourselves, as well as our loved ones, unless we are able to create some balance between work and play, between obligations and personal desires, we will hardly flourish in our leadership role for very long, much less enjoy a satisfying and fulfilling life.

5

Really, Really Bad Leadership and What We Learn from Our Mistakes

BY THE TIME Carole walked in the front door of her home, her blood pressure was bubbling through the roof of her brain. Or at least it felt as if her head was going to explode from the pressure. She had not eaten most of her lunch so she was hungry, as well as tired and overwhelmed. It had been a tough day in every way possible. Her division head was barely tolerable during his best days, but today he had been even more out of control than usual. She had been concentrating hard on an inscrutable spreadsheet when all of a sudden it felt like a brisk breeze had scattered the papers on her desk. She looked up to find "Evil Boss" standing by her desk, arms folded, and that distressing look of scorn on his face.

"Just what exactly do you think you're doing?" he asked her.

What the hell do you *think* I'm doing?, she thought to herself, but decided it would be best to keep her mouth shut. Carole looked up at him with an innocent expression that was hardly insincere; she had no idea what he wanted from her this time. It seemed that whenever she, or any of her colleagues, completed any assigned project or task they were in for a humiliating tongue lashing, usually a rather spectacular performance in front of an audience pretending they were busy with their own work. The one today had been worse than normal, a diatribe that went on forever, even though she was still unclear about what she'd done wrong.

Carole was fuming as she walked in the door, still trying to metabolize the anger and frustration from work, exacerbated by the stress of rush-hour traffic on the way home. The first thing she noticed as she threw her things on the table, harder than she had intended, is that the house seemed like a mess. That's all it took for her to go ballistic, screaming at their Labrador for blocking her path, and then letting go with a barrage of complaints directed at her husband and two children who had been quietly watching cartoons on the couch. "What the hell is wrong with you people?" she yelled at them in disgust, raging because there were toys all over the floor and she could tell that no attempt had been made to organize dinner. Her family members cowered on the couch, confused by this crazy woman who no longer resembled their mother or wife.

It's Time to Talk Openly About Bad Leadership

We know that work affects family life just as family life impacts satisfaction and performance on the job. So it isn't particularly surprising that bad leader behavior would have contagious effects on everyone else in a variety of ways. First and foremost, productivity is reduced, people withdraw or quit, health problems increase, anxiety and stress become unrelenting, and employees or followers are even more inclined to steal and cheat within the organization as a form of payback for perceived abuse.[1]

Specifically related to one of the themes of this book, when followers are subjected to bad leaders at work, there are consequences for every other aspect of life, especially related to the quality of time with loved ones. A number of studies have found that when a subordinate is treated poorly by a boss or supervisor, he or she is far more likely to take frustrations out on others, especially those at home.[2] Such employees are also more likely to act out within the organization in a variety of ways, following the dysfunctional template established by their leaders. This has been described as the "kick the dog" phenomenon since those who are subjected to bad behavior at work often take their sense of powerlessness home, treating their friends and family members as abysmally as they have been treated.[3] This displaced aggression, which cannot be expressed at work because of the hostile and oppressive environment, may frequently surface in unexpected ways that undermine other personal relationships. Most commonly, it is expressed as increased anger, annoyance, unpleasantness, criticism, and psychological distress, just as the vignette describing Carole that opened this chapter.

This isn't an excuse for bad behavior as much as an explanation, but aggression certainly comes with the territory of being a leader since in almost any setting or context that person must protect precious resources, hold on to or expand territory, or defeat rivals. Whether in sport, war, commerce, academia, or the animal kingdom, aggressive behavior can be not only appropriate but also essential to survival. Yet in other cases, aggression leads to mistrust, escalation of threats, and even chaos.

A leader's aggressive behavior does the most damage when it represents an impulsive, vindictive, or angry reaction to a perceived threat. As shown in the previous example, it can become an indirect, displaced behavior that results from feeling humiliated, shamed, or bullied by someone else. According to Robert Sapolsky, who studied this broad landscape, "giving ulcers can help you avoid getting them." In other words, it's been found that displaced aggression toward another target actually does work to lower one's stress hormones.[4] That's why it is not uncommon that a leader who has suffered an indignity from someone else may lash out at others who are conveniently in range. It turns out that aggression is contagious for whoever happens to be in the vicinity.

There are examples of really bad leadership everywhere we look considering that over one-quarter of all leaders are described by their followers or employees as "toxic," meaning they are inconsiderate, uncommunicative, and ineffectual bullies.[5] As already mentioned, it has been estimated that more than half of all corporate managers are considered incompetent in their jobs and end up failing.[6] Even more disturbing, less than 10 percent of senior executives believe their companies develop competent leaders on a global scale, and less than 2 percent think that any kind of training or development programs improved things at all.[7] If you think about it, that's a rather incredible figure attesting to poor professionalism. Just imagine if half of all physicians or plumbers were considered incompetent at their jobs?

The news cycle thrives on publicizing the latest instance of deceptive, unscrupulous behavior on the part of some public figure, executive, or coach. And whenever someone in a position of responsibility does make some error in judgment or a mistake, there is a cover-up because of the apparent expectation that leaders are infallible. Admitting mistakes and apologizing are not an option. Failure is shameful and inexcusable, evidence of essential incompetence. Indeed, *repeated* failures may very well indicate essential ineptitude, especially if the individual doesn't learn valuable lessons from those lapses. Yet almost all eventual successes in arenas of sports, battle, or business arise from previous failures and the mistakes that were learned.

Leadership is usually framed as stories of spectacular success in which some heroic figure saved a company, organization, battle, nation, perhaps the world, because of some incredibly courageous or brilliant strategy. We celebrate these victories and deify the figures associated with them. Yet studying leadership is just as much about failure as it is about triumphs, and ignoring the latter is likened to studying only health in medical school but nothing about disease.[8] Even though most of the literature on leadership is focused on success, it behooves us to study failure with equal vigor considering how common it is that things don't work out as planned.[9] This usually occurs for several reasons:

1. *Tactical errors.* There was evidence of poor judgment, as well as impulsive or ill-advised decision-making. This can occur because of excessive caution as well as risky choices.
2. *Relationship troubles.* The executives managed to alienate members of the staff or engaged in behavior that led to ongoing conflicts and disagreements. Often they were viewed as aloof and unapproachable.
3. *Personality defects.* This was by far the most frequent reason for difficulties, especially when leaders manifested traits of arrogance, narcissism, and an inability to manage their own behavior because of emotional volatility.
4. *Attitudes.* Leaders are observed carefully for the slightest signs of their true feelings. Those who are viewed as pessimistic, or see themselves as special and above everyone else, have a discouraging effect on others. This is especially the case when they lack awareness of their impact, tending to blame others when things go wrong.[10]

When discussing the nature of bad leadership, and its accompanying causes, we can move way past any jargon or psychological diagnoses since almost anyone can describe a really bad leader with the same eloquent terms as Stanford researcher Robert Sutton, who characterizes such individuals as "assholes."[11] Indeed, they are, especially as the label describes the disrespectful and misguided ways in which they treat others and elevate themselves at the expense of others. Of course, it's also possible to be a fabulous person, admired and loved by everyone, and still spectacularly clueless and incompetent when it comes to taking care of business. Similarly, there are also very unpleasant individuals in leadership roles whose obnoxious behavior is excused because they are so damn good at their jobs.

In all fairness, toxic leaders are not usually born that way but are "trained" to be annoying and difficult. Ironically, it is the organizational culture that even permits such behavior in the first place, including the established norms. In addition, you can't have a bad leader without conspiring overseers, team members, and complacent followers. And when the organization does fall apart, as it most likely will, the toxicity will have seeped into almost every crevice, making the mess all that more difficult to clean up.

When You Really Believe You Are the Greatest

There are many different pathways to leadership, but most of them are driven by ambition and the need for achievement. Let's just say that most leaders tend not to be the most modest, self-effacing individuals, but rather often have a high degree of self-confidence and a sense of mission. As we've covered, this is a good thing some of the time considering that a leader's job frequently involves influencing, persuading, and inspiring others. In order to be effective in this role, it is obviously important to believe in yourself, as well as your ability to make a difference.

Any human trait can become both a gift and a burden. Individuals who are impatient, for instance, can be both impulsive and action-oriented; they get things done in a timely way. Likewise, narcissism receives a lot of attention because of its prevalence among media-hungry celebrity leaders who crave the spotlight. Since leadership is primarily about serving others rather than oneself, it may appear as if this kind of personality would be at odds with positions of authority. Leadership clearly has a dark side, one that manifests itself in several prominent themes that begin with an abuse of power.[12] When leaders are perceived to behave in ways that favor cronyism, inequity, and "tribal loyalty," this often creates difficulties among those who feel marginalized. Second, there is usually some damage inflicted on followers since the leader may be seen as overly aggressive, insensitive, and a bully who may even appear to enjoy dominating others. There is, thus, a certain amount of overcontrol, obsession with meaningless details, micromanagement, and perfectionism. Such individuals have a lot at stake in terms of their image and so may respond aggressively to any perceived slight or threat.

Narcissistic leaders tend to do well for a limited period of time precisely because of some of the functional benefits of their personality style. There is a cumulative effect that results from their selfishness and ego-driven behavior, eventually leading to decreased performance, poor morale, limited motivation, fractured loyalty, and compromised job satisfaction.[13] That is one reason why narcissism was originally conceived by Sigmund Freud as a pathological condition characterized by constant self-aggrandizement and a tendency to view others as "objects" to be controlled and used for one's own personal goals. Narcissism is no longer viewed solely as a "disorder," but rather as a personality "construct" that also has functional components.[14]

Whereas generally self-absorbed individuals tend to leave a wake of casualties and damage behind them, they also find themselves in leadership positions because of some of these same traits. They likely have very high self-esteem. They are extraordinarily self-confident and charming. Their competitive and aggressive nature serves them well with respect to attaining and holding on to power with desperate single-mindedness.

It has also been found that those who score high on the traits described above may also enjoy a kind of "productive narcissism."[15] If you think about some of the coaches of popular sports franchises, you would immediately recognize their tendency toward explosiveness, excessive perfectionism, domineering and controlling behavior, and eccentricities that are forgiven as long as they are successful. Indeed, there is some adaptive value in being "a little narcissistic" since it is often associated with courage, vision, charisma, and the desperate need for achievement and recognition. They are frequently seen as creative and bold thinkers. That is one reason why leadership experts have such a difficult time deciding whether narcissistic traits are necessarily destructive or can, in fact, be quite helpful.

Among the few attempts to determine the relative effects of narcissistic leaders, one study examined the behavior of over 100 CEOs rated high in this dimension.[16] The researchers measured the trait in an interesting way, looking at indicators such as: (1) the frequency with which their image was included in promotional material, (2) the prominence of their photo in the annual report, (3) how often they are mentioned in company press releases, (4) how frequently they use the pronoun "I" during interviews, (5) how disproportionately they are compensated compared to other employees. Whether you agree with these measures or not, they do tend to indicate a pattern of self-indulgence. The researchers found that whereas it was true these leaders were seen as bold and innovative, powerful leadership figures, there were rather extreme fluctuations in the performance of their organizations.

Once a narcissistic leader is in power, it's often too late to control the damage because such a person would install protective safeguards that insulate him or her from attacks or criticism. Yet there are also notable cases in which particular leaders learned from their earlier self-centered mistakes and adapted accordingly to transform themselves. Steve Jobs is an excellent example of this phenomenon whereby he had to work through the tough lesson of being dismissed from Apple. He became what is known as a more "tempered narcissist" who was able to change his ways to become more collaborative, humble, less abusive and critical, and far more measured in his responses to colleagues. It would appear as if it is precisely the characteristic of humility that moderates the more distasteful parts of flamboyant personalities and makes leaders appear more attractive and accessible.[17]

The question then becomes how does one learn such humility. As is so often the case, Steve Jobs learned the lesson the hard way—through abject failure, disappointment, and rejection—unceremoniously dismissed by the company he founded. It was during his years in "exile" that he forcibly came to terms with his personality issues that others found so off-putting. He was able to reinvent himself during later life, to enjoy a rare do-over, because he finally found he had no choice but to accept that what he had been doing did not work. He alienated everyone around him. He created and maintained an atmosphere of intimidation. He stifled creativity. And he made some really bad, misinformed decisions because he trusted the judgment of so few others. After experimenting first with NeXT (another misguided failure), and later with Pixar (one of the greatest successes ever), Jobs eventually remolded himself into a leader who retained his charisma and self-confidence but also learned to adapt his style to become more responsive to others.[18] In other examples of a similar transformation, two of the most charismatic leaders of the 20th century, Franklin Roosevelt and Mahatma Gandhi, both struggled with their sense of self-importance before realizing there were ways they could use their celebrity status to serve a greater good.

The Shadow Side

Psychoanalyst Carl Jung talked about the dark side of every personality, a shadow that is both primitive and very, very dark. This shadow disguises the shame and guilt we feel about our basest human instincts such as lust, greed, envy, rage, selfishness, and dominance. It is the distasteful or even "evil" part of ourselves that we hide or deny, although we tend to project those traits onto visible leaders who represent the embodiment of evil, such as Hitler, Pol Pot, Stalin, Charles Manson, or Darth Vader.

When leaders' personal characteristics result in dysfunctional organizational practices or toxic interactions, the result is often an atmosphere in which their followers feel harassed, bullied, and unappreciated. This isn't just a case of incompetence or someone operating way over his or her head, but rather represents a serious breach of integrity and professionalism. There is no circumstance I can think of in which one adult will respond well to another who screams or becomes verbally abusive. In fact, one of the only instances I can think of in which raising one's voice is a preferred and effective response is when a leader in battle yells, "Charge!"

Otherwise, yelling at someone, anyone, usually provokes one of several predictable reactions—shame, remorse, guilt, self-blame, inadequacy, followed by anger and a desire to seek revenge. I can't think of a time when anyone has felt immediately grateful for a leader (or teacher) saying in a public meeting (much less a private conversation), "That is one of the stupidest ideas I've ever heard! What the hell is wrong with you? Can't you see that we have to fix this thing, not make it even worse?"

There are individuals who seek leadership positions in the first place because they really do get off on dominating others and putting them in their rightful place. When they can claim that their bad temper is the result of some personality trait, one they just can't help, they have a ready excuse for saying or doing whatever they want and then excusing themselves afterwards: "Sorry about that. You know I have a bad temper," meaning it's really *your* fault for triggering the outburst.

Regardless of our own weaknesses, limitations, and flaws, they do sometimes offer great excuses for avoiding change or action. These are referred to as "secondary gains," and imply that people receive benefits as a result of their self-defeating behaviors. For instance, the leader with the bad temper claims that because he has an Irish mother and Italian father, he just can't control his rage. "Everyone in my family has a temper," he says with a laugh and a shrug, as if this gives him a license to abuse anyone he wants, whenever he wants— which is exactly the case. It is, in fact, quite advantageous to convince those around you that you occasionally go out of control, but you really can't help it, so they better just get accustomed to such behavior. Imagine how often you would get your way if others around you fear that something they might say or do would set you off.

Famous leaders—whether CEOs, politicians, or football coaches—are frequently portrayed in the media as overly emotional, arrogant, and mercurial in their outbursts. They are even described as bullies who are both malevolent and malicious in their single-minded pursuit of personal ambition and notoriety. Their self-aggrandizing behavior leads to varying degrees of organizational dysfunction, especially temper tantrums and deceit, as well as employee/follower annoyance (undermining, lying) and even personal trauma leading to addictions, workaholism, depression, and debilitating stress. Much of this results from relying on a favored interpersonal style that rules by fear and retribution, public criticism and ridicule, silencing voices of discontent, inequitable policies, and the use of bribes, blackmail, and threats to ensure compliance.

Dark side characteristics, including dimensions of narcissism, are a matter of degree and fall along a continuum. The degree to which the shadow side actually results in lousy leadership depends on several factors.[19] Obviously, the first consideration is how extreme the particular personality trait is manifested in the person. A little bit (or even a moderate amount) of obsessive-compulsive behavior leads to exacting, excellent performance. The second issue has to do with the extent to which the personality traits threaten and intimidate others, or the degree to which others find the behavior offensive. Finally, and perhaps most importantly, it is related to how well leaders can regulate their emotions and manage their own behavior. It is one thing to have a propensity to lash out at others and quite another to give in to this impulse. This helps to explain why potentially toxic personal characteristics can be either helpful or harmful, depending on how they are expressed and controlled, in addition to how well the leader learns from past mistakes.

We Have Bad Leaders Because We Tolerate Them

Graham thinks he is just about the greatest boss in the world. You would know that immediately after meeting him because it would be one of the first things he would tell you, "Did I mention that there are over 1,800 employees who report to me?" Then he would talk with self-importance about how much everyone depends on him. If he trusted you, he might also mention that some people just don't get him, which is a code implying that he is insanely disliked by almost everyone who comes into contact with him. The one thing he has going for him, which earned him this lofty position in the first place, is that it feels to him as if his life depends on his willingness to do almost anything to stay on top of everyone else. He has always been game to do whatever it takes to get ahead: say anything, do anything, make whatever deals were necessary to hold on to power. The one thing that he doesn't seem to understand is how oblivious he is to the ways in which others actually view him. His primary defense mechanism is to pretend he doesn't care. But he cares deeply.

There are many reasons why leaders like Graham fail so miserably at their jobs. It is a paradox that some who aspire most desperately for positions of power are precisely those who are doing so for selfish and self-promoting reasons that are at odds with their primary role to serve others. Sometimes they lack the requisite skills and experience that might be needed to succeed in the job. They may also not have had good role models to mentor them during their rise in power.

It is hardly surprising that those who aspire to leadership positions do so in order to control and manipulate others for their own purposes. Let's be brutally honest with ourselves: Anyone who achieves leadership status does so not just to save the organization, or the world, but to help him- or herself.

Almost without exception, there are intensely personal motives for tolerating all the responsibility, aggravation, and pressure of being in charge. Certainly, there are privileges and numerous advantages, luxuries that are not afforded to others that make some of the sacrifices a reasonable trade-off. But there is also a price to be paid for all the extra time, effort, and commitment that usually involves working harder and feeling more pressure than anyone else. Anyone who says they are taking on the job purely as an altruistic act to serve others is lying to him- or herself, and everyone else. Whether in the military, politics, corporations, or academia, even religious-based organizations, *everyone* has some personal motive that drives them to achieve recognition, approval, power, control, and material benefits that are not afforded to others. Even Gandhi had his demons, given his chronic shyness and underachievement as a young man, the neglect of his family in the pursuit of his dream for India to become an independent nation. And whereas he aspired to chastity and forbid others to sleep with their spouses, he made an exception for himself to sleep with young, naked women as an "experiment" to tempt himself. He was also notoriously insensitive and disrespectful toward women in general, an attitude that was certainly prevalent in the period and cultural environment in which he lived. It is hardly surprising that any human leader, even the father of a nation and "living god," would also have flaws and desires that drive personal ambition.

There have been notoriously toxic leaders over the last few years, whether political figures who have literally ruined their countries, corporate executives who drove their companies into oblivion, or leaders who were so corrupt that the whole culture of their organization became poisonous and completely dysfunctional. One rather dramatic example of this was the several decades long reign of terror orchestrated by Sepp Blatter, the president of FIFA, the governing body of world futbol (soccer). After dozens of indictments were handed down, it was discovered that the entire foundation behind the organization was rotten and corrupt, and an old boys' club in which all business was conducted via bribes under the table.

Why do leaders get away with self-indulgent actions that are clearly not in the best interests of those they serve? Because they can. And because we allow them to. In some cases, they are rewarded generously, perhaps spectacularly, not as a result of their actual performance on the job, but rather by the deals they were granted by overzealous boards. Tens of thousands of employees may be laid off, stock values tank, or the football team may have a consistently losing record, and yet the CEO, coach, or leader is given millions of dollars in bonuses. The takeaway from many of these lessons is that it really doesn't matter much whether you can deliver on your promises, merely that you can make them in a convincing fashion.

Learning from Failures

When leaders are inclined to talk about their failures, admit wrongdoing, apologize for mistakes or miscalculations—and do so sincerely—they are generally perceived to be far more accessible and responsible.[20] Of course, such disclosures should be both selective and appropriate, so one does not appear weak, incompetent, or clueless.[21] In one instance of this reported in a book about the diagnostic errors that physicians make, a famous cardiologist kept a detailed log throughout his distinguished career of every mistake, misdiagnosis, and error of judgment he'd ever made.[22] He would then spend hours revisiting and studying the records of his failures in order to remind himself of his own fallibility, as well as to protect against repeating the same mistakes. He believed that it was only through such honest and critical self-scrutiny that he was in the best position to significantly improve his skills and knowledge.

So much depends on how failure is defined in the first place. It can indeed be framed as an unintended mistake, disastrous consequence, or disappointing result, but also viewed as merely an unexpected outcome or new information about the consequences of an action or decision. In a previous research project, I once interviewed the most noted luminaries in the field of psychotherapy, those who have had the most influence and impact during the past century.[23] I asked them to share stories of their most miserable failures, perhaps the single greatest mistake they'd ever made—and more importantly—what they learned from the experience. I was surprised how many different ways these leaders defined failure in the first place. Some of them were naturally outcome-based in that if a patient didn't improve or became worse, then that was clearly a failure. But others conceptualized the phenomenon more in terms of their own inflexibility and refusal to adapt to changing circumstances, regardless of the result. Still others based the assessment more on their own internal feelings of ineptitude, once again irrespective of what actually happened. But those who were most forgiving, most inclined to regard failures simply as ongoing feedback, rather than an ultimate result, preferred to treat unexpected or unsatisfactory outcomes as an unfinished process that provided important lessons for increased effectiveness.

There are, thus, both bad failures as well as "good" ones. Bad failures are end results that can't be repaired or rectified; even apologies and excuses won't do. Good failures, on the other hand, are unfinished products. They provide meaningful and useful information about the impact of behavior and, therefore, are absolutely crucial input to make adjustments to better achieve a desired objective. It isn't necessarily a failure if you don't hit the bull's-eye, as long as you can adjust your aim to hit the target. The likes of Albert Einstein and Thomas Edison failed constantly in their endeavors and experiments, which is why Edison claimed he never failed but just discovered 10,000 ways that things didn't work out as he'd anticipated. In a book on failures in science, and what they have taught us, the point was made that nature has a pitiful batting average when it comes to preparing its creatures to survive given that 99 percent of species are now extinct.[24]

Failure Promotes Reflection

"What the heck was *that* all about?" Megyn walks away from an interaction with two members of her team who had been assigned a specific task to complete by the end of the week. But when she checked in with both of them, they acted as if they had no idea what she was talking about. She remembers distinctly sitting down with both of them to explain what needed to be done and the deadline that was non-negotiable. Yet not only had they failed to complete the work, but they both also pretended ignorance about the task.

Megyn had considered all kinds of ways she wanted to respond to them in the moment, to call them out on their neglect and unprofessionalism. But she sensed something else was going on, perhaps something that she had missed. Like so many human interactions, this one was a mystery, one in which it was clear there was more to the encounter than first met the eye. Had her instructions been unclear? Were these two team members conspiring to undermine her in some way? Maybe they had actually completed the task but intended to take credit for all the work? Or perhaps the opposite: Perhaps they were protecting her in some way, insulating her from the fallout if things went wrong? The point is that Megyn spent an inordinate amount of time thinking about and considering the various meanings of the incident, as much to make sense of the confusion as to work out an alternative approach to the problem. Eventually, of course, she would talk to the two of them again to find out what happened, but prior to this, she wanted to better understand her own possible role in the confusion so as to prevent a similar situation in the future.

Most of us remain haunted by our worst mistakes in life, often holding on to regrets and wishing we had behaved differently. Yet it is precisely this critical thinking, when brought under reasonable control, that helps us to learn from what happened, forgive ourselves for lapses, and move forward in such a way to stop the same mistakes from re-occurring. Of course, there is a difference between reviewing mistakes of the past and obsessing over them with shame and regret, versus using them as object lessons to improve performance in the future.

Failure Provides Useful Information

One way to conceptualize failure is simply to see it as valuable information about the impact of any action. It tells you that efforts are not producing desired outcomes, at least as they are currently structured. As such, the input is telling you loudly and clearly—if you are paying close attention—that it is time to stop doing what you are doing and to try something else instead. It is thus the impetus for much greater flexibility and experimentation and often leads to creative breakthroughs, but only if you are prepared to give up the status quo for the risk of improved results.

Prior to the invasion of Normandy in which the Allies turned the course of World War II, there was a catastrophic defeat on the beaches of Dieppe in France resulting in a loss of two-thirds of all forces that attempted a landing. The number of accumulative mistakes was overwhelming, beginning with spotty and inaccurate intelligence about German fortifications, poor training and preparation of the troops, inadequate air support for the invasion, and even allowing the enemy to discover the plans for the attack. The Germans used the invasion attempt as a propaganda bonanza, calling it a "military joke" that bolstered their own overconfidence and set up perfectly the next actions that would follow on the beaches of Normandy.

"Failure is simply the opportunity to begin again," Henry Ford once observed, "but more intelligently." And he knew a few things about the subject considering his own string of disappointments. Winston Churchill insisted that in spite of the tragic loss of lives at Dieppe, there was so much learned from the failed expedition that the Allies were better equipped to plan and implement their subsequent landings in France and North Africa. Communication between units was significantly improved during future operations and Allied forces learned a tough lesson: that it was not advisable to attack heavily fortified positions (an interesting insight in the context of business as well).

The nature of scientific investigations also elevates failure, or "non-significant results," to a place of prominence. We learn as much when predictions and information are wrong as when they are absolutely accurate. The "scientific method" can be simply reduced to the following procedure: (1) You have an idea or plan; (2) you test the idea to see if it works out as anticipated; (3) if it doesn't work the first time, you try again to see if you get the same result; (4) if it fails again, you review your procedures to see if you followed the plan as originally conceived; (5) you make some adjustments and perhaps try again, often with the same disappointing outcome; (6) you learn from this effort and decide to try something else, reporting to others on the lessons that resulted. This is the essence of science and the vast majority of times that experiments result in the "null hypothesis," meaning that the original hypothesis was rejected and another explanation or course of action followed.[25]

Many of the most important breakthroughs in medicine occurred when predictions were made and hypotheses tested that failed miserably, leading to alternative pathways that never would have been considered otherwise. Sidney Farber, who is responsible for some of the earliest successes in treating childhood leukemia and developing the first effective chemotherapy treatments, found his initial efforts to be tragic mistakes. He reasoned that synthetic folic acid, injected directly into the bloodstream of cancer patients, would kill malignant white blood cells that were exploding throughout the system. What he discovered instead is that this treatment actually *accelerated* the rate of cancerous growth, killing the children in the experiment. Farber was dismissed from his job and became a pariah among his colleagues. But the story did not end just yet.

Farber adjusted his thinking in light of this horrific miscalculation. If folic acid increased the rate of uncontrolled white cell growth, what effect would an *anti*folate have? And, would such a compound that blocked the proliferation of white blood cells actually send the leukemia into remission? It turned out that this catastrophic failure became the first groundbreaking advancement in treating cancer with chemical treatments and led to the first optimism within the medical profession that this terrible disease might someday be cured.[26]

Failure Teaches Humility

When Michael Skelly (mentioned in Chapter 2) ran one of the most expensive congressional campaigns in history, and lost the election, he had no choice but to consider a reassessment of his life and career. There must be other ways he could make a difference—and Skelly was that rare species of politician who really was in it for the greater good, rather than his own ambition. He recognized and accepted some of his own limitations that might have doomed his campaign, but he also understood other realities that were more related to his chosen political party in the geographical region of the country where he ran for office. He determined that he could sponsor, mentor, and support candidates running for office in other local elections. He volunteered for community projects, leading efforts to build green spaces and walking/cycling trails throughout the city. Then he applied what he learned from past experiences in business to launch a completely new project.

Skelly had been CEO of an energy company in the past, enjoyed a degree of success, then made some mistakes in selling the enterprise to a larger conglomerate that had a very different vision. He vowed he would never make that mistake again and also learned a few things during his political campaign about empowering others within the organization to redistribute leadership responsibilities.

If you would visit the corporate offices of his wind energy company, you would see rows of desks that butt against one another in a huge room. Skelly's desk is on the end but very much integrated into the work space of the other employees. He has learned over time, from previous mistakes, that it is best to help followers feel a sense of ownership and responsibility for the company, that it belongs to all of them, that they all share a commitment to the mission—not just to him. It is loyalty to a vision, not just to an individual, that inspires people. Whereas Skelly is quite the charismatic man in his soft-spoken way, he also understands from experience that by decentralizing power, he actually protects the company far better than if he controlled everything himself. This requires a degree of personal humility, as well as trust in others.

Process Failures Constructively

The whole point of our discussion is that you really can't stop failures from occurring. Failure in leadership, like almost everything else in life, does not result from a single mistake or misjudgment, no matter how vigilant you might be. Rather, there are a series of errors never corrected as a result of inadequate feedback and meaningful data as things proceed. Even life expectancy and health problems fail the way all complex systems fall apart, including those within organizations—because of random and gradual factors that are barely noticed.[27]

Many leaders are absolutely delusional about their own performance, referred to as *illusory superiority*, the so-called Lake Wobegon effect, named after the fictitious town in Garrison Keillor's stories where "all the women are strong, all the men are good-looking, and all the children are above average." There have been so many fascinating—and hilarious—studies of people's self-judgments about their abilities that are not at all consistent with reality. Something like 98 percent of American high school students believe they are better qualified than their peers to serve in leadership positions. We don't seem to outgrow this self-inflated vision of our behavior considering that 80 percent of drivers consider themselves more skilled than anyone else on the road and 93 percent of college professors view themselves as far better teachers and researchers than their colleagues. And lest we think that the degree of self-deception among leaders is going to vastly improve, in one study of Stanford MBA students, it was discovered that 90 percent believed themselves better qualified and smarter than their classmates.[28]

If mistakes are not exactly preventable, then the real question relates to how best to recover and learn from the experience. Recovering from mistakes has been described as the new most important leadership competency.[29] It certainly helps not to believe in your own infallibility so that you can recognize the times that you mess up. It is also useful to question yourself constantly, as well as to recruit trusted advisers who will be similarly honest and forthright in their observations.

In a review of the empirical research on leadership failures, one author concludes that "what differentiates wonderful and less-than-wonderful leaders is not whether they make mistakes or not, but what they do afterwards."[30] The errors that leaders make, after making a mistake, include the failure to recognize or acknowledge that they messed up in the first place. Second, there is often a marked reluctance to apologize for the error because of fears that doing so will be seen as weakness or incompetence, even though often the opposite is true since contriteness is viewed as a strength if it is not excessive.

The key to leadership success is not related to avoiding failures and mistakes, but rather processing them in such a way that they become important lessons that are not repeated. There are a series of questions to consider that help with this task.

1. *What are the signs that what I'm doing isn't working?* If you aren't able to recognize when things are going wrong, and aren't willing to honestly admit this, the process ends right away. It certainly helps to have trusted colleagues who will tell you the "truth," or at least their version of it so as to compare with your own perceptions.

2. *What are people celebrating as a result of the failure?* Sometimes there is a "conspiracy" of sorts in that people have a vested interest in maintaining

the status quo even when it isn't working. It is important to sort out exactly who is profiting from an ineffective policy or strategy so that it is possible to alter the contingencies in more enhancing ways.

3. *Has the problem been defined in such a way that it cannot be resolved?* Within the field of psychotherapy, there is a diagnostic technique called "reframing" that takes a problem which seems insurmountable and redefines it—puts it in a different frame—in such a way that it becomes much easier to address. An employee who describes herself as shy presents a relatively entrenched self-identity that is impervious to change. After all, if one is shy, that sounds very much like a permanent state of being. There is a difference, however, in seeing this not as a stable personality characteristic, but rather as a situational condition: After all, nobody is shy in every situation and there are likely many instances in which this same person does not behave shyly at all. In a similar vein, when an organizational challenge feels too difficult to effectively confront, one first option is to simply redefine it in a different way: "It isn't so much that our profits are down because of the economic downturn (which can't be controlled), but rather because we have not altered our strategy to fit the new realities."

4. *What interventions have been most and least helpful?* It helps to take inventory of what has worked best in the past, and what hasn't worked well at all. It is sometimes extraordinarily difficult to stop doing something that is obviously not working. Yet until such time that an ineffective strategy or policy is suspended, it's very hard to discover alternatives that may work far better.

5. *How have I been negligent?* It's important to "own" responsibility for mistakes; if nothing else, it models the kind of courage and transparency that you may wish others to embrace. Until such time that you are willing to acknowledge mistakes, it's not likely they are going to be repaired. In addition, as mentioned earlier, selectively disclosing failures often results in increased regard and respect from others. It isn't just about an apology and attributing blame accurately, but also making it clear there are a recovery plan and better strategies to prevent similar problems in the future.

6. *What can I learn from this to help me grow?* If mistakes and failures are viewed as nothing more than feedback about how things are going so far, then the input is invaluable for making adjustments and do-overs. If you enjoy solid relationships with team members, they are likely forgiving of errors, unless they are chronic and excessive. You have the opportunity to tap a number of outside resources whether they are colleagues, literature

and research, or consultants. The key question to be considered is what lessons can be gleaned from the experience.

Although these questions offer some general prompts to help unravel the reasons for failure and possible causes of mistakes, it's important to realize that recovery depends very much on the particular kind of error or misjudgment that was made, each signaling a different strategy. Some mistakes involve poor decision-making or impulsive, misguided actions requiring an immediate apology. Keep in mind that leaders are generally terrible at this skill, which ideally involves: (1) an acknowledgment of the mistake or miscalculation; (2) recognition of the impact and damage that resulted; (3) acceptance of responsibility; (4) avoidance of excuses or "buts"; (5) demonstrated sincerity, honesty, and authenticity; (6) a plan to rectify the problem; and (7) asking for forgiveness.

Compare this "formula" for the perfectly executed apology to the typical kinds that leaders offer reluctantly, petulantly, and insincerely. General George Patton famously slapped and humiliated two soldiers during World War II, berating them as cowards and "gutless bastards" even though they were debilitated, exhibiting symptoms of battle fatigue and posttraumatic stress disorder. When word of this incident leaked out, General Dwight Eisenhower ordered Patton to apologize. He did so by claiming his actions were "wholly impersonal" and that, basically, he hadn't been able to restrain himself from his "loud talking." Patton violated just about every one of the basic rules, leading to his eventual downfall.

By contrast, when a passenger was unceremoniously and literally dragged off a United Airlines plane, leading to a spectacular public relations disaster, CEO Oscar Munoz went on an apology tour. But it wasn't just his intention that helped to calm the waters, it was the way he chose to address the problem by avoiding excuses or blaming others. He accepted full responsibility for the incident in ways that are highly unusual for leaders, who often look for scapegoats. First, he said, "It's never too late to do the right thing," immediately acknowledging the problem rather than making excuses. Next, he agreed that it was a "system failure" for which he felt shame. "We had not provided our front-line supervisors and managers and individuals with the proper tools, policies and procedures that allow them to use common sense," Munoz asserted. "That's on me. I have to fix that." Then, he offered both retribution to those who had been present, as well as a plan to prevent such an event from ever happening again.

In addition, when reporters gave him an easy out and asked whether the passenger in question was, in fact, "belligerent," or in any way shared some responsibility for the incident, Munoz instead replied, "No, he can't be. He was a paying passenger sitting in a seat in our aircraft, and no one should be treated that way."[31] Now *that* is a perfect example of an apology by a leader who seeks to move forward and learn from failure.

One consistent theme within this chapter is that failures and mistakes need not derail a career or sabotage the best-laid plans. In fact, if leaders are risk averse and timid, and avoid failure at all costs, they are likely not moving things forward. "You want people to make mistakes," one CEO explained, "people who don't make mistakes probably aren't doing enough."[32]

The ways that others interpret and respond to defeats depend a great deal on the resilience that the leader shows immediately afterward. In studies of how leaders recover from their mistakes, researchers concluded that people tend to remember the excuses you might have offered but forget the apology over time.[33] That's why it is so important to act with humility, transparency, authenticity, and courage. After all, people are not only watching closely, they desperately want to follow in your footsteps.

6

It's Not About the Agenda, It's All About Relationships

ADMIRAL HORATIO NELSON is considered one of Britain's greatest military leaders, a fierce and unconventional commander during the Napoleonic Wars. He was known as much for the loyalty he commanded among his troops as he was for his naval victories. This was especially surprising given the total obedience he demanded of others even though he was inclined to break every established rule that existed. One reason for this was his willingness to do anything to ensure the safety and welfare of his men.[1]

Within his naval fleet during the Battles of Nile and Trafalgar, he borrowed a term from Shakespeare's *Henry V* to describe his officers, the "Band of Brothers," denoting the mutual closeness of his men. Nelson was able to create such a high degree of relational engagement with his officers and sailors that he had built reserves of "social capital" that helped to immunize him against excessive criticism and second-guessing, as well as deal with inevitable mistakes. "Yet, if I know my own thoughts," Nelson mused, "it is not for myself, or on my own account chiefly, that I feel the sting and the disappointment! No! it is for my brave officers; for my noble-minded friends and comrades. Such a gallant set of fellows! Such a band of brothers! My heart swells at the thought of them."[2]

You would no doubt predict his officers and men would have followed him to Hell and back, which they did in the terribly bloody naval engagements as part of the Mediterranean Fleet. Rather than micromanaging and controlling every aspect of his command, he delegated as much as possible to his captains, allowing them to make decisions during the heat of battle. This is one of the major differences between a manager and an inspirational leader who values relationships above all else. Their roles are differentiated in the sense that managers deal with circumstances they've seen before, resorting to standard operating procedures, whereas leaders respond to situations that up to that point have yet to be experienced. It's the difference between certainty and uncertainty.

This can be explained as the distinction between relatively simple, straightforward problems versus "wicked" problems that are not just complex, but also complicated in that there is no clear understanding of what is causing the difficulty, nor a clear path to identify the culprits. Examples of these intractable problems are things like global warming, mental illness, terrorism, obesity, and addictions, all of which have confounded scholars and leaders for some time.

How does one approach, much less attack, such a complex, challenging problem within an organization? One pathway is to function as a psychologist and anthropologist, using empathy in order to understand more clearly what others are experiencing and the meaning of their behavior. You can't recruit, mobilize, and inspire others to jump on board unless you understand the unique ways in which they view what is going on. Among all the leadership skills briefly mentioned in the *Army Field Manual*, one of the most critical is the kind of empathy and interpersonal sensitivity that is characteristic of high emotional intelligence. This means being able to walk in the shoes of followers, to truly know and understand their experiences—from their own point of view. Although this ability is given much less attention than decisiveness and authority-based leader interventions, it turns out that being able to empathize with the experience of subordinates is absolutely critical to leadership success.[3]

This should not be all that surprising considering the overwhelming body of research to support the idea that the single most important ingredient—by far—to promote lasting changes in people's lives is the development of a trusting and supportive relationship. Techniques, strategies, and specific interventions account for less than 15 percent of successful outcomes; the balance of positive results derive from relational factors, as well as personal characteristics of the leader—and the followers.[4] As obvious as this might appear, even professional therapists and counselors rely way too much on their interventions and techniques, instead of focusing on the quality of the relationships between members and within the group setting. That is one reason why it is so important to create the kinds of relationships with colleagues, peers, subordinates, and overseers that are *mutually* supportive and encouraging.

Earning Social Capital

The concept of "social capital" that was evident in the story of Admiral Nelson's ability to inspire his followers is far more important than most leaders imagine, especially within hierarchical organizations in which there are extreme inequities of power, resources, and compensation. That is part of the rationale for why a company like Ben and Jerry's instituted an original policy of limiting its CEO's salary to a 5 to 1 ratio, compared to the lowest-paid employee. Of course, this was later increased to 7 to 1, then 17 to 1, and now is no longer publicized. Nevertheless, given that most Fortune 500 CEOs currently make 300 times more compensation than their lowest-paid employees, this produces considerable inequality, whether deserved or not. It exacerbates the perceived relational distance between leaders and their followers or employees.

We know from research that when organizations or cultures allow extreme inequities in compensation, and have job specialization, a relative surplus of resources, strict chains of command, and some degree of technological sophistication, this fosters considerable resentment, demoralization, and minimal social capital. The latter is usually defined as a high degree or reciprocity, trust, and active engagement within a group.

Those organizations, groups, and cultures that have low social capital and relational engagement are characterized by the following conditions: (1) high rates of bullying, antisocial behavior, and toxic aggression; (2) increased crime, violence, and acting out; (3) beliefs by those in power that subordinates are less than worthy and deserving of their lower status; (4) people within the group tend to be less kind and helpful to, and respectful of, others; (5) those lower on the hierarchy tend to have more health problems and a shorter lifespan. In other words, morale, cooperation, and collaboration are severely compromised when people are forced to continually confront the fact that they are treated poorly compared to others.

One example of this phenomenon that we have all experienced is what it's like to board a plane, when you are required to shuffle through the first-class section on your way to squeeze into an economy seat. In one fascinating study, it was found that such "social inequity" leads to increased passenger air rage than in conditions when the different passenger classes are separated into different directions.[5] In addition, the privileged individuals tend to feel a greater sense of entitlement and become more demanding of flight attendants. After all, who doesn't feel a little special and smug enjoying a cocktail and nuts as the "peasants" walk by staring enviously at the extra legroom?

But here's the really interesting thing: It doesn't matter as much as people think that *being* poor or disadvantaged necessarily leads to despair, discouragement, and bad health, but rather like most things in life, it's about *feeling* poor. So once again, we revisit the importance of leaders helping their followers to feel valued in order to build increased social capital within the group. This means that, ideally, it is far better in many organizations to perpetuate an atmosphere of relative equality; when such is not possible or realistic, it is critical to increase social capital as much as one can. This occurs primarily by encouraging trust and healthy interpersonal engagement within an organization. This begins with the congruent image and reassuring mood that leaders project (and hopefully demonstrate) during their daily interactions.

The Leader's Mood Is Contagious

In earlier chapters, I mentioned Jeremy Gaffney, who has launched a number of start-ups in the technology field. He recognizes that so much a part of his job has been to help some very talented but eccentric superstars remain focused, as well as level-headed. The focused part isn't that difficult because the workers are all passionately obsessed with their work, but the emotional stability part is challenging, he offers to me, "because these are people who had a tough time fitting in somewhere else. A lot of us, and I'll include myself in this, we're oddballs."

Gaffney sees his role within the various companies as being the stable figure to whom others can look for grounding, especially when things aren't going well, when money is short, or when the firm has to interact with equity partners who are less than supportive. "My job is to provide an environment that is flexible, but also one that provides sufficient structure. But just as importantly is that I have to communicate the passion of my dream. I want to make the best games in the world and that dream is infectious. If I can find others who share that dream, then we can all chase it together."

Of course, such a vision is much easier to articulate than accomplish, especially with a bunch of "oddballs" who are each accustomed to playing his or her own tunes, some of whom play very dissonant chords and seemingly incoherent lyrics. "If I can articulate a vision that is broadly appealing to these creative people, say to them, 'Hey look, we need to go in this direction together,' that's attractive to them because they are often so isolated and alone. It's all about us running together in roughly the same direction, with the same basic purpose."

One of the things that would immediately strike you about Gaffney is that he presents himself as very level-headed and logical. The world can be collapsing around him but he will calmly and rationally present a hypothesis about what he believes will happen next, supported by some fairly convincing evidence. That is soothing and reassuring to those who often feel as if they are operating without a net, without much financial or emotional stability. He is as much a benevolent brother or father to his employees as he is a boss, always calm and collected no matter what crisis or obstacles they may be facing next.

Of course, benevolence—or its corresponding opposite, aggressive malevolence—is perceived and experienced in different ways, contexts, and relationships. There are times when those in leadership positions must display decisive action to defeat a rival, protect precious resources, or even expand territory. Whether in sport, war, commerce, or academia, aggressive behavior can be not only appropriate but also absolutely critical for survival. Yet in other cases, aggression leads to mistrust, escalation of tensions, or even chaos, affecting the behavior of everyone else within the vicinity.

When Daniel Goleman and his research team investigated the emotional landscape of leaders, their results were unexpected; after reflection, they made perfect sense. "The leader's mood and behaviors," according to Goleman, "drive the moods and behaviors of everyone else. . . . To be more specific, the leader's mood is quite literally contagious, spreading quickly and inexorably throughout the business."[6]

The Boss's Moods

While there are all kinds of attention directed at leaders' capability for managing finances, budget, production, and profitability, there is precious little attention on the ways in which they manage themselves, especially their moods and the effects on their relationships. This is as true for what happens when a stressed-out leader returns home and dumps on his family or friends, or when personal issues trigger exaggerated emotional responses at work. Although the most florid example might be a leader displaying abusive anger and losing his or her temper, it can be just as impactful if that same person is seen walking around *appearing* sullen and preoccupied.

Biologist Lewis Thomas, who spent his life studying the social behavior of ants and termites, noted that rather than functioning as separate individuals, these creatures are really just a single animal interconnected through their communication system to share a single thought and pursue a common goal.[7] Before we write off this observation, concluding that we are hardly similar to ants, consider that just like us, these insects farm their food in the form of fungi, raise their own livestock as aphids, raise and send armies into combat to defeat enemies, use chemical weapons, confuse enemies through misdirection, even engage in child labor. About the only thing ants don't do, Thomas noted, is watch television.

Similar to social insects, the neurological systems of human workers are also "wired" together through ceaseless communication—and I'm not talking about the Internet or texting. The brain's limbic system has evolved into an open loop system that is intimately connected to the emotional responses of those around us, especially those in charge. This development occurred largely as a means by which people could signal one another for help in times of danger or need. We are thus equipped with empathic skills that allow us to read others' emotional states with exquisite sensitivity. Some researchers have even discovered that you can watch 30-second videos of couples engaged in conversation with one another—with the sound turned off—and still predict which ones will eventually divorce.[8] Hint: It is about subtle, nonverbal "micro-expressions" revealing contempt that last only milliseconds.

Crying, unique within the human species, is one example of how certain behaviors have evolved over time to command attention from others and act as a plea for assistance.[9] There are far less dramatic signs of emotional inner states that are also fairly easy to detect, and followers become experts at reading carefully any nuance in a leader's mood to predict the behavior that might follow. "I had this one boss," a senior executive recalled to me about one of his first jobs, "and we would all huddle near the entranceway when the dude walked in first thing in the morning. We could all tell just by his stride what kind of day it was going to be; we'd even take bets with one another as a kind of office pool to refine our assessments."

This sounds amusing to the executive now, but he also admitted how absolutely terrifying it was to wait and watch for the day's verdict. If the walk was slow and languid, accompanied by the boss avoiding all eye contact, they knew they were in trouble. If, on the other hand, he walked in briskly with his head nodding, he would smile reassuringly, virtually announcing it was safe to talk to him. One can readily see that a leader's mood and emotional expressiveness (or lack thereof) have a profound effect on all the other "ants" that are interconnected to him or her, and everyone else.

Infants learn during their first months of life to read the moods and expressions of caregivers in order to hone and refine their survival skills and the means by which to ask for help. They can literally feel tension in a room or from the person holding them. Over time, we become more and more attuned to the feelings of others, especially of those who are in a position to help or hurt us. It is also obvious why relationships become so important in any team, unit, tribe, or organization that hopes to function optimally. And it all begins with the leader's state of mind and how those signals are visibly displayed to others.

This has profound implications for understanding the importance of congruence between how leaders behave at work versus their everyday life. It just isn't possible to show up at work every day, or even occasionally, and fake a good mood; we just aren't as good at covering up our inner emotional states as we may think. In spite of how eager leaders are to augment their skills with the latest technology innovations, leadership theories, or other breakthroughs, it would appear that the single most important area for improvement might very well be to focus on our own mental health and relational engagement with others.

Caring, Compassionate, and Relational Leaders

Although we constantly applaud and celebrate leaders who are successful as a function of the brute force they wield to make their visions a reality, we rarely acknowledge other key interpersonal components of inspiring and guiding others that involve relational qualities of compassion and caring. This is what truly inspires loyalty and commitment, not only to an organization but also faith in leaders themselves. Southwest Airlines' success has been partially the result of its budget pricing and novel approach to service, but is also the outcome of its leader's relational style. From Southwest's inception, Herb Kelleher believed that his company wasn't about airplanes, or even serving customers—it was about creating a culture in which his followers would be nurtured and have fun on their jobs. He has avoided laying employees off, introduced profit sharing, created as much flexibility as possible, viewed the union as an ally instead of a nemesis, and created a spirit of collaboration such that even the pilots help the flight attendants pick up trash before deplaning. Everything was about relationships to Kelleher, whether with his board, managers, suppliers, or union, creating a culture of mutual respect.

This stands in contrast to the typically male-dominated, authoritarian model of leadership through explicit power and control that gets all the attention, even with its considerable negative side effects of sparking fear and resentment. One reason why relational aspects of leadership are so often ignored is because so many of the positions have been controlled by dominant men who yearn for more power and control. I mentioned in Chapter 4 how so few women lead multinational companies, even though they make up half the workforce.[10] The figures are only a bit higher for women serving as state governors or senators. And this means that male dominance still is the norm when we think of leadership.

Gender differences are actually quite interesting when we consider the common conception of humankind's evolution as sparking a "fight or flight" reflex when faced with stressful or crisis situations, whether a saber-toothed tiger, irate subordinate, or dangerous competitor, one in which we are programmed to protect ourselves by either doing battle or fleeing from the risk. And yet, it turns out that women have evolved in a distinctly different pattern that emphasizes "tend and befriend" over dominance, meaning to use support, compassion, caring, and empathic resonance in order to build coalitions and lead others.[11]

One classic example of a woman's style of leadership might be exemplified in a figure like Oprah Winfrey, who rules an empire of media-based products and services originally spawned from her talk show that was broadcast to 150 countries and has since expanded to include websites, social media, workshops, trade shows, magazines, books, and even her own television network. What she is "selling" in so many of these formats is self-empowerment for women; her signature pitch is communicated through her own sense of compassion and empathy for others. She has devoted many of her shows to causes that speak directly to those who are suffering or oppressed, whether covering themes related to mental illness, healthy lifestyle, addictions, the environment, workaholism, and abuse. She has used her influence and power to try to make a difference in the areas to which she feels most committed.

Sure, she is a billionaire celebrity, but also one with an image of caring for others, as evidenced by the ways in which she not only presents herself on media but also walks through life, distinguished by her philanthropy and charitable foundations. Likewise, Bill Gates reinvented himself in the latter part of his career, transforming the image (and practice) of his life from that of a ruthless, computer geek with few interpersonal skills to that of perhaps the most generous advocate of social causes in the history of the world. He has literally vowed to put most of his money where his mouth is, donating billions of dollars to address health and safety issues around the world. He has evolved over time from the consummate model of male, authoritarian, technologically based leadership to someone who best represents the moral obligations of privilege. His actions have inspired a handful of other billionaires like Warren Buffett, Michael Bloomberg, and Mark Zuckerberg to ante up, signifying the ways in which an inspirational leader can influence and invite others to get involved in a worthy cause.

Even with their many critics, Oprah and Gates have made sincere attempts to use their power, fortunes, and influence for greater good. They are both relational in their leadership approach, relying on friends, family, colleagues, and followers to make their dreams into reality. Like many other relationally oriented leaders, such as Admiral Horatio Nelson, they inspire the kind of loyalty and commitment among passionate followers that will help to immunize them against the inevitable missteps and mistakes that will sometimes occur.

There is one other significant advantage of this more empathic, relational style of leadership in that it helps to bond *mutual* loyalty and commitment, not just to the leader's vision but also to one another's welfare and collective satisfaction. After all, human beings are essentially tribal beings, built to function optimally in cooperative groups. In studies of the disbanding of our tribal heritage, people have become far more independent but also considerably isolated and estranged from one another.[12] Depression and suicide were quite rare phenomena among indigenous people with collectivistic cultures, and yet nowadays the highest risks of such emotional disorders occur within the most affluent and urban populations. It is, thus, one of the principal functions of a leader in any contemporary organization to help others to guide, support, and nurture one another, especially during times of difficulty when compassion and empathy are, in fact, what are most needed.

Mentoring Others

When asked what it is about the subject of leadership that most people don't understand, an executive and general counsel for an energy company believes that potential success is all about the relationships that are created with their equity partners, public officials, local landowners, and most of all, employees within the company. "Building our project is important," Cary admitted, "but just as important is molding and growing a whole group of people who will do well for the rest of their careers."

Cary has major responsibility for legal matters within the company, negotiating contracts, overseeing all the outside legal work that must be done, meeting with government officials, but he actually views his most important job as mentoring the young employees within the company. Ultimately, he feels responsible for people in the early stages of their careers: His job isn't just about building a successful project, it is also about mentoring people along the way. That is one reason why he is so relationally focused, even though his training occurred in an arcane specialty field within international law.

"It's not just what I do that matters, but how I say or do something, and how others interpret those actions," Cary explains. "I try to be as thoughtful and generous with others whenever possible. I make myself as accessible as I can." These aren't just words to him as he makes his home available to his colleagues and staff to drop by, visit with his children, stop by for an impromptu meal, consult with him about personal matters in their lives. More than anything else, Cary views his most important leadership attribute as being conscientious and thoughtful toward others at all times.

This sounds easy in theory, or as a goal, but it is incredibly difficult in practice, especially given all the other demands that life places on us. At the time I interviewed Cary, he was absolutely exhausted, having stayed up most of the night caring for his infant and toddler. "Sleep just isn't in the picture these days," he said with a laugh, "and discretionary time is somewhat limited. I try to exercise whenever I have a spare seven minutes. Yesterday my workout was doing push-ups with my daughter sitting on my back, yelling 'Giddy up Daddy, Giddy up.' She thought that was fun and I did too until she started standing on my back trying to surf." Again, a good-natured laugh ensued, but you could also see the fatigue in his face.

In order to keep mentoring relationships as one of his major priorities, whether at work or in daily life, he has surrendered all excuses for not having—or making—time with his wife, his children, his closest friends, and his co-workers. Everyone knows this about him, and it is precisely this commitment so evident in his behavior every day that inspires his staff and colleagues to follow his lead. "Leadership is about prioritizing what's important," Cary summarized, "and then to avoid any excuses for why you didn't follow through on those things. You say no to what doesn't really matter." He makes this a guiding principle for not only his own life but also all those employees and colleagues whom he mentors.

Cary sees one of his main roles within the organization as helping others to find greater meaning and responsibility in their work. He believes that what they do together is not only a public service but also such incredible fun, and he tries to make this enthusiasm and passion as contagious as possible. The goal is for these feelings to not just be present when staff are in the office but to permeate every other aspect of their lives. "I truly enjoy the people I work with. They are my friends. And I care deeply about them. I have to know what is important to them and make sure that they have time to do the things they enjoy the most. Rather than a distraction, I think this makes us all more committed to one another, and ultimately more responsible."

It may appear as if this philosophy is a means to an end—building their project—but Cary feels strongly that the relationships he maintains with colleagues are the glue that holds everything else together. "The point of leadership," he says succinctly, "is to inspire others to do good, and provide them with the resources and support to get that done. After all, we are fighting climate change one carbon molecule at a time. That's got to be worth something."

Cary's company has come up against so many insurmountable obstacles related to government regulations, self-serving political manipulations, obsolete laws that were never intended to apply to our current environmental predicament, scrambling for money, among others. Almost every month, there is some new crisis that threatens the very viability of the firm's project. Cary sees his job as keeping everyone as centered and optimistic as possible, given all the disappointments and hurdles they have faced.

Not every leader aspires to this kind of leadership philosophy, much less is even interested in investing so much time and energy in others' lives, but regardless of one's style, goals, and situation, the more skilled you are at reading and responding to people's priorities and needs, the more willing they will be to follow you into battle—and forgive you when things don't go as anticipated.

Facilitating High-Functioning Groups

People work together in all kinds of ways, as partners or collaborators on a project, as part of a team, community, or extended network. Although such groups all share in common some level of relational engagement, they have some significant differences that also require varied kinds of leadership configurations.[13] In a partnership between two collaborators, trust and openness is a key issue that modulates reasonably equal participation; otherwise, one or both partners will become frustrated with what is perceived as an unfair distribution of responsibility or the workload. In work groups, each member is typically assigned particular tasks that relate to the overall group goals. Teams are created for the purposes of some operational objective, and the relationships formed are optimized to accomplish assigned tasks. Within a community, or larger organizational structure, there are complex interrelationships between coalitions, teams, and other units that have been formed, based on convenience or personal interests. Finally, networks are composed of those who wish to remain connected in an ongoing way, whether as alumni of a school or members of a listserv.

Groups that are high functioning, regardless of their structure, have certain features in common that act to build relational connections and closeness between members.[14] Many of these principles have been derived from decades of research on optimal group performance, whether on the job, battlefield, or social encounters.

Cohesion and Trust

Nothing much happens in any group without mutual trust. Participants will be cautious and guarded, reluctant to do or say anything that puts them at possible risk for censure or humiliation. The atmosphere will either be rather formal, passive, and withdrawn, or else aggressive and competitive with people trying to score points and establish dominance.

As we've discussed within the context of leading meetings, any high-functioning group must feel safe enough for participants to respectfully disagree, to even support conflict when it leads to some resolution. The key is always trust—trusting yourself to speak your mind without fear of reprimand, trusting one another to be supportive even when there are sticky areas of contention, trusting the leader to protect member dignity. The most spirited, interesting, and productive groups are often those in which the relational engagement between members operates at the highest level.

"I'm usually the outlier," one senior staff member described herself to me. "I'm like the kid in the *Emperor's New Clothes* who yells out the guy is naked. I sometimes see people roll their eyes when I speak up but I also see them smiling affectionately. People appreciate me even though I'm a pain in the ass at times. But I think I serve an important role challenging the way we do things just because we always do them that way."

What this woman did not mention explicitly, but that clearly explains why and how she can get away with being a rebel and "speaker of the truth," at least *her* truth, is that the leader not only indulges her behavior but also encourages it. He actually likes opposing arguments and believes that it fortifies the strength of the unit. This could only be possible when there are consistently enforced norms that emphasize building solid cohesion within the group.

Consensual Goals

Given the point raised earlier about the importance of allowing as many people as possible to have a voice, the corresponding goal is even more challenging to achieve—seeking consensus. This, in itself, can become a group norm that is absolutely imperative so everyone ends up at the same place even if they chose different routes to get there. This means helping everyone involved feel committed to the objectives that have been decided; without that, you end up with a lukewarm response from some people not sufficiently motivated to complete the tasks. It is thus important that the goals not "belong" to the leader, but rather represent an organizational priority supported by members.

This objective sounds good in theory, but it is quite difficult to achieve in practice given the competing agendas and preferences that diverse groups of people hold. Some are cautious and timid, others aggressive and reckless. Some with excessive ambition have aspirations to move up the power spectrum and so seek opportunities to control the proceedings. Some just want as low a profile as possible. The leader's job is to bring together the different perspectives into a unified vision that is also consistent with the organizational goals that have already been debated by those in highest authority. "That's an interesting idea," or "You've thought a lot about this," or "I like the way you care so much about this issue" are all subtle, gentle ways of saying, "Thanks for your contribution but there's no way in hell we are doing that!"

Effective groups and organizations thus feel mutual and shared responsibility for outcomes. Members develop a deep and abiding interest in helping to make things work. There is a sense of loyalty inspired precisely because people believe they are pursuing their own best interests, instead of working on behalf of someone else who doesn't even know they exist.

Compassion and Caring

This category is usually optional in many work settings, especially domains where interpersonal responsiveness is not particularly valued, but it is still highly desirable. Who wouldn't want to be part of a group in which the members care deeply for one another, watch each other's back, and genuinely look forward to time together?

Although there is plenty of research indicating that relatively homogeneous groups tend to be more cohesive and cooperative since they have so many shared qualities and interests, frequently the most spirited, creative teams include quite diverse members in terms of their skills, abilities, interests, backgrounds, and experiences. Abraham Lincoln was renowned for inviting rivals and competitors, even traditional enemies, to serve in his Cabinet. As he was the first Republican presidential candidate ever elected, he had few allies or colleagues on whom he could rely, so he recruited those who had opposed him to join the administration, including his Secretary of State William Seward, a Whig; his Secretary of the Treasury Salmon Chase, who was a big supporter of slavery and a member of the Free Soil Party; and Secretary of War Edwin Stanton, a Democrat. Needless to say, this was a courageous idea on Lincoln's part, but it led to all kinds of crazy conflicts among these men. Lincoln has also been credited with pure genius for bringing his enemies closer so he could disarm them.[15] It would be difficult to underestimate, however, how challenging it was for Lincoln, or any leader, to negotiate and mediate disagreements among such opposing points of view.

Bill Clinton loved to observe his advisers arguing with one another, even encouraging them to disagree with him, in order to clarify his own views on issues. It is one thing to tell people you want to hear their honest opinions and quite another to actually reinforce and reward that behavior, even when doing so leads to increased tension and personal challenges that must be managed. The key to making this approach work appears to relate back to the cohesion and trust within the group, as well as how well the leader is perceived as benevolent and caring. This became a problem during Trump's administration because of the mistrust and backstabbing that took place among various advisers who all had their own self-serving agendas.

Access Specialized Expertise

One of the factors that makes groups so potentially effective, and powerful, in making decisions is the opportunity to rely on such a variety of experiences and specialized expertise. Each voice in a room or organization is not created equal, even in the most democratic of institutions. There are certain people who just know and understand things so much better than everyone else. Even though the most eager and boastful voices are heard the most frequently, that doesn't mean they offer the most useful input.

A leader's job is to know not just the capabilities and special contributions of each team member, but also how to draw out those who are best equipped to provide useful input. Sometimes the quietest individuals are precisely those who have the most important things to say.

Accountability Between and Among Members

Whereas all followers are ultimately accountable to the leader, an even more powerful incentive occurs when they feel a great sense of loyalty and commitment to one another. That is why brothers (or sisters) in arms are willing to sacrifice their lives for a "noble cause," though such a reason does not necessarily relate to abstractions like freedom or democracy; soldiers are willing to die to save their friends.

Coalitions form within any human organization, based on shared interests and priorities. Friendships, even romances, develop as well, creating their own alliances that can become insular and self-serving, rather than ultimately helpful to everyone. Whenever a leader can structure things such that team members follow one another, power is (seemingly) decentralized and responsibilities are more evenly distributed. This is the hallmark of high-functioning groups.

Remember: You Are Not Just a Person but Also an Object

If you remember one of the basic ideas of Sigmund Freud, you will recall that he devised the idea of "transference" to capture the phenomenon in which patients (and all other humans) "project" onto their therapist (or other authority figures) strong feelings and reactions that have been shifted because of unresolved issues with parental-type figures from the past. More simply, we sometimes experience leaders in very personal ways that reflect distortions, blind spots, or exaggerations, resulting in feelings we have had toward others who remind us of those in leadership positions. We sometimes see leaders not as they are, but as we imagine—or even need—them to be.

This realization is profound, even if sometimes obvious. It means that leaders are not really judged based solely on their actual performance, but rather assessed according to fantasy, myth, projection, and transference reactions. To some within an organization, the leader is viewed as a paternal object, a mother or grandfather figure. For others, a leader reminds them of an older brother, an annoying neighbor, a former teacher, or that guy on TV who is always trying to sell us something. Leaders are thus cast in certain roles, especially by the media, as villains, heroes, frauds, white knights, tricksters, or fools. Those within the organization form their own fantasy characterizations of the leader based on what they think they want and need most.[16] If feeling helpless or powerless, they want someone who appears omnipotent. If recently burned by some authority figure, their resentments might spill over, so to speak, transferring feelings of suspicion and anger to view the leader as fraudulent. And if feeling needy or emotionally bereft, someone might see the leader as a potential rescuer.

At each developmental stage of life, we are searching for something quite different. Those in their 20s are seeking mentors who really do resemble benevolent parental figures, endlessly patient, brilliant, and always support-ive and validating—all the things that their actual mother or father perhaps could not, or would not, provide. Once in their 30s, followers might be more in the market for a leader who is like an older sibling, meaning continued deference and respect but also more informality. And so on throughout the life span.

Whether justified or not, whether you think it is part of your job or not, leaders are still put in the position of acting as if they are parental objects or authority figures. This means, of course, that even the most careless ges-ture or inadvertent facial expression will be interpreted in a dozen different ways, depending on what others imagine it means. I've been told over and over again that when I'm concentrating really, really hard, listening with com-plete focus, I have this blank expression on my face. Time and time again, people have told me that it appears as if I'm judging them. Almost every time (sometimes I really am judging) I try to explain that I was just listening, the offended parties will once again still insist that the expression doesn't look that way to them. Now I've practiced this expression in the mirror and seen it in a photo, and I'm pretty sure it appears genuinely "blank," but others, espe-cially much younger junior staff, feel intimidated not by what I'm actually doing or saying, but rather by what they are projecting onto me.

So, how do you fix this?

I'm glad you asked. We have been exploring the power of compassion and caring as exemplified by some of the prototypical paternalistic or maternalis-tic leaders like Pope Francis, Oprah Winfrey, and the Dalai Lama. Whether others want or need validation, support, affection, or parental approval, it doesn't matter because good leadership involves providing them as often as possible and as warranted. That is the hallmark of leaders who are perceived as benevolent: They are accessible to followers and provide a moral grounding to the organizational operation beyond a profit-and-loss statement. They are seen as visible symbols of what the company stands for. That is one reason why so many prominent executives resign from presidential advisory boards when they so vehemently disagree with decisions they believe are directly oppositional to their basic core values.

Compare two university presidents with and for whom I've worked. Magda is rarely seen on campus except riding around in her air-conditioned golf cart with an entourage. Her face is plastered on the school's website sev-eral times each week, proclaiming every little accomplishment; such overtures are looked upon with scorn by most faculty, who find her arrogant and self-promoting. Whether she really cares about students, staff, and faculty is beside the point because perception is everything, and when you insulate yourself behind a wall of assistants blocking access, it may restrict any bothersome intrusions but at a cost.

Dirk was one of the most incredible leaders I've ever known. He had an open-door policy whereby any student or staff member could come by his office to chat, at any hour without an appointment, as long as he was not otherwise occupied. Of course, he *was* busy most of the time, but it's the thought that counts. Second, he made a point to eat lunch each day in the student cafeteria, as well as to be seen walking around campus, looking in on folks while they were at work. He volunteered to teach a class each semester even though that was hardly part of his job; nevertheless, it kept him closely in touch with the students. Finally, and most remarkably, he recognized every single one of the 400 faculty members on campus—by name—and would greet each one as he strolled by. Adding to this perception of deep caring, he would send a personally written and signed note to each faculty member whenever he or she published a book or article, or presented a paper at a professional conference.

But here's the irony: Although Dirk was viewed by almost everyone on campus as accessible, caring, compassionate, a relationship wizard, he was eventually fired by the board of trustees for failing to get a handle on the budget and mismanaging finances. And Magda? She is despised by almost everyone on campus for her inaccessibility and self-serving ways, firing anyone who is not completely loyal to her and her agenda, yet the university's chancellor just renewed her term of service. So, what's the moral of the story?

Relationships are certainly important. Compassion and caring are indeed highly desirable characteristics in a leader who values accessibility and follower approval. But such is not necessarily nearly enough to succeed in an organization when there is also a bottom line of fiscal responsibility. Caring leaders are often idealized to the point that they become paralyzed because they may block initiative and autonomy and promote dependency. They may also "care" too much about things that feel good but don't necessarily lead to growth and productivity.

It's Not Just What You Know, but Who You Know

Knowledge and skills are critically important to leaders for sure, but just as critical are the social networks from which to draw support, guidance, and alliances in times of need. This, of course, is how the world works—and it has always been that way. In fact, it could be said that one of main functions of leaders throughout the ages has been to build a set of alliances with other "neighboring tribes" to promote collaboration and cooperation with competitors, as well as to create trade opportunities in all the ways that an exchange of goods, services, and information is possible.[17]

Successful leaders have carefully recruited and nurtured a set of allies over the years, exchanging favors, building coalitions, collecting and paying off debts. This has been described as "Legos for grown-ups," developing all kinds of personal relationships that allow them to access private information and data that may be unavailable to others.[18] They develop rich sources of intelligence across a spectrum of settings and contexts, and they do so not just for personal gain but because they truly believe that everyone deserves to be treated with respect and consideration.

Tom Kolditz, a former army general and leader of a leadership institute mentioned in a previous chapter, makes an effort to engage anyone he can within his organization, regardless of their position. Many evenings when he might stay late to work in his office, the maintenance person comes in to empty trash. Although Kolditz may often feel rushed to finish up his work and head home, he always takes time to talk with the trash collector about her life. Over time, he has found that he looks forward to these brief encounters, sometimes even lingering a bit so they can continue their ritual dialogue. Kolditz does this not for any particular agenda except that he enjoys getting to know everyone around him, regardless of their position and responsibility. While it is true that he learns a lot of fascinating gossip from this woman, he is not consciously aware of any systematic attempt on her part to gather data. They just talk about their lives.

Kolditz learned from his time in the military that his ability to do his job well was based on the accuracy and deep knowledge he gained about the soldiers under his command. This is no less true today when his "troops" consist mostly of ambitious students who want to make a difference in the world.

Leaders who value social networking have developed exceptional relational skills that permit them to put others at ease, quickly establish trust and intimacy, and engage people in ways that make them feel heard and understood. It requires systematically reaching out to others who have specialized expertise and knowledge or skills that may someday prove useful. It means cultivating these relationships over time, not just for any eventual benefit that may be needed, but rather because such individuals so enjoy this process of getting to know others.

Social networks become their own valuable resources and commodities that can be shared with allies and exchanged as currency. One administrator I know is part of a road cycling group that includes a member of his company who is known as notoriously tightlipped about anything that goes on within his unit that controls budgets and the allocation of resources. The time the two of them spend riding together has loosened up their relationship in such a way that this administrator has access to all kinds of secrets. But just as important is that they now swap referrals when one or the other needs access to someone else in the company who may be in the best position to help him.

Networking for leaders often begins during their university days when we first begin to form allegiances that help us to navigate the complex dynamics of a competitive academic environment. Wendy Kopp first conceived of the idea of Teach for America when she was an undergraduate at Princeton University.[19] She recruited other student leaders on campus to join her vision and eventually devoted her senior thesis to the topic of creating a national teacher corps that eventually became a reality years later. She broadened her networking to include possible corporate sponsors for her vision, eventually building a big enough coalition that she launched this audacious project soon after graduation. And as you'd expect with an organization that is focused on mentoring and teaching disadvantaged young people, the success of the operation depended so much on finding and training followers with solid relationship skills.

One more nuance of the networking phenomenon among leaders isn't related to simply *who* they know but *how* they know them in terms of the level of engagement. In describing what has been called an "entrusting style" of relational leadership, one researcher relates how symphony conductor Michael Tilson Thomas conceives of his role in directing an orchestra.[20] He had been called upon as a guest conductor to lead the Chicago Symphony in a rendition of Tchaikovsky's Sixth Symphony, and he wanted to inspire them to go beyond their perceived limits of the notes on the page. A conductor's relationship with his musicians largely determines the relative freedom they feel to improvise versus following the established script that they have performed hundreds of times previously. "Let's breathe together," Tilson Thomas instructed the orchestra during a rehearsal in which they seemed confused by his permissive style that was quite at odds with that of their regular conductor. "Hold the first note slightly longer, and then let the melody gracefully fall away from it," he instructed them. "I couldn't make the music happen alone," Tilson Thomas explained, "We needed to share the feeling, we had to find that shape together, and we did. It was miraculous."

Miraculous things can—and do—happen in settings in which the leader trusts his or her followers enough to set them free. There is by no means universal agreement on what leads to greater productivity. Some claim it is all about the talent you recruit, finding the best and brightest people. Others believe, based on different evidence, that it isn't always who is on your team that matters as much as how well they function and collaborate together. It is relationships that bind people together for a common cause, especially when they are built on trust and mutual respect.

PART III

Skills and Interventions

7

Some Neglected Leadership Skills and Strategies

"SO, WHAT SHOULD WE DO?"

The question, asked by someone in the room, hangs in agonizing silence. Everyone present is scrupulously studying the conference table's grain of wood. A few participants appear to be taking notes, but if you looked more closely, you'd see they were just doodling nervously.

At this juncture, the leader is flooded with choices about what to say or do next. Silence can mean so many different things, each of which signals a very different intervention or response. If the silence signals that people are just reflecting on what was asked, and are thinking about what they want to say, then it is best to wait things out as patiently as possible even though doing so may be uncomfortable. But what if the reason why people are not saying anything is that they don't know what is really being asked? Besides possible confusion, perhaps they are afraid of saying something wrong that will result in censure or humiliation? In the case of confusion, it would be best to provide additional clarification, but if the reason for the reluctance to speak is related to fear of criticism, then considerable reassurance is necessary.

If these were the only possible explanations for the collective silence, it would be like a multiple choice exam with four supplied choices, only one of which is correct. But in the realities of leadership, there are sometimes an infinite number of options or explanations, none of which may be a definitive answer, or perhaps *all* of them play a part in the phenomenon. In this example, for instance, the silence could mean that people are resistant and pouting. Or perhaps they are expressing disapproval through withdrawal. Or maybe they honestly don't have a clue about what should be done and are waiting for more information or direction.

All Responses Are Contextual

It is clear from this situation, and so many others, that before we can take action, whether on the smallest scale, such as responding to someone in a meeting or conversation, or else launching a whole new enterprise, we first must accurately assess what is going on, what is most needed, and what might be most helpful. I use the word "might" deliberately because there is almost never a way to truly know for sure ahead of time what is going to produce the best outcome. We may have our hunches and hypotheses, but the ultimate best choice is based only on available—and always insufficient—information. This, of course, sometimes leads to wildly inaccurate predictions regarding the future, even among the most accomplished leaders. Darryl Zanuck, CEO of 20th Century Fox, predicted in 1946: "Television won't be able to hold on to any market it captures after the first six months. People will soon get tired of staring at a plywood box." Ken Olsen, founder of Digital Equipment Corporation, proclaimed in 1977 at the World Future Society that "there is no reason anyone would want a computer in their home." More recently, in 2007, Steve Ballmer, Microsoft's CEO, asserted, "There's no chance that the iPhone is going to get any significant market share." No matter how good any of us are at our jobs, we still make poor choices based on inaccurate or unreliable readings of a situation.

I have been teaching graduate courses in group leadership for over 40 years, and I still find it to be among the most complex, confusing, overwhelming jobs imaginable. It isn't just the responsibility for others' welfare, or the usual complexity and chaos of organizations, that makes the job difficult. Neither may this be solely attributed to the ongoing stress of tracking so many variables simultaneously, nor the uncertainty of where things are heading and why. The overall challenge is being able to simply figure out what is really happening on any given day or at any given moment.

There's a myth circulating in popular media, and even within academic journals, that leadership involves certain universal skills and behaviors that can be consistently applied in similar situations. Yet every context is quite different, not only in terms of the goals of the organization, the personnel on board, the cultural environment, but also the unique interaction among all these variables.

A team member fails to complete an assignment that is an integral component of an overall project. The particular intervention chosen to address this issue depends very much on a variety of factors, including: (1) this individual's prior history; (2) the interpreted meaning of the noncompliance (neglect, forgetfulness, overscheduled, acting out); and (3) the kind of relationship that exists between the employee and leader. The person could conceivably be privately confronted, publicly challenged, supportively encouraged, ignored, or even dismissed. It would appear that rather than leader skills conceived as being somewhat universal and stable across settings and situations, the skills are actually discontinuous in the sense that they vary considerably across roles and responsibilities. This helps explain why some extraordinarily competent leaders find themselves in great difficulty when they change jobs or are promoted, continuing to rely on the skills that worked for them before rather than adapting to quite different circumstances.

Soft and Hard Skills

Leadership skills are often organized (or "stuffed") into four broad categories that involve problem-solving, political maneuvering, instruction/teaching, and persuasive/warrior abilities.[1] Other researchers have insisted that leaders actually employ additional critical skills that include problem identification, which is absolutely necessary before problem-solving given that critical issues can be conceptualized in many different ways.[2] Once a problem is clearly identified and analyzed, other skills call for planning future goals and forecasting likely trends—which we've seen are often based on flawed assumptions and incomplete data.

With all the attention directed toward specific management techniques, leadership strategies, and simplistic skills, often ignored are some far subtler factors that make for excellence in almost any domain. Most executive, management, and leadership programs have traditionally concentrated on providing what it takes to manage, control, and direct others, without necessarily teaching alternative ways to empower and facilitate followers' initiative. Thus, so-called hard skills are often featured most prominently in the curriculum, assuming that if someone is adequately prepared in accounting, finance, budgeting, forecasting, marketing, inferential statistics, inventory logistics, and other areas, that's about all the person needs to be an effective manager. What's missing, of course, are the "soft skills," the kinds of relational and personal attributes that facilitate trust, loyalty, and commitment by followers.[3] Leaders certainly know things, and can complete various tasks better than others, but they also inspire followers through their sense of morality, integrity, respect, and caring.

There is indeed a set of discrete skills and behaviors that almost all great leaders have developed, which is very good news for those of us who wish to become better at our craft. It means that each of us has the opportunity and capability to become so much more effective in what we do as we add to and refine our skill set to provide more options and more successful outcomes. Yet many would agree that leadership ability is not really acquired as a skill, but rather represents a way of being.

As discussed earlier, there has been considerable debate within the leadership literature on whether excellence in this role, or even competence, is primarily the result of personal traits or skills that have been developed over time. With regard to the latter, it does appear that the most important abilities are part of an evolutional process that begins during adolescence with intrapersonal skills that enable the regulation of emotion. This is when we learn to control outbursts, moodiness, and inappropriate social behavior that may be off-putting to others. It is also the time when our awareness of strengths and weaknesses becomes critically important to capitalize on signature abilities and compensate for potential blind spots.

Such personality attributes are frequently defined in two distinctly different ways that may be at significant odds with each other. The first perspective is guided by the ways we see ourselves; this is defined as *self-identity* and may, or may not, be an accurate representation of some semblance of reality. The second perspective involves the ways in which you are viewed and experienced by others, and this consists of your reputation among followers or in the community.[4]

It is a leap of misguided faith to assume there is perfect congruence between the ways you see yourself and the ways you are viewed by others. What we think we see in so-called reality is just an approximation of what may actually exist. We "reconstruct" a version of reality based on our own perceptual filters, one that is sometimes wildly distorted, inaccurate, and illusional.[5] Even the most basic assessments and decisions that are made are so strongly influenced by a biased internal framework. Imagine, for example, three umpires having a few beers after a game and sharing their approach to calling balls and strikes.[6] The first umpire says, quite simply, "There's balls and there's strikes and I call them the way they are." The second umpire nods his head in understanding, but offers instead, "There's balls and there's strikes, and I call them the way I *see* them." The third umpire, recognizing that his two colleagues represent *objectivist* and *constructivist* perspectives in their philosophies, announces, "There really aren't any balls and strikes until I call them!" In other words, this postmodern, *radical constructionist* umpire recognizes that reality only exists, not as any objective reality, but rather as a construction of our own imagination and perceptions. If this is truly the case, then that means we must be very cautious and tentative when we assume that others see and experience the world in the same ways we do.

If this flexible perceptual worldview is an example of one's soft skills, then a second set is characterized by the development of interpersonal skills that are considered essential for building trust, loyalty, and support. It isn't until higher education, and entrance into the world of work, that so-called business skills follow, which include the necessary requirements of understanding budgeting, marketing, and such. Finally, actual organizational leadership skills evolve that integrate the key components of each of these domains.

Again, we must consider the difference between what leaders believe is important versus what their followers consider significant, since there is sometimes considerable disagreement regarding goals and the processes used to achieve them. Leaders talk a lot about paradigm shifts, profitability, market share, branding, outcome accountability, certainly important objectives, but followers almost never mention those as nearly as important to them as the leader's integrity and fairness, his or her competence and composure during crises, a vision and goals that have been collaboratively developed, and finally decisiveness.[7] This purposefulness would be qualified in terms of "good" versus "bad" decisions for the organization, and also those for individuals, since almost everyone examines decisions and actions in terms of how such choices will affect them and their own needs. Competence is thus identified when others feel like things are getting better—for them and their own constituents.

Pushing and Pulling

Different situations, contexts, and challenges often require quite varied styles of leadership, depending on the particular needs of followers, not to mention the overarching problem. Investigating the nature of leadership within tribal traditions, the Iroquois Nation employed two parallel systems of governance, depending on whether they were facing the crisis of war or conditions of relative peace and prosperity.[8] In other words, they believed two very different styles of leadership were optimal for these opposing circumstances. During emergency situations, war chiefs stepped up because of their courage, fierceness, and loyalty, not because of such virtues as justice, harmony, and caring. Once hostilities ended, peacetime leaders were chosen by the women to preside over a civilian population that was more in need of support and social services. It was considered rare, if not improbable, that a single leader could operate effectively during both stable and crisis situations.

Leaders often find themselves frustrated and stymied when they persist in following the same pattern just because it is comfortable and familiar, perhaps having worked well in the past. In a study of leadership under adversity, coal miners who had been trapped underground during an explosion were interviewed.[9] They had limited water, food, oxygen, and light sources, and they were completely cut off from the outside world. The first leaders to emerge sought only a means to escape and survive, admonishing others to search for a water source and try to dig their way out. They saw their roles during this "survival stage" as one of pushing and cajoling followers to take decisive action. They were autocratic, controlling, single-minded, and stubborn, seemingly uninterested in anyone else's opinions; if someone began crying or begging or complaining, these survival leaders would immediately shut them up. It was during the second stage, when the trapped miners had to wait for days in the dark without losing their minds or hope, that far more empathic, emotionally resonant leaders emerged. They worked to soothe and reassure others, relying on what might be described as a far more empathic, compassionate style. It must seem evident that these two very different leadership styles actually differentiated typically gendered ways of relating during crises.

It is important for leaders to have developed a broad range of skills and styles, those that can be adapted to different circumstances and follower needs. It is also incredibly advantageous to be able to draw upon the signature strengths of both maternal (empathic) and paternal (authoritarian) patterns in order to support and nurture others, as well as to motivate them or take charge when that is what is most needed. This frequently means increasing one's capacity for uncertainty and ambiguity, becoming far more flexible and adaptable, and learning multiple ways to approach problems when favored strategies are not effective.

It is one of the enduring frustrations of therapists, coaches, or any other agent of change that people insist on continuing to do things that are clearly counterproductive, even when there is consistent, overwhelming data that these approaches are not working, or perhaps making things worse. In other words, people remain stuck because they keep doing the same things over and over again, without noticeable improvement. And they do so because once upon a time, in another situation, with other people, the same approach worked just fine.

So to get "unstuck," sometimes the best course of action is to stop whatever you are already doing and try something else. And usually a good place to start is trying the exact *opposite* approach. If pulling on the door doesn't work, try pushing it. If arguing doesn't work with someone, try reasoning.

If challenging someone isn't effective, and you've tried that several times with the same results, try backing off. I'm not suggesting that any of these approaches would be more helpful, but they at least offer the *possibility* of working, whereas the prior strategy will most likely never work, especially if it has already been tried a few times with the same dismal results.

This point may seem rather obvious, but you'd be amazed how often people resort to doing things that are clearly ineffective, and yet they keep repeating these actions over and over again. This willingness to let go of favored or comfortable strategies when they are clearly not working is one of the most crucial "soft" skills because it is the primary means by which we can ever discern more effective alternatives.

Motivation Is Almost Everything

Speaking of more effective alternative strategies, beyond all else we could discuss, leaders are in the business of motivating others, whether to further their own interests or for some greater good. After all, one of the leader's essential jobs is to make work meaningful for others, and we are failing miserably at this task considering that the vast majority (less than one-third) report feeling truly "engaged" in their jobs.[10] Why? Because most leaders don't really understand what's most important to those they are paid to serve.

Sure, fair compensation matters to a certain degree, but so does recognition, pride, social interaction, freedom, and a sense of personal control. It's all about validation and appreciation. "Acknowledgement is a kind of magic," observes behavioral economist Dan Ariely, "a small human connection, a gift from one person to another that translates into a much larger, more meaningful outcome".[11] And "meaningful" is indeed almost everything, sometimes even far more critical than any financial remuneration or other perks.

In a series of experiments, Ariely set out to investigate what really drives people to perform their best at work and in daily life. When assigned specific tasks to complete, he discovered that monetary compensation means very little should the effort not feel as if it has some larger purpose and meaning. People take pride in what they do; they aren't all that happy just to go through the motions for a paycheck no matter how generous it might be.

I remember being introduced to a classic psychology experiment decades ago that has forever become embedded in whatever I understand and practice as a leader. The researchers selected a group of preschoolers and divided them into two groups. In the first control group, the kids were handed art materials and let loose to draw or create whatever they liked. In the second experimental group, the children were paid a "salary" to produce artworks. Then the researchers followed up with the children some time afterward to see which ones continued to have an interest in art. It turns out that the intrinsic reward of painting for its own pure joy was far more rewarding—and those children who were paid to draw lost interest once the financial incentives were withdrawn.

Since then, numerous other experiments have investigated what people find most motivating, whether applied to corporate leadership, teaching, or parenting. In many cases, throwing more money at followers can actually demotivate and discourage them.[12] Consistently, bonuses, stock options, even promotions have been found to be much less effective rewards and forms of encouragement than those strategies that provide: (1) a sense of deep connection among coworkers; (2) emotional pride and satisfaction in a sense of accomplishment; (3) recognition and validation by leaders and peers; (4) ownership of the results; and (5) deeper meaning derived from the work that extends to satisfaction in other areas of daily life.

These conclusions, of course, fly in the face of what most people *say* is most important to them. So often, they complain about feeling underpaid or poorly compensated for the amount of time and energy that they put into a job, although often those circumstances result from deficits in other areas just described. We know, for example, from studies of well-being and happiness that life satisfaction is not appreciably affected by greater income beyond a certain moderate set point ($75,000 in most southern U.S. states and above $100,000 in California, Hawaii, and cities in the Northeast).[13] After all, billionaires like Warren Buffett, Larry Ellison, Mark Zuckerberg, Michael Dell, Mark Cuban, and Jeff Bezos, who already have more money than they could possibly spend in a hundred lifetimes, are hardly driven by the need to accumulate greater wealth (except as a marker of success), but rather by the satisfaction they derive from the meaning of their work.

Many leaders appear relatively clueless about how critical it is for followers to feel valued and appreciated, and how little time or effort is required to do so. Ariely cites as an example the case of software engineers who labored tirelessly on a project for weeks, investing extraordinary energy into their work.[14] Then the boss abruptly announced that the project had been cancelled, leading the engineers and designers to feel dispirited and discouraged, to the point that they significantly reduced their investment in their job. When they were asked what might have led to a different outcome, they offered lots of actions that would have required so little effort—allowing them to present their work to their peers, using it as a pilot project for a future prototype, and so on. The point is that leaders don't spend nearly enough time figuring out simple ways to let others know their work is meaningful.

There are hundreds of popular articles and blogs spread all over media that purport to offer "6 Secrets to Motivate Employees" or "15 Effective Ways to Motivate Teams," and they certainly do advance sound ideas. But they often miss the point that inspiring and influencing others is not based on following a formula; it is about infusing a core attitude that people deserve to be valued for the important things they do to make an organization function well and produce quality products or services. When a leader demonstrates essential kindness and respect to all those within his or her purview, such an attitude becomes contagious.

One other interesting nuance of this motivation challenge is that, physiologically speaking, the anticipation of rewards is just as important (if not more so) than the actual delivery of the bonus, recognition, or pat on the back. The endocrine system kicks into gear with a flood of internal happiness and satisfaction not after receiving a reward, but according to neurobiologist Robert Sapolsky, during pursuit of that reward.[15] People spend an inordinate amount of time thinking about what might likely occur and relishing the possibility of improved circumstances, which is one reason why gambling is so addictive. Dopamine receptors in the brain light up most intensely when people engage in behavior directly related to the anticipated jackpot.

The kind of leader praise that is experienced as most rewarding and motivating is not the kind that highlights innate ability ("You're so brilliant!"), but rather determined, extraordinary effort ("You worked so hard!"). When followers (or children) are praised and reinforced for their perseverance and grit, they tend to work harder in the future, as well as report greater satisfaction, demonstrate more resilience, and value their own work more enthusiastically.[16] Thus, the lessons to be learned include these:

1. It's really, really important to conceptualize the leader's job as a motivator.
2. Maintain conditions in which followers know and anticipate that superior work will be acknowledged and appreciated.
3. Create a culture in which superior work is appreciated by not only the leader but also peers (meaning a cooperative rather than competitive atmosphere exists).
4. Make sure to focus on people's effort and commitment, rather than just their skills and abilities.

5. Whereas people certainly value monetary and extrinsic rewards for their work, especially when it is perceived as fair and equitable, just as important (if not more so) is instilling a sense of pride in a job well done—and consistently letting employees know their effort has been recognized.
6. More than ever, people are searching for greater meaning in their work—and lives. Anything leaders can do to help them find such satisfaction in their daily labors is going to inspire greater commitment.

Leaders Are Mostly Made Rather Than Born

Organizations spend something like $30 billion each year on leadership development, so there seems to be some kind of general agreement that the most important skills can be learned over time. In other words, although certain people may be born with particular qualities that make them more likely to aspire to, or be chosen for, leadership positions, most of the capability (more than 70 percent) is actually developed through experience and shaped by one's upbringing.[17] The challenge is that since there have been no less than 70 such skills that are considered significant, covering everything from managing stress, learning to say no, processing negative feedback, and so on, what focus should become the greatest priority?[18]

Listening, Really, *Really* Listening

When leaders in various settings and environments were asked what they considered the most important skills to master, both now and in the future, about the only one that ranked most consistently in the same place—number one—was interpersonal and relationship-building skills (which was why it deserved its own chapter). Those interviewed also predicted that the ability to persuade and influence others will only become more important in the future, replacing many traditional "management" skills.[19]

Leaders are known primarily for being good talkers. We are persuasive, articulate, and inspirational. We know how to convince others to do things they'd prefer not to. We know how to discuss, debate, argue, cajole—and do it louder than anyone else. But the most important secret of an exceptional leader is knowing how to listen deeply to others, and then being able to communicate an accurate understanding of what has been said.

Since leaders are accustomed to being the most important person in the room, it is often difficult for us to shut up and listen. But it is more than listening skills that are appreciated most by subordinates (and family members);

it is also the ability to respond in such a way that people feel heard and understood. It is absolutely useless, for example, to reassure someone with "I know what you mean," or "Yes, I understand." You must prove the depth of your understanding by showing others that you actually got what they were *trying* to say. I emphasize "trying" in the previous sentence because frequently people don't say what they really mean and are looking for help clarifying their thoughts and feelings during an interaction.

Being interpersonally responsive to others is, in fact, one of the most crucial leader skills. In spite of most available training focusing on all kinds of simplistic or arcane business strategies and techniques, it is really the most basic relational skills that build loyalty and trust.

Getting Stuff Done

Many leaders talk a good game, make all kinds of promises, present any number of projections and plans, but don't follow through on the delivery. It may be that their ambition was out of control or that they were less than honest about what they could accomplish, but the bottom line is they weren't able to do what others counted on. This is more than just disappointing; it is a betrayal of trust.

One other variation of this theme is related to ongoing communication with colleagues, subordinates, and other stakeholders. There are different standards with regard to follow-up once someone sends or leaves you a message, but generally speaking, the expectation is that you will offer some kind of timely response, usually within a day or two. There's nothing more frustrating to any of us than sending someone a message, to ask an important question, solicit input, or request information, and it appears as if the communiqué slipped into a black hole. We are left to wonder whether the message was actually received, was accidentally deleted, a response is forthcoming, or whether the recipient is just hopelessly backlogged and can't keep up with requests. It is thus both a priority, and a kind of skill, when leaders make a commitment to others, and themselves, to respond to inquiries promptly and responsibly. This is even more of a challenge if you are one of those workers bombarded with hundreds of messages each day.

Building a Team

It is one of the most challenging tasks for anyone to recruit and select the most qualified people to be part of a working team. References may provide relatively meaningless statements of support, or worse, they often gloss over someone's performance issues, with the supervisor contacted eager to be rid of an employee who has been a problem. During interviews, people present their best possible behavior, and it is only much later, perhaps months, before you learn what someone is really like on the job when the honeymoon period ends.

No matter who is assigned or selected for a team, and what they bring to the table in terms of abilities, expertise, skills, and resources, the leader's main job is to help everyone perform collaboratively and cooperatively in their functions, differentiated tasks, interpersonal sensitivity, and ongoing communication. This is especially the case in extreme environments, whether during crises, when climbing mountains, or in combat.

Ultimately, for a team to work well together, they must have access to crucial information that allows them to function as a unit, rather than as individuals going their own way, without regard to collective goals. So, first of all, it's important that the leader state clearly and exactly what the goals of the task, mission, or assignment are, and make certain that everyone is onboard and committed to this objective. In addition, team members need to know: (1) what specific tasks will be required of them to achieve the desired goals, (2) what challenges or obstacles they might likely encounter along the way, (3) what each member knows and can do to contribute to the collective effort, (4) how everyone will work together, and (5) what steps should be taken if (or when) the original intentions become derailed.[20]

These conditions are established not merely by informing members of the rules, but rather by setting a tone and climate through one's own behavior, and building a sense of group cohesion. In fact, ultimate performance by a group is directly related to their perceived cohesion, although it's not clear whether it is the achievements that lead them to feel pride and closeness to one another, or their collective goodwill that motivates them to work harder for one another.[21]

When Sara Safari was part of a climbing team scaling 27,000-foot Cho Oyu in the Chinese Himalayas, the expedition fell apart at times because of the fractured relationships among some of the climbers and guides. "There was one guide who was constantly on my case," she reported to me. "He was always playing us against one another, encouraging us to be competitive with one another. But the worst part is that he'd always wait for me to do something wrong, something completely inconsequential like not eating or drinking at the same time he thought I should, and then he'd humiliate me in front of the group."

Sara spent quite a few nights in her tent, recovering as much from the emotional abuse as the physical challenges that ravaged her body, sometimes even crying herself to sleep. The hardest part for her was that the team became splintered, and rather than feeling supported during this arduous and dangerous expedition, she constantly felt under fire. That she was able to summit the peak was more a testimony to her stubbornness and resilience than anything offered by her leader and the toxic culture he created.

A few months later, Sara joined an Everest summit attempt that would eventually end in disaster because of earthquakes and avalanches that killed dozens of climbers. But during this climb, she had a very different team experience in which the lead guide made certain that everyone clearly understood their primary job was to help everyone else. Quite a bit of time was invested in building cohesive relationships so that the climbers felt very much like a family, not just members of a working team. Although they ended up trapped at Camp 2 above the Khumbu Icefall before they could be rescued several days later, it was precisely because the climbers were so committed to one another that they were able to survive and assist each other.[22]

Stretching Goals

There's a fair bit of evidence to indicate that reaching for ambitious, even seemingly unrealistic, goals significantly increases the likelihood of dramatically improving progress and productivity. When engineers, teachers, or managers are encouraged to formulate seemingly outrageous objectives, they are far more likely to achieve greater outcomes in a significantly shorter period of time.[23] I'm not talking about just *any* impossible goal, but rather those that are constructed to achieve specific outcomes within certain time parameters and with logical, successive steps.

Stretch goals are as potentially transformative in everyday life as they may be within organizations. When Sara Safari attended a leadership workshop, the instructor invited everyone in attendance to declare out loud a ridiculously improbable goal for themselves. She overheard someone behind her share that she intended to trek to Everest Base Camp in the Himalayas. Impulsively, Safari upped the ante and blurted out loud that she intended to *summit* Mount Everest to bring increased attention to, and raise money for, the children she was supporting in Nepal. After everyone applauded this decidedly ambitious stretch goal, reality set in. It turns out that she had never climbed, or even been in the mountains in her life; she had never even gone camping before and she hated cold weather.

Nevertheless, once making this public commitment, Safari devoted her life for two years into transforming herself into a world-class mountaineer, scaling some of the highest peaks in the Andes and Himalayas. Although her goal of reaching the summit of Everest was initially stymied, she got close enough to her objective that it completely changed her life, not to mention that she raised triple the amount of money originally intended. It was also a series of summit failures that pushed her to work harder to an even more audacious stretch goal—to become the first Persian woman to scale the highest mountain on each of the seven continents.

One note of caution about stretch goals: They can also be rather discouraging if you aren't prepared for disappointment. I used to run weight-loss groups whose sessions would end with each participant declaring how much weight he or she was going to lose the following week. I remember one woman who became so carried away she declared she would lose six pounds during the following week. Unfortunately, I didn't take the time to negotiate something more realistic for her. I later heard from a friend of hers that the reason she never returned to the group again was because she *only* lost four pounds and was ashamed to face everyone because she believed she had "failed."

Mastering Ever-Changing Technology

In the olden days, the business of leadership used to take place face-to-face, with everyone in the same room, cave, or field. It is now the case that almost anyone can have some degree of influence by posting something on social media, publishing a blog, even launching a revolution or starting a civil war with a tweet distributed to millions of followers. Leaders no longer wear three-piece suits and sit in fashionable offices; as long as they have Wi-Fi coverage, a call to action can be sent while literally sitting on the toilet. Corporate decisions by Netflix, Facebook, Verizon, Uber, Gap, United Airlines, GoDaddy, and Bank of America were all reversed after consumers and the public protested rate hikes or other unpopular choices on social media.

It begs the question of whether the power of formal leaders is being eroded now that everyone is directly connected. Anyone can post a YouTube video or tweet that goes viral to millions of viewers in a few days. Anyone can launch a call to action online, whether to announce a meet-up, to find a rave, to locate a new gourmet food truck, or to form a political movement to overthrow the government. Most of us now have the power to not only express displeasure at some decision made by an employer or government, but also try to block or defy the order or law. During the time of Thomas Paine before the American

Revolution, one had to write a pamphlet protesting some unjust law, then print and distribute it by hand (or via horseback). Now it takes less than 30 seconds for some movie star or athlete to express an opinion to 10 million followers. Justin Bieber has over 100 million Twitter followers who closely watch his everyday movements. Katy Perry, Taylor Swift, and other celebrities have more followers than the president of the United States. And if they are unhappy about something, these stars let the world know it, such as the time Swift initiated a civil war against Apple because of the computer giant's policy on royalty payments for streaming music, forcing them to change it.

It is increasingly clear that traditional leadership roles, as we have previously known and understood them, are obsolete.[24] The power of leaders has been somewhat weakened and "tarnished" by the alternative means of instant communication via social media so that we now need a complete reconceptualization of what it means to influence others within organizations or the wider world. Anyone can gain instant information online that is often more accurate than whatever sanitized messages are officially distributed by leaders.

With this ever-changing set of circumstances, coupled with the relentless advancements of technology, today's leaders must be, above all else, flexible and up-to-date with every alternative means by which to touch and communicate with followers on a regular basis. In addition, they must be prepared to harness, if not counteract, the new, far more democratic world order with instant access online.

Dealing with Uncertainty

Leadership, above all else, is about dealing with uncertainty rather than known variables. Surprises are the order of the day. The job involves not just managing risk but capitalizing on opportunities. There are all kinds of risks in every organization related to the marketplace, financial matters, operating issues, and strategic decisions. Some of the perils are known and predicted but many are not, especially considering that most forecasting of economics, business, and markets is not necessarily very accurate.[25]

It is the anomalies and exceptions to the rules that kill us. When Nicholas Taleb wrote about the so-called "black swan phenomenon," he was talking about the improbable events occurring in the landscape that not only catch us off guard, but also begin a cascade of miscalculations that, if unrecognized and unchecked, can have devastating outcomes.[26] These are the outliers that we didn't see coming, the economic collapses, political upheavals, scandals, strikes, and earthquakes. Because such events are both unanticipated and extreme, they carry with them a kind of tsunami-like impact. Examples of such circumstances can be something as pedestrian as losing an important client or customer, or catastrophic national or world events such as the assassination of Archduke Ferdinand that launched the First World War, the economic collapse of the Great Depression or recession of 2008, the fall of the Soviet Union, or the attacks on Pearl Harbor or the World Trade Center towers. In every case, it would appear as if the events came "out of nowhere," even though each displayed signs of impending disaster that were long ignored.

It is the leader's job to at least be aware of the potential for such black swan events and prepare for a decisive response. This is often compromised by too much devotion to maintaining the status quo, thus denying that a burgeoning problem truly exists. As such, it is often too late to mount a defense against destabilizing forces, which is why it is so important to build intelligence networks from a variety of sources that provide the most reliable and up-to-date information on any contingency or possibility that could arise.[27]

When the Empower Nepali Girls Foundation mobilized an effort to organize relief programs after the devastating series of earthquakes that struck Nepal in 2015, the news media and scientists were reporting that the aftershocks of the 7.8 event would soon dissipate, with life returning to normal. The day that I arrived in Kathmandu with a medical team to head toward the epicenter as first responders, another quake literally knocked us to the ground, collapsing buildings everywhere and sending the population into another round of terror. There were so many things that we had never anticipated and planned for since the best intelligence told us that recovery was already underway. Once we arrived on the scene, however, we discovered a very different scenario. The Nepali government was blocking attempts by charitable organizations to deliver survival and medical equipment. Millions of dollars of supplies were stacked up at the airport, not allowed to pass through customs. There were no other relief agencies in operation or visible government officials (many politicians were in hiding because of threats against their lives due to their incompetence, corruption, and complacency). Very few enforceable construction codes were in effect, so buildings fell like dominoes once the Earth buckled. The government was also ordering all foreign aid workers to leave the country. It was complete chaos, with thousands of people dying and no help in sight.

Everything we did, and all that we accomplished during our visits, were based on improvisation and the most flexible responsiveness to ever-changing events on a daily basis. When the monsoon rains and floods began, we had to move our operation inside mobile tents. When people were too sick or injured to visit our aid stations, we made house calls as needed. Every day, the government continued to issue new and different regulations, requiring us to alter our strategies or remain under the radar. The whole operation was an exercise in continuous adaptation in light of new surprises that became so commonplace we stopped trying to predict anything that the government or Nature would next throw at us. The single most important leadership skill was helping the volunteers and team members to take inevitable changes in stride, without breaking their momentum and morale. It became an annoying, but also amusing, part of our work that made all of us so much more flexible in terms of future challenges.

The skill required to deal with uncertainty represents as much an adjustment in attitude as anything that we might do differently. So much of the work that leaders do takes place internally, inside our heads, where we plan and strategize, as well as let go of things that are getting in our way.

Self-Talk and Inner Life

We all suffer slights, injustices, and feel haunted by the past. We hold grudges and relive annoying conversations. Over and over. Especially when we are trying to fall asleep at night, tossing and turning, grumbling and planning fantasies of retribution. There is a saying in 12-step programs like Alcoholics Anonymous about allowing certain people, usually a perceived nemesis, to live in our heads rent-free. The only thing worse than being subjected to an indignity or perceived slight is allowing ourselves to relive those moments over and over and over again.

I mentioned previously how one of the premier skills of exceptional leaders is the ability to manage their emotional reactions. This is something that is actually learned over time and takes considerable practice, considering it is the most natural thing in the world to give free rein to our feelings of anger, frustration, disappointment, jealousy, and resentment.

Among all the major life skills that go far beyond leadership, we might include emotional regulation of one's inner life at the top of the list. This involves not just the ways we react to events on the outside in terms of emotional expressiveness, but also the ways we metabolize and process them on the inside. Every day, every hour of each day, regardless of what you are doing and where you are doing it, there are instances when you are called upon to react in some way. Perhaps "called upon" is less than accurate since there is clearly a choice in the matter—and that is the point. It may not seem that way in times of crisis or evocative circumstances, but prior to almost every feeling, a particular thought precedes it.

Imagine, for instance, as you dress in the morning, you break a shoelace and have no spare to replace it. Then, as you commute to work, the traffic is unusually insane, taking you twice as long as normal to get to your destination. Once you arrive, you learn the conference call that you specifically planned and prepared for has been cancelled, and for a reason that makes no sense. Whoever was supposed to set up the coffee machine apparently forgot to do so. It's 8 in the morning, and the day already feels like a challenge before it truly begins.

Each of these relatively minor disappointments and setbacks offers a number of possible emotional reactions, from a shrug of annoyance to a major hissy fit. The question we are exploring, however, is that what determines this particular response is hardly an automatic reaction. The answer is found not in the circumstances themselves, but rather in the way they are interpreted and how you talk to yourself about what happened. Compare, for example, that in the preceding instances of disappointment, one's reactions could be either measured ("Oh well, sometimes these things happen") or exaggerated ("This ruins my whole day").

The examples of bad traffic, no coffee, a cancelled meeting, or a broken shoelace might seem rather insignificant, but these are exactly the kinds of experiences that people may become unreasonably upset about. They are usually circumstances that: (1) can't be controlled, (2) don't really matter, and (3) don't get any better after whining and complaining about them. These are also the typical kinds of incidents that send some people you know into fits of rage. The overnight package doesn't arrive on time and the boss goes crazy. Someone forgets to handle a matter, or does it in a way that is different from what was expected, and it results in a major dressing down in public.

There are some people in power who have managed to get away with their abusive or otherwise emotionally overwrought behavior precisely because they deliver strong doses of intimidation that appear to make resistance futile. In the short run, ruling through terror may very well motivate people, but as we've learned, it also comes with a number of negative side effects that eventually sabotage many of the things that keep followers loyal and satisfied.

Talking to Yourself Differently

There is a popular branch of psychotherapy called cognitive therapy that was originally developed simultaneously by two theorists working independently.[28] Although some differences characterize their approaches, the main idea is something pinpointed in the preceding section: that the ways in which we respond to experiences depend not so much on the events themselves, but rather how we choose to interpret them. All experiences, all events in our lives, all happenings on the job, are intrinsically neutral, their ultimate effect determined by the ways we perceive them.

When leaders feel discouraged, frustrated, or blocked, they can either make a choice (and it is a choice) to blame external factors such as others' incompetence, the economy, inclement weather, market changes, bad luck (even if they do play a role), or to accept responsibility for what is within their control. It may very well be the case that subordinates did a substandard job, competitors didn't play fair, or unforeseen circumstances played a part in the failure, and it's certainly helpful to assess such factors accurately, but externalizing blame is usually not all that helpful in the long run. Blaming "fake news," the media, ruthless enemies, and other scapegoats may help a leader to sidestep responsibility for his troubles, but it ultimately does very little to alter the trajectory of his or her failure to get things done.

So many of the difficulties and challenges in life can be minimized not necessarily through dramatic changes in structure, but rather by altering the ways in which people view things. When humans complained about long waits for elevators in high-rise buildings or for subway trains, engineers found that they could significantly reduce such complaints not by adding more cars, but rather by giving people more to do while they wait (installing mirrors next to doors so people could admire themselves) or providing an illusion of more control (adding displays that provide precise information on arrival times). Similarly, traffic accidents, road rage, and general impatience can be reduced simply by installing countdown delay screens so drivers and pedestrians experience a greater sense (or illusion) of control over their movements.

Meaning-making concerns just about everything in life; it is the attitude and interpretations that people bring to their experiences. A mistake can be defined as a failure or learning experience. Negotiations that don't end up as anticipated can be viewed as a loss or an unexpected outcome. Conflicts in relationships can be experienced as breaches of trust or opportunities for closer intimacy. Likewise, stressful experiences can be internalized as interesting challenges or devastating emotional turmoil, depending on how they are metabolized. It is now understood that a leader's moods, emotional energy, and responses determine to a great extent the ways in which followers subsequently respond. So it isn't just our own mental health and life satisfaction that are at stake when we overreact to situations, but the whole well-being of the organization.

Depending on what we tell ourselves about evolving circumstances, we can respond in a multitude of ways that lead to very different outcomes. A deal falls through after months of painstaking work, a sizable investment of time and resources, and big plans for the future. Whether you'd go into a tailspin, or demonstrate resilience and immediate recovery, is not only based on what was at stake, but also on the ways you processed what occurred and made sense of it.

People tend to resort to self-defeating ways of thinking out of laziness and/or a lack of precision. The reality is that external events and circumstances can rarely make us feel anything—we alone do that to ourselves. Of course, unforeseen events occur in the world, often disappointing ones, and other people can behave in obscenely stupid ways, but that does not necessarily predetermine a particular response. We have the ability to *choose* the way we interpret events and experiences, and *that* is what creates particular feelings.

The process by which negative emotions are neutralized begins with recognizing them in the first place, followed by identification of the underlying thoughts that preceded them—and there is almost always evidence of irrational or disordered thought patterns if the emotional reaction is extreme. Many of the most common belief patterns that consistently result in exaggerated negative responses and abject misery include some form of *exaggeration* in which you imagine the worst possible outcome. Just because one thing happens that is disappointing doesn't mean the world is ending (even though it may initially feel that way).

A second common cognitive error that leads to negative emotions is *overpersonalizing* what happened, believing that everything is a direct assault on you. Leaders are especially prone to feeling like they have special status, leading to a level of self-importance that makes everything appear personally directed, even though the universe, fate, or God hardly has you in mind when your shoelace breaks or a conference call is cancelled.

A third example is *dichotomous thinking*, referring to some people's tendency to look at things in extremes, often failing to see middle ground: "Because this deal fell through, our situation is hopeless and I'll never get anything going." You would recognize several kinds of distortion in that assumption, beginning with an expressed certainty that is inappropriately pessimistic and the use of an exaggerated modifier, "never," to imply the future is utterly doomed.

In these and other examples of distorted thinking, cognitive tendencies may be challenged by examining the beliefs critically:

- What is it that makes *you* so special you are immune to the daily disappointments that afflict everyone else in the world? Shit happens. Get over it.
- Who says the world is fair and that you—and everyone else—should get exactly what they deserve? Clearly, the world is unfair in all kinds of ways. Otherwise, you wouldn't lock your doors at night. You would be even more fairly compensated for your time. And everyone would love and appreciate you almost all the time.
- Just because this one thing happened, where is the evidence that this means everything else will fall apart? This is a gross overgeneralization for which there is scant rationale for your distorted, pouty assumption.
- This is clearly disappointing, as well as annoying, but what makes it absolutely *terrible*? If this is considered the worst possible outcome, then what would you call it if something *really* tragic occurred, something life-threatening to you and everyone you love?
- Just because you made a mistake or miscalculation, how does that label you as incompetent or a failure? Granted, making a series of mistakes that escalate in severity, and refusing to learn from these errors, probably does qualify as a degree of incompetence, but describing yourself—or someone else—in absolute terms because of some specific behavior is hardly justified.

It isn't the specifics of these examples that matter as much as the underlying principle, which is actually quite simple and a lesson you learned when you were a child: Sticks and stones may break your bones, but names can never hurt you. Well, sometimes name-calling can be rather hurtful, but once again, that is determined by how the behavior is interpreted. If a mentally ill, homeless person yells some obscenity at you on the street, you would hardly take that personally, or perhaps even blame the person for erratic behavior that cannot be controlled.

The main idea, however, is somewhat magical and utterly transformative: *What you feel is based on what you think.* If you don't like how you are feeling, then change the way you think about what happened. That sounds easy but, of course, is quite difficult when in the throes of emotional upset. It does take remarkable self-control and commitment to manage emotional reactions when feeling threatened or disappointed or fearful, but that is why being a leader isn't for everyone. It is one of the most important parts of our job to model the kind of emotional resilience and centeredness that we wish for others, whether followers or loved ones.

Self-Talk When You Most Desperately Need Wise Counsel

It is interesting that even when the skills and tools are readily available to minimize emotional unsettledness and process disappointments and stressful situations far more constructively, most people shun the power of self-control. They prefer to blame fate, bad luck, bad breaks, the economy, the weather, the business climate, limited resources, and especially others' behavior.

Most people don't want to take responsibility for the ways they feel all the time. Doing so is sometimes exhausting, and it is far more fun and easier to blame others when things go wrong. In spite of constant complaints and occasional feelings of helplessness, many simply prefer to externalize problems for a variety of reasons, most of which are related to reducing their own responsibility and taking on the role of a victim.

Perhaps this helps explain why some leaders, even those whose very livelihood and effectiveness depend on their ability to remain calm, controlled, and rational during times of difficulty, still become emotionally volatile during situations when it is hardly in their own best interests or those they are serving. Of course, there are times when intimidation and even abusive behavior can be useful in that it keeps others at a distance and protects against anticipated attacks. Nevertheless, a dear price is paid for stoking up rage and indignation because of the corrosive flood of cortisol and other hormones that wear down body systems. Sleep is disrupted. A host of stress-related symptoms result, many of which could be reduced significantly if people made different internal choices.

Imagine, for example, that a manager is staring at a draft report still sitting in his inbox. He is ultimately responsible for making sure that it is distributed by the deadline and will be held accountable for any significant mistake made. Here is what he says to himself as he shakes his head, glaring at the offending document:

> *God damn it! These people are just damn incompetent. This sort of thing happens all the time. Why can't these people get their shit together? This is going to ruin everything and probably destroy my whole friggin' career in this place. Nobody will ever take me seriously if I can't even make sure that a report is filed properly. I promise that some heads will roll because I just can't stand it when they act like idiots. The people around here just don't respect me and this is how they express it.*

I'm guessing that you can recognize some aspects of this internal rant that are highly exaggerated and irrational, representing extreme overreactions and leading to the kind of self-talk that is virtually guaranteed to make almost anyone a basket case. As you look back over the passage above, you notice the extent of the exaggerations ("This sort of thing happens *all the time*"); distortions ("This is going to ruin everything and probably destroy my whole friggin' career in this place"); absolute, inaccurate judgments ("These people are just damn incompetent"); and overreactions ("I promise that some heads will roll"). In fact, there is little evidence to support any of these interpretations or assumptions.

Notice that we are talking about evidence, as well as challenging assumptions and beliefs, to determine the extent to which they may be distorting and exaggerating current circumstances. It is all determined by how you choose to think about what happens around (or within) you.

When people react with strong negative emotions to events, this may often be the result of subscribing to irrational beliefs and counterproductive self-talk. It is important to become far more aware of what you find yourself thinking during times of stress or strong emotional reactions. It is at this point that you can either decide to give into anger, anxiety, depression, or frustration, or do something constructive to challenge the beliefs that are most getting in your way. Certainly, there are some serious mood disorders (panic attacks, chronic anxiety or depression) that are more the result of underlying organic causes than situational responses, but even these can be reduced a bit by talking to yourself, especially if your symptoms are being treated with medications and psychotherapy.

There are a few common ways in which people distort and exaggerate experiences to make them far more disruptive and uncomfortable than they ever need to be, many of which you would have recognized in the previous example. For example, a leader facing an unexpected problem says to herself, "This is absolutely a disaster, the worst thing that could happen right now on top of everything else." Of course, short of being diagnosed with Stage IV terminal cancer with only one month to live, everything else is only disappointing or annoying. But we tend to overreact to things that happen, often telling ourselves that it was a complete and total disaster (which is actually quite rare). If something is *merely* disappointing, or *only* a small setback, then it doesn't feel like a "complete disaster" or "major catastrophe."

There are other similar kinds of distorted, exaggerated, or otherwise irrational assumptions and beliefs that most consistently land us in emotional trouble. When we mutter "It's not fair," or "I deserve this," or "It's just the way

I am," we are subscribing to beliefs that are not often based in reality. After all, the world is clearly not fair, you are never truly entitled to anything, and not much really defines you as a static being.

With regard to this last point, we often rely on self-defining statements to label who we are and what we can—and can't—do. This usually takes place through the use of language that labels us in absolute terms: "I'm shy," "I'm not good at math," "I suck at budgeting." In each of these examples, the person is casting him- or herself in a particular mold without considering that *all* behavior is situational and contextual. Nobody is shy in all circumstances. There are always exceptions to any absolute self-judgment. Whereas it might be the case that you really don't have a gift for numbers, forecasting, public speaking, or providing critical feedback, there are surely times when this is not true at all and you are able to demonstrate reasonable competence. These are examples of irrational overgeneralizations that often get us in trouble with ourselves, and others, by failing to recognize that one case does not lead to a rule.

The process by which to challenge counterproductive and self-defeating self-talk begins first with recognizing when it is occurring. This means catching yourself thinking internally, or even hearing yourself say aloud, statements like "He *made me* so angry," "This *always* happens to me," or "This is so unfair."

It turns out that nobody can really get inside our heads without our permission, nobody can really make us feel anything without our cooperation, and nothing automatically impacts us without our own interpretations and chosen beliefs. It is by examining the self-talk inside our own heads that we identify the most important clues to what may be causing self-inflicted discomfort or even misery.

There may be another life and leadership skill more important than self-talk, but I can't imagine what that might be—unless it is related to the ability to tell the kind of stories that persuade, influence, instruct, and inspire others.

8

The Power of Storytelling to Inspire, Influence, and Persuade Others

I WANT YOU to come with me on a journey. Imagine that we are traveling to the other side of the world (assuming you live in the Western Hemisphere) to a remote village in Nepal near the Indian border. We are standing in the schoolyard of a rural village of Dalit, or "untouchable caste" people, who survive by subsistence farming, mostly rice, lentils, and a few vegetables. We've also learned that girls in the village are disappearing somewhere but, so far, it is hard to figure out what that means. Girls disappearing? Where do they go?

As we are standing around watching the kids play, we see them kicking balls of string as pretend soccer balls or playing "hacky sack" with spools of rubber bands. The school principal approaches to chat with us, and during the conversation, we probe a bit to find out what happens to the girls who "disappear." Reluctantly, the principal explains that the families in the village can't afford to feed all their children or send them to school. Their annual income is less than a few hundred dollars and school is an unnecessary expense for them. They consider girls worthless considering they will only end up "belonging" to another family after they are married off. So it is not that difficult of a decision to keep the girls at home and send the boys to school.

"And what happens to the girls who disappear?"

The principal shrugs. "Sometimes their families find a husband for them but they have no dowry so that is, how do you say, a limitation?"

"What about the others?"

"They go to India."

"India? What do they do there?" Another shrug. Eventually, we learn that the girls, some as young as 10 years old, are sold to brothels because their families can't afford to feed them. Over 10,000 Nepali girls each year are smuggled across the border to become sex slaves. It seems that some Indian men who are HIV positive believe that if they have sex with a virgin, it will cure their AIDS. So there is a burgeoning demand for young girls as commodities to be exploited. They are raped two dozen times each day and have an average lifespan of a few years.

I don't know about you, but this is just about the most horrifying story I've ever heard. But it gets worse, much, much worse, because the principal points to a little girl standing on the edge of the playground by herself. "See that girl over there," he says, pointing to a girl who may be about 11 or 12 years old. "She will be disappeared next. She has two older brothers and the father is a drunk so there is no money."

Here's the question: What would you do?

It was not an act of generosity, or courage, but rather an impulsive gesture when I asked the principal how much it would cost to keep the girl in school and out of harm's way.

The principal shook his head in that characteristic head waggle that is so common in this part of the world. It means yes, no, and maybe—all at once. "It is too much expensive. The girl, she needs two school uniforms. And you can see she needs shoes," he said, pointing at her bare feet. "She must pay school fees each month and she needs books and supplies. It is all too much."

"What are we talking about? How much would this cost for a year?"

"Three thousand rupees," he answers right away, knowing where the question was headed.

"Three thousand rupees? That's like, what? Fifty dollars?"

So, let me ask you again: What would *you* do?

Probably the same thing I did at that seminal moment 15 years ago, a moment that changed everything in my life. I reached into my pocket, pulled out a few bills, and gave them to the principal. Then I turned my back and walked away as quickly as I could to hide my tears and the sobs that were building in my throat. I completely lost control: I had just saved a girl's life for $50. It felt like the single greatest thing I'd ever done. Although I help people for a living, nothing comes close to the feeling I had knowing that without me, this girl would be . . . disappeared.

One of my Nepali colleagues approached me gingerly, seeing I was in extreme distress. "You are feeling proud, Jeffrey sir, that you gave that principal money, yes?"

I nodded my head because I couldn't yet speak.

"What do you think happens now?" she asked me.

"Excuse me? What do you mean?"

"That principal over there? He put the money in his pocket and that is where it will stay."

"Wait a minute. What are you saying?"

She then proceeded to explain to me that the girl was going to India anyway. Unless I told the principal I planned to return to the village to check on the girl, and actually did so, he would keep the money for himself. This is a country in which corruption is often the norm and those in power make sure they stay in their leadership positions.

"So you're saying I have to come back here? If I don't return to this place, that girl is going to be sold into slavery?"

Again, that waggle of the head, the equivalent of a helpless shrug.

So, now what? It is one thing to hand over the price of a dinner out to save a girl's life, but what about the prospect of taking four planes, a bus, a truck, and a long trek across endless rice fields to get to this place. And did I mention this is not the beautiful part of Nepal with Himalayan snow-covered peaks? This was jungle and rice paddies, and it cost thousands of dollars and a week's worth of travel to reach. So, *now* what would you do?

Stuck by my impulsive gesture, trapped into returning, I decided that if I had to come all the way back to this godforsaken place, then what the heck, show me a few more girls to help. Since that time, we have expanded our foundation to more than 15 different villages across the country, and now mentor and support hundreds of girls who are at risk of being trafficked into slavery or forced into early marriage. Our first girl, the one who had been standing barefoot in the schoolyard? She is now an oncology nurse, the first girl in her village to ever complete higher education and the first lower-caste girl to work in the local hospital. Several other girls are now in medical school, and dozens of others are attending university. It all began with the rather impetuous offer of a few dollars and has now grown into a whole movement.

Seminal Stories of Organizations

This story is called a "founding myth," or the seminal story of an organization that started almost two decades ago. It contains within the narrative all the features designed to move an audience and get them onboard with our mission. It communicates a "transcendent purpose," rather than merely a "transactional" one that provides products and services to needy children. As such, it appeals to the moral high ground and invites empathic resonance. It is also impactful and persuasive precisely because it is emotionally arousing. Of all the material presented in this chapter, this story may be the only thing you remember years from now.

It has long been recognized that the most inspirational and effective leaders are consummate storytellers. They become students of the craft, viewing themselves as performers, entertainers, and actors, as much as anything else. Start with a story and listeners immediately go into a trance: "Once upon a time . . ."

Richard Branson, CEO of Virgin Airlines, is known for his openness and willingness to share stories about his life, just as political candidates have learned to do so as a way to build connections to constituents. Within the music industry, troubadours like Bob Dylan, Bruce Springsteen, Jay-Z, or Taylor Swift feature lyrics that offer stories of conflict and resolution. Comic geniuses like George Carlin, Richard Pryor, Ellen DeGeneres, John Oliver, Sarah Silverman, Dave Chappelle, among so many others, tell the self-deprecating stories of their lives that are so entertaining precisely because they are brutal and real. And, of course, Ronald Reagan, Bill Clinton, and Barack Obama were all fabulous storytellers. Political speechwriters understand all too well that their best work includes powerful stories that trigger emotional resonance.

Steve Jobs was the consummate storyteller as the primary means by which to introduce his radical new products and recruit followers. One of the greatest corporate speeches ever delivered occurred when he stood on stage and announced with a flourish, "This little device holds 1,000 songs and it goes right in my pocket." That was the "vision thing," the imagining of a future that few others would have considered. This was the dream that Jobs had for his company, perhaps best exemplified in the famous Super Bowl ad "1984" that was first aired on the last day of 1983: "Here's to the crazy ones, the misfits, the rebels, the troublemakers, the round pegs in the square holes. . . . The ones who see things differently—they're not fond of rules. . . . They push the human race forward, and while some may see them as the crazy ones, we see genius, because the ones who are crazy enough to think that they can change the world, are the ones who do." This was the slogan and vision of the company, the story they wanted the world to embrace as their brand, that Apple "thinks different."

On the other hand, a lack of vision—or even that perception—can quickly undermine a leader, as George H. W. Bush discovered when journalists kept asking him, "Where is the real George Bush?" He continued to be pressed with regard to his vision for the country, and for his administration, and he would just slough it off as unimportant. He would complain about "the vision thing" that did not matter much to him. Unfortunately, this communicated an image of a leader without direction or goals, regardless if that was really the case. This became a problem for Donald Trump as well when he was perceived to lack a coherent policy vision that seemed to change by whim and circumstances.

Recognizing the critical importance of a narrative slogan that defines a presidential run, many successful candidates have defined their core message with a very short story—among them, Abraham Lincoln ("Don't swap horses in the middle of a stream"), Calvin Coolidge ("A chicken in every pot and a car in every garage"), Dwight Eisenhower ("Peace and prosperity"), Ronald Reagan ("It's morning again in America"), Bill Clinton ("It's the economy, stupid"), Barack Obama ("Yes, we can!"), Donald Trump ("Make America great again"). There are even whole approaches to leadership that primarily define the role as one in which a shared central narrative guides organizational values, presents a unified mission, and reduces uncertainty and ambiguity.[1] Yet this isn't so much a story that the leader creates as one that represents a collaborative process among all those within the organization. And, naturally, there is usually more than a single narrative and all kinds of other stories circulating that may directly contradict the "official" version. So, for example, Google's original narrative slogan, "Don't be evil," was meant to imply a code of conduct devoted to the greater good, but counterstories also circulated in response to privacy concerns and the negative associations with being an "empire." It is for this reason that the company slogan was changed to the more benign "Do the right thing." But regardless of the wording, the message was intended primarily as a unifying value for employees that their mission wasn't just about making money or taking over the world.

For many years, the flagship slogan of Southwest Airlines has been "You are now free to move about the country." But the story of origin, or founding myth, of the company has become a legend among employees, a story that has been passed on from one "generation" to the next.[2] When Herb Kelleher first launched his rebellious little aviation company, he used a catchy slogan in its advertising, "Just plane smart!" The only problem was that one of his competitors was also using a very similar slogan, "Plane Smart." You can easily predict what happened next: The two parties spent millions of dollars in litigation, battling it out in courtrooms to determine who was entitled to the spoils of victory.

But this story has a twist. It appalled Kelleher that both sides would end up paying lawyers so much money to wage a conflict that might be resolved in some other way. So instead, he proposed to his competitor that they engage in an arm wrestling tournament—with the winner getting to keep the slogan. It was an event that was viewed by their employees, as well as the media. It is now a story told over and over by Southwest employees as an example of how they think and operate differently (and this isn't meant to trigger another lawsuit with Apple).

Although there have been many novelists and playwrights interested in the ways that stories can influence and transform the psyche and behavior of listeners/readers, German novelist Gustav Freytag was among the first to explore this process systematically through the works of Shakespeare. Since that time, marketing and advertising agencies have studied how their 30- and 60-second "stories" can persuade consumers to purchase their products and services. Cute animals, babies, and sexual images are obviously successful attention triggers, but so are those that feature intimacy or relational connections.

The most influential stories tend to follow similar patterns, presenting a problem or challenge, describing conflict or tension that rises to a climax before resolution. The types of stories that are most often favored by leaders generally fall into several categories (see Box 8-1).

Among the kinds of stories frequently told by leaders, it is the "great works" variety that may be the most important of all, focusing on the appreciation and recognition of contributions. Most of us crave some degree of approval

---

BOX 8-1

Types of Stories Favored by Leaders

Type of Story	Effects and Influences
Founding Story	Instills pride and loyalty, inspires and motivates followers
Pivotal Story	Captures historical legacy and branding, reviews previous triumphs and failures, presents organizational worldview
Teamwork	Emphasizes relational and collegial bonding, mutual sacrifices, shared challenges and breakthroughs
Great Work	Recognizing and celebrating achievements, shared gratitude for performance

and acknowledgment by authority figures and surrogate parental figures. As mentioned previously, the vast majority of people who quit their jobs say their main reason for doing so is that they felt their effort wasn't appreciated by their bosses or the organization.[3]

A counterpoint to this perspective (and, of course, there will always be an alternative point of view) argues that such overreliance on authority-based validation may solidify the power and control of the leaders at the top of the organization, but at the expense of employee initiative and work satisfaction.[4] After all, there is a mountain of research that supports the importance of intrinsic motivation and self-efficacy to maintain feelings of well-being, conditions that are compromised when so much depends on external validation. Morale in almost any human group is fueled by creating a culture of mutual respect and shared accountability for performance and outcomes.

Leaders Primarily Exist Within Stories

As many leaders have learned the hard way, it isn't just what you do that matters most, but rather the stories people tell about your actions. How leaders are viewed is thus directly connected to the classic stories associated with them. Such tales may not capture a meaningful piece of a leader's accomplishments or failures, but represent some symbolic, simplistic anecdote that supposedly describes a signature trait.

George Washington crossed the Delaware and chopped down a cherry tree, confessing his crime. Ergo: He was courageous and honest.

Kenneth Lay was a corrupt and abusive corporate leader who put tens of thousands of people out of work and compromised the vitality of the energy grid.

Donald Trump is a failed (or successful, depending on the story) real estate mogul—or reality show actor—or political figure—or visionary—or self-promoting charlatan. It all depends on the story, as we well know from the example of Steve Jobs, who has been alternatively characterized in films and biographies as a mercurial tyrant or creative genius.

Consumers, colleagues, followers, competitors, and enemies tell stories about us that promote a particular image that may burnish our reputations or compromise them. It's all about the narrative that becomes the official, if not the most popular, version. And, of course, there are so many different stories that could be told, highlighting courage or spinelessness, resourcefulness or cluelessness, integrity or dishonesty. Was Lyndon Johnson a hero or a villain? Again, it depends on the story told, and by whom. His eventual capitulation to the appeal of Martin Luther King led to his signing the Civil Rights Act.

Yet visit the War Remnants Museum in Vietnam, and he is portrayed as a war criminal who was never brought to justice.

In his book about the cognitive processes of famous leaders like Margaret Mead, Robert Oppenheimer, Eleanor Roosevelt, and Alfred Sloan, psychologist Howard Gardner explored the ways in which different stories about these and other figures compete with one another until a single version takes hold. He summarized the "dominant" story associated with each figure who played an important role during the Second World War, and then contrasted it with "counterstories" that were also circulated about them. Chiang Kai-shek fought for China's independence and revolution, versus the narrative that he was an elitist and corrupt dictator who deserved his ultimate fate of exile. Winston Churchill patterned his personal biography as a fearless advocate for the "English race," versus the alternative version that he was an imperialist warmonger. Josef Stalin was either a champion of the common worker, or else a terrorist who committed genocide. Franklin Roosevelt was an activist during crisis, or a greedy, power-hungry megalomaniac who betrayed the upper class into which he was born.

Likewise, many of the figures of this era worked hard to "publish" their own versions of the preferred story. Adolf Hitler demanded of his subordinates that they show uncommon courage and sacrifice, yet he was actually quite self-indulgent and preferred to remain safely in a bunker in his final days. Benito Mussolini portrayed himself as a tireless worker but was actually inclined toward laziness at times and working irregular hours.

One example of exemplary leadership that Gardner presents is the work of Robert Oppenheimer, who was the director of Princeton's Institute for Advanced Study before being recruited to run the Manhattan Project that built the atomic bombs dropped over Hiroshima and Nagasaki. With Gardner arguing that the keys to leadership involve collecting cooperative and eager followers, as well as communicating a story of personal and group identity, Oppenheimer's life serves as a cautionary tale of two competing stories. He was clearly a genius and perhaps the one person on the planet who could have herded physicists, chemists, engineers, professors, staff, politicians, and military personnel into some kind of cohesive and effective team, given the complexity of their mission. "What was called for from the director of Los Alamos at the time," one of the prominent physicists explained, "was to get a lot of prima donnas to work together, to understand all the technical work that was going on, to make it fit together, and to make decisions between various possible lines of development. I have never seen anyone who performed these functions as brilliantly as Oppenheimer."[5] The public obviously agreed since his face was eventually emblazoned on the cover of *Life* magazine and he was generally regarded as the savior of the project that ended the Second World War in the Pacific.

That's one version of his story. The other is far more tragic, with him later branded as a Communist and security risk during the McCarthy era, discredited of his extraordinary accomplishments, stripped of all responsibilities, and sent into exile, resuming his directorship at Princeton. His reputation was eventually rehabilitated when President Johnson awarded him the Enrico Fermi Award shortly before his death, but these two competing stories, of him being a heroic leader versus a traitor, shadowed Oppenheimer throughout his life. Ever the diplomat and restrained leader, he never publicly commented on the disgraceful way he had been treated after devoting so much of his life to what he considered a noble cause.

The reality is that many of the stories offered about prominent leaders are, in fact, myths and fables, rather than accurate portrayals. While it may be true that the most favored books about leadership are biographies, autobiographies, or anecdotal accounts of victories or successes, most of them are incomplete, biased, and primarily designed to bolster an image, legend, and legacy. They are, thus, distortions of what really occurred and tend to over-romanticize heroic figures and exaggerate their roles. In a scathing indictment of such "unscientific" literature, one researcher cites a number of examples in which leaders have been portrayed as saviors when they were actually quite different than described. He doesn't necessarily have a problem with the stories themselves, however unreliable and slanted they might be, lauding successes but ignoring or covering up failures, but rather that the fabrications and exaggerations are rarely challenged or fact-checked. This often leads to a number of misperceptions and wildly inaccurate versions of events that we would never want to emulate if we knew the whole story. It also contributes to contaminating any evidence-based practices that are actually supported by empirical research.

The reason why stories about leaders, and told by leaders, are so popular is precisely because they often follow a dramatic arc that both commands attention and acts as a powerfully persuasive object lesson. The truth is we remember stories in ways that don't allow us to hold on to other information and data. And one more truth is that these stories can be myths and legends rather than factual and still take hold as an alternative reality that supplants a leader's actual behavior. The public doesn't even seem to care whether the self-serving embellishments are accurate or not, as long as it makes for a good story that confirms their own opinions. In addition, the media has been trained not to expect much truth or authenticity from those in charge, especially during the Trump era when *The New York Times* started to keep a running tally of the number of public lies the president uttered (averaging four every day).[6]

Stories Are Real

The architecture of the human brain is designed to organize information in the form of a story. This is true whether we are talking about simple themes, complex ideas, or even the appeal of musical lyrics. A story is simply a way to remember things that we consider worth holding on to, which is why most of our interactions with others involve swapping stories back and forth. We do this naturally and constantly precisely because it is the optimal way to convey ideas so they will have some impact. This is especially true in leadership scenarios in which we ask followers to consider new ways of operating, first guiding them through their imaginations to places they could soon inhabit.

"It's *only* a story," you might sometimes hear a person say. And, of course, he or she would be technically correct since what we say about events is hardly the same as what actually happened. And yet . . . and yet, a well-told story can *feel* as real as almost anything we might directly encounter, as if it was our own lived experience.

If you question whether stories are real or not to viewers or listeners, consider what happens when a popular television show is dropped or kills off a beloved character, sometimes leading to national riots or strikes, such as what happened in India when a popular soap opera was cancelled. People sometimes become so attached to fictional characters that it feels as if they are among our circle of intimate friends.

Perhaps this is one reason why leaders interviewed in one study rarely mentioned an influential book among the so-called classic business and leadership offerings. Think about that. It means that although there are thousands of books on leadership like this one published each year, purporting to offer important secrets—and they are certainly purchased and consumed—they don't appear to have much impact. Instead, leaders who were surveyed mentioned novels that presented characters who demonstrated strong leadership and inventive problem-solving when faced with struggles that were resonant of their own personal daily conflicts. Such books as *The Old Man and the Sea*, *To Kill a Mockingbird*, or *East of Eden* are hardly standard texts in business school or management seminars, but the leaders found them more inspiring and instructive than popular volumes on the subject of leadership. Likewise, they preferred non-fiction books like *Into Thin Air*, *Tuesdays with Morrie*, or

Nickel and Dimed that told inspiring stories of leaders dealing with adversity, or putting themselves at risk in order to discover something significant.[7] Our future leaders, the so-called Generation Z (those born after 1995), consider Katniss Everdeen, the protagonist from *The Hunger Games*, to be their most inspirational role model. They also check social media for stories an average of 100 times each day.[8]

Consider who, or what, have been your own most helpful and influential mentors and teachers throughout your career. What is it that you remember about them and the impact they had on you? First of all, it was probably a special relationship, one in which you felt valued and respected and trusted. Second, they told amazing stories that you still remember.

Nowadays, we tend to privilege data over stories in all kinds of ways. We are constantly asked for supportive data, empirical evidence, statistical measurements, key performance indicators, sales figures, profit margins, linear regression analyses, probability distributions, compliance metrics, implied equity risk premiums, capital costs, debt ratios, benchmarks, and standards within the industry. This certainly helps to bolster actions, not to mention fortify the rationale for such decisions. It's also interesting to consider that storytelling influences and persuades people in ways that data can't touch. This is true with respect to working with an individual, a large group, or even if the goal is to change the world.

It is startling to consider how stories have had such a major impact on world events. Just consider how stories from the Bible, the Qur'an, and other religious texts have shaped the lives of literally billions of people in terms of their core beliefs. Machiavelli's *The Prince* helped free Italy from oppression during the 16th century. Henry David Thoreau's personal story of exploration in *On Civil Disobedience* was taken as a manifesto of freedom and inspired Gandhi's own revolution of disobedience that launched India's independence movement. Abraham Lincoln once teased Harriet Beecher Stowe that *Uncle Tom's Cabin* helped start the Civil War and he wasn't far wrong. Upton Sinclair's *The Jungle* led to an activist movement that began the call for workers' rights to unionize. Rachel Carson's *Silent Spring* was instrumental in sparking the environmental activism movement of the 1960s.

In addition to inspiring social or political movements, or even provoking civil unrest or wars, stories have been known to be among the most seminal influences in the lives of great leaders. A number of famous leaders have disclosed examples of how their lives were forever transformed by a particular story. Bill Clinton mentioned *One Hundred Years of Solitude* as the story that affected him the most. John McCain cited Hemingway's *For Whom the Bell*

Tolls, and Barack Obama revealed that Joseph Conrad's *Heart of Darkness* was most memorable.

Before we delve further into the subject, the most compelling evidence I could possibly present is to reflect on your *own* experiences with stories. As you consider a few questions below, pay attention to what immediately comes to mind.

1. What is a (or *the*) story that had a powerful influence or impact on your life? This could have been a fairy tale, myth, or legend you encountered as a child. It could have been sparked by a comic book, puppet show, song lyrics, play, opera, documentary film, movie, television show, short story, novel, or story told to you by someone else. Regardless of its source, this story continues to haunt you to this day, perhaps in some way responsible for who you have become.

2. What is a story that you frequently tell someone whom you've just befriended, someone whom you want to truly *know* you? In other words, what does this story say about you, your values and priorities, what is most meaningful to you?

3. What is a story that you frequently find yourself telling others, whether in your family, work, or community, to illustrate some favored idea, to inspire, motivate, or support them in some way? This could include a metaphor, teaching tale, self-disclosure, or other anecdote.

It turns out that our world is not only constructed of atoms, just as our experiences are not shaped only by events that occurred; each of us represents the sum total of all the stories we've heard and lived, as well as those we've told to others. Elon Musk of Tesla has even wondered if, in fact, we won't all be living someday in a simulation of virtual reality. In just 40 years, we've evolved from playing Pong to multiplayer online games that involve millions of participants. Acting as a provocateur, Musk asks how long it will be before we are all inhabiting another kind of storied reality. "Either we're going to create simulations that are indistinguishable from reality," he suggests, "or civilization will cease to exist."[9]

Stories to Influence and Persuade

The first "novels" ever written were the Nordic sagas that told stories of heroic exploits by the Viking warriors and prominent Icelandic families. These tales were so poignant and influential that even today Icelanders speak about characters from the sagas in the present tense, as if they were still alive. Within the context of organizations, sagas are stories with a different purpose: They are designed to influence those who are involved in the collective work.[10]

As mentioned, one of the main jobs of any leader involves communication to followers, the sort that is persuasive, visionary, influential, designed to help them to work collaboratively to reach common goals. This is most often accomplished through three main avenues,[11] the first of which involves *rational arguments* that include logical statements with empirical evidence, hard data, and an appeal to rational thinking: "Our surveys indicate that customers are likely to increase their orders exponentially when allowed to customize their own configurations."

The second style of *hard persuasion* relies most often on a punishment orientation, using threats, blame, and retribution for those who don't comply with leader expectations: "Anyone who can't or won't show up for work this weekend shouldn't bother showing up again on Monday." Whereas appeals to logic are sometimes less than impactful, this threatening communication style does force compliance but with all sorts of undesirable side effects, such as perpetuating caution, conservativeness, avoidance of risk, suppression of criticism, not to mention a certain amount of anxiety, fear, and resentment.

The third means of influencing others, *soft persuasion*, appeals to emotion and can frequently be the most powerful communication style of all. This is where storytelling comes into play because of the ways in which it elicits emotional arousal and conveys ideas with subtlety, which require more active forms of engagement by others. It is obviously a favorite approach of litigators to persuade a jury through an emotionally evocative anecdote.

Moe Levine, a noted trial lawyer, shared his strategy for closing arguments in a case where his client sought damages for a catastrophic injury.[12] Rather than presenting a lengthy summary of the case, hitting key points, reviewing all the critical messages he wanted to get across, he instead stood up, faced the jury, and told a one-minute story. He began by mentioning that he couldn't help noticing that the bailiff brought lunch to all the jurors during recess. Then he observed the judge and clerk going to lunch, as well as the other attorney and his client. "So I turned to my client, Harold, and said, 'Why don't you and I go to lunch together?' We went across the street to that little restaurant and had lunch."

Levine paused for a bit, letting that image sink in before he continued. "Ladies and gentlemen, I just had lunch with my client. He has no arms. He had to eat like a dog. Thank you very much."

The transformation of Steve Jobs in later life can be partially explained by new dimensions in his abilities as a storyteller, one who learned to appeal to emotional resonance. Whatever previous skill he had had as a storyteller to inspire others, his interest in the craft was magnified a hundred-fold once he added Pixar to his portfolio. Consider some of the earliest wildly successful films that were produced under his watch—*Toy Story, WALL-E, Brave, Monsters, Inc.*—all so richly resonant with emotionally powerful narratives that were combined with technologically groundbreaking art. This was a lesson that Jobs took even more to heart during a time when his competitors were essentially viewed as identical clones with no soul. It's also more than a little interesting how the narrative of *Toy Story* parallels Jobs' own life, as well as setting a template for so many of the Pixar films.[13] An endearing character becomes embroiled in conflict and danger because of overconfidence and personality flaws, eventually coming to terms with his or her own weaknesses and relying on courage, risk-taking, and relational connections to seek some kind of redemption after return from exile.

Toy Story single-handedly resurrected Jobs' career during a time when his other new enterprises were failing miserably. But the lesson learned was one that Jobs more fully integrated into his persona and became the driving force for every product he and his companies ever produced: People respond best to emotionally moving stories that touch them deeply. Jobs further enhanced his storytelling ability with mentoring from a few of the most talented sages in the business—John Lasseter, Andrew Stanton, and the rest of the crew that produced some of the most memorable animated feature films in history.

The Neurobiology of Stories

If you focus once again on a story that has had a huge impact on your life, it's entirely possible that the result may have been as profound as anything that could happen in psychotherapy.[14] Even more intriguing is that fictional stories are usually more influential than non-fiction.[15] This is more than a little ironic when you consider that the stated purpose of self-help books is to produce lasting change. Any guesses why novels or dramatic films are often more impactful than non-fiction?

Fiction creates another reality, a parallel universe, in which you agree to immerse yourself. As such, you suspend disbelief and your critical voice, or you will lose the magic. If you are watching a movie and start to make comments about the lighting, direction, or acting, then you aren't actually *in* the story; you remain outside of the experience. Likewise, when you are reading a good story, you generally try not to interrupt the flow by pointing out, "Zombies would *never* do that," or "I can't believe that he set the scene in Rome, of all places." Once that happens, you are no longer honoring your contract with the author, storyteller, or filmmaker to join the journey. Compare this experience to that of reading any non-fiction book like this one, where you may be constantly arguing with me, pointing out ideas you disagree with, quibbling about certain things that you don't think are quite accurate, countering viewpoints with your own that you believe are more valid. This represents a kind of active engagement with the author, but it also interrupts the flow of the overall experience.

Fictional stories not only draw the listener, reader, or viewer in, they also provoke high levels of emotional arousal. The human brain has evolved *mirror neurons* that provide vicarious experiences as if they are real.[16] This makes it possible to have all kinds of dangerous adventures, learning all sorts of adaptive survival strategies for dispatching zombies, vampires, aliens, or talk show hosts, all without ever being in personal jeopardy.

Storytelling kicks in many kinds of chemical reactions in the nervous system.[17] During tension, conflict, or aggressive acts that are described or shown visually, the hormonal system floods the body with cortisol, just as it would if you were actually face-to-face with a life-threatening situation. At various times in the narrative that elicit relief or joy, oxytocin is released to improve empathic resonance with the characters. And if the story ends well—as good stories tend to do—then the limbic system releases dopamine as a reward, leaving you feeling elated, optimistic, and hopeful at the tale's conclusion.

A case in point: Viewers watching the 2014 Super Bowl were asked to select what they considered the single best commercial aired during the game. The winner? It was a Budweiser commercial called "Puppy Love" that told a 60-second story about a Clydesdale horse and yellow Labrador retriever who become best friends, then were forcibly separated before they reunited at the conclusion. The commercial had all the elements of a perfect story—tension, drama, conflict, emotional activation, and resolution since the two animals lived happily ever after together. In one study, it was found, regardless of the content of an advertisement or the product it promotes, when some dramatic arc is included as a "mini-film," one that appeals to deep feelings, the ad is more likely to be remembered. Great ads also tend to follow the same five-act structure as any play by Shakespeare.[18]

What this means for our purposes is that if you can somehow tell stories that draw people in with vivid descriptions, metaphorical allusions, and

BOX 8-2

Features and Functions of Storytelling in Leadership

- Captures attention and interest through provocation and entertainment
- Follows the natural structural and functional properties of memory
- Presents "coded" information in an efficient package
- Provides a different form of "direct experience" through vicarious identification
- Evokes strong emotional reactions that inspire, motivate, or ignite passion
- Induces altered states of consciousness and hypnotic inductions through immersion in narrative
- Resonates with cultural and historical traditions within the organization or community
- Bypasses resistance and defensiveness through the subtle introduction of concepts and ideas
- Appeals to multiple dimensions of complexity and cognitive processing
- Facilitates recognition of patterns across life experiences
- Introduces overarching, organizing scaffolds to understand phenomena and life experiences
- Introduces alternative realities (fantasy) that facilitate creative thinking
- Teaches significant adaptation and problem-solving skills through vicarious experiences
- Presents alternative pathways and options for viewing problems and their solutions
- Provides opportunities for the rehearsal of new behavior through surrogates and simulations
- Diminishes power imbalance between leaders and followers through self-disclosures and personal sharing
- Reframes and reconstructs disappointments, setbacks, and failures as object lessons and learning opportunities
- Fosters a higher level of moral development and ethical decision-making
- Creates "secret" passwords that act as reminders and reinforcements of prior insights
- Leads to the critical evaluation of parallel issues that might otherwise feel threatening
- Promotes wisdom, tolerance, and flexibility in thinking about oneself, others, and the world

interesting detail, then you develop one of the most powerful means to influence them in subtle ways. The goal of such anecdotes, whether a personal disclosure, parable, or case example, is to evoke a strong emotional response. They provide the opportunity for listeners to identify with the protagonists in such a way that it leads to greater empathy. If you stayed with me in the story about Nepal that opened this chapter, if you could vividly imagine the situation and picture yourself in my shoes, then the device was effective in triggering your own caring and compassion.

It is also primarily through stories that we build and sustain relationships with people. Almost every conversation we have during the day involves telling stories about ourselves and others. Part of this is related to image management (enhancing our own reputation), part is connected to regulating gossip (that reports outliers and slackers), and part involves sharing stories from the past. Box 8-2 summarizes some of the other functions and possibilities for telling stories in a leadership context.[19]

In optimal circumstances, the best stories offered by leaders become infectious, meaning that they begin to circulate among followers. The most influential examples evolve into virus-like entities that spread among followers.

A Catalogue of Stories

There are obviously different kinds of stories that leaders might employ for different purposes. Some are created for entertainment value, others to impart particular kinds of messages or reinforce particular values. In all their various forms, a number of experts on the subject have suggested that any great story, or speech for that matter, avoids certain "deadly sins" that leaders often rely on as a default position, such as blaming or criticizing others, complaining about things that are beyond one's control, constantly making excuses, all of which lead to "viral misery."[20] Instead, the best storytellers are those who have mastered certain basic principles:[21]

1. Focusing on one major idea that is most important and sticking with that single theme
2. Offering something that others care deeply about, not just something that matters to you
3. Being authentic and developing a unique, signature style that is personal and recognizable
4. Using one's voice, gestures, and very being as instruments to express passion, excitement, and drama

5. Evoking strong emotional reactions to the narrative, ideally designed to make people both laugh and cry
6. Remembering that stories are designed to connect with the audience and build relationships, thus minimizing the use of slides whenever possible

It's interesting that leadership and management programs regularly equip future professionals with all kinds of crucial skills related to their jobs, but rarely include perhaps the most important one of all—which is learning to become a charismatic and persuasive storyteller. While briefly covering this neglected territory, it's also important to understand the different ways in which stories may be put to the most productive use.[22]

Sharing Knowledge

At the simplest level, stories can provide an example of a problem or challenge that parallels similar obstacles within the organization or larger arena. Long ago, Joseph Campbell traced the salient themes across all human cultures since the beginning of recorded history (and beyond).[23] He reviewed the common themes of Roman or Greek mythology, ancient fairy tales, myths of indigenous cultures, as well as the plotlines of contemporary plays, films, and novels, concluding that almost all such narratives contain within them familiar patterns. The hero(ine) may have "a thousand different faces," but the story is much the same whether in the Old Testament, *Grimm's Fairy Tales*, or *Star Wars*. The protagonist is faced with a life-threatening quest to obtain some desired prize, which could be a hand in marriage, magic power, or coveted object. There are many battles and obstacles along the way, but eventually the protagonist discovers a secret strategy or method from a mentor who usually has some special magical skill.

Hidden within every such tale is a nugget of information intended to be imparted. These are often cautionary tales that broadcast potential dangers of the current situation and offer possible suggestions for a plan of action. I have a favorite story I tell about two frogs who become trapped in a deep hole and can't jump out in spite of the encouragement of their peers yelling down at them. One frog dies of exhaustion but the other one, after a final, herculean effort, manages to propel himself to safety. Lying on his back in exhaustion, his peers wonder why he tried so hard to save himself when, in fact, they had been yelling at him to give up because his situation was so precarious and pitiful. When he finally gathered his breath, the surviving frog explained that he was deaf and so believed that the others were actually cheering, rather than discouraging, him.

I could explain what I believe is the moral of this story, but it is usually preferable to let the audience decide that since there isn't actually any *intrinsic* meaning to this—or any other—story except what you take from it. This embedded knowledge is incomplete and ambiguous, but contains within it the stimulus for further thought, discussion, and action. After all, how often do we think we are encouraging someone when, in fact, he experiences our input as critical judgment? How often do we believe we are giving someone constructive feedback when she doesn't hear that? How often is there a disconnect between intentions and how behavior is received? You could simply *tell* people this important insight, but it is more likely to be remembered in the context of a story.

Springboard Story

Most of the time, leaders are primarily concerned that any discussions lead directly to action. This is quite different from social situations where the pure pleasure and satisfaction derived from interpersonal engagement are themselves sufficiently rewarding. We can talk endlessly about sports, politics, cooking, movies, or books without it necessarily leading anywhere, except greater intimacy and a personal connection. While working, however, we are interested in moving discussions to some desired outcome.

There are a number of direct ways that we might attempt to initiate change within an organization or group, such as simply providing a clear directive about what must be done. Ah, if only things were that simple! There are all kinds of unanticipated reactions to a straightforward order, including anything from absolute obedience and reasonable compliance, to downright disobedience and rebellion. Generally speaking, most people aren't all that happy with authoritarian leaders.

In a story designed to motivate action, the structure usually involves sharing an example of a significant change that occurred in the past, even with considerable challenges and obstacles along the way. The change is clearly evident in the narrative, the protagonist is someone with whom the audience can identify, and there is almost always a satisfying ending that implies some course of action. Once the story is told, the audience is asked to picture how *they* might move things along with regard to the current transition or crisis.

Who I Am

These are the personal stories that leaders share about themselves, often the most misused and misunderstood variety of storytelling. Given that those in responsible positions frequently believe they are special, better, and more important than others, there is a temptation to tell stories that are overly self-congratulatory, variations of the theme "Ain't I great?" This can, and does, inspire confidence among followers if used judiciously, but just as often, it creates greater psychological distance with followers. While it is true that people prefer their leaders to be somewhat omnipotent and hold special powers that they may covet for themselves, it is also the case that they appreciate a certain degree of modesty and humility.

When you do reveal stories about yourself, it is as important to demonstrate examples of compassion, caring, and especially resilience in the face of difficulties, as well as to talk about heroic successes of the past. One's image is burnished by advertising not only stories of extreme competence, but also those that feature uncertainty and make you appear more human and accessible. A rule of thumb for most professional speakers is to begin with a story that presents oneself in a self-deprecating light, thus making it easier for the audience to identify with the challenges presented.

Who *We* Are

Branding is just another name for the "title" of a company's story. The value of a brand is usually assessed in terms of its investment in marketing and advertising, its measured public goodwill, and its recognition among consumers. Companies like Lego, Red Bull, Disney, Apple, Microsoft, Coca-Cola, McDonald's, Starbucks, and the Red Cross have immediately recognized names, not only for their products but also because of their essential purpose.

"We stories," the kind of branding meant for internal consumption, present a symbol of the corporate or organizational culture, which is essentially a collection of stories told by people. It is the "official" worldview, augmented by underground versions told in less public settings. It could be variations of the theme "This is the way we do things here."

One researcher, operating under a grant from the Centers for Disease Control, investigated ways to prevent bullying in schools. He described to me one example of his team's effort; it concerned what happened when a new kid showed up at school for his first day. The other children were all standing in line waiting to enter the cafeteria when the new boy slipped into the front, "taking cuts" rather than waiting his turn at the back of the line. The girl standing in front of him turned around and said, "Hey, you're new in this school. But that's not the way we do things here." In other words, the norms and culture of the school were actually enforced by the children themselves. This was *their* branding, and they were damn proud of it.

Branding stories represent attempts by organizations, or political figures, to circulate their own versions of a story that they prefer consumers or voters to swallow. In today's climate of 24-hour news cycles, many celebrities and leaders use social media to send out capsulized stories in the form of a tweet or post. These are distributed in order to control image management in the face of critics. It also explains why 13-year-olds so obsessed with the way they are "branded" by others check social media as many as 300 times each day to immediately correct or react to any perceived slight, assess their relative popularity among others, respond to criticism or misrepresentation, or just to see what others are saying about them. One girl, for example, felt she had to immediately reply to a post by someone critical of her: "Go die. Stop trying to be popular. Holy shit you are ugly." Another junior high school boy disclosed why he constantly checked Facebook or Twitter: "I want to see what they're talking about and if they're talking about me. Because if they're talking about me, I'm going to talk about them."

If this sounds like war, that's what it has begun to feel like, not just to adolescents who feel under attack, but also any organization that operates in the public sector. It is critical to (try to) control the stories that people share by distributing our own versions that are more accurate and measured.

Imparting Values

Every organization has core values they consider sacrosanct. These involve more than just serving customers, making profits for shareholders, providing a needed service or product, serving constituents; they convey what the central mission and purpose of the organization are all about. Companies like Patagonia, North Face, and other outdoor clothing manufacturers demonstrate a strong commitment to environmental causes. Red Bull screams "adventure" and "risk-taking" as an association with its adrenaline-branded beverages. Southwest Airlines conveys its "story" by focusing on fun and customer value. Starbucks, Ben and Jerry's, TOMS Shoes, and other companies demonstrate a commitment to certain social causes.

Value stories are not just intended for customers, clients, or public consumption, but also to solidify employee morale. The goal is to emphasize cohesion through a sense of collective pride. When I first took over an academic department at a university, I hired new faculty and staff to rebuild a dying unit from the ground up. Universities are often ruled by so-called faculty governance by which decisions are made through elaborately complex democratic policies. Meetings are often controlled through Robert's "rules of order," in which subcommittees report on issues that are then discussed and voted on to determine majority rule. However, whenever you vote on things, there are winners and losers, so I decided to establish a value in our department whereby we would make all decisions through consensus, rather than voting. Consensus-seeking takes longer, for sure, but the result is a feeling afterward that all parties involved were able to negotiate with one another until agreement was reached. It's been a long time since I left that leadership position, but I still hear from others around campus, "Oh, you're from that department that never votes." This has become one of the core values of the unit in which the members proudly communicate through their behavior that they have high levels of cohesion and mutual respect. This is what increases the possibilities for collaboration and cooperation in relationships.

Relational Engagement

Stories don't really have to serve any purpose other than to promote deeper intimacy, closeness, and respect. Many of the conversations around the water cooler, copy machine, printer, staff lounge, coffee or lunch breaks are focused on comparing notes about opinions, sharing information, talking about ideas, sharing interests.

If you were to listen to a group of people hanging out together, you'd quickly catch on to the almost frantic effort to make oneself known to others, often without much mutual listening. I recently overheard two executives talking to each other during a break. It went something like this:

> "I just got back from Scotland and finally got to play both Muirfield and St. Andrews. I couldn't believe how . . ."
>
> "Yeah, I was there a few years ago but I don't know, I'll take Pebble Beach. Better weather and more challenging . . ."
>
> "So, I was telling you about Scotland. I got a chance to see some of the ancestral lands that my grandmother . . ."
>
> "I still think Pebble Beach has a much more pristine feel, if you know what I mean."

They were obviously more interested in talking rather than listening, with a desperate need to be heard even if they weren't able to give that acknowledgment to each other. Nevertheless, many of the stories that are told throughout the day are intended to promote greater closeness. This is how we build coalitions and support, how we recruit allies to our favorite cause.

All these types of stories project into the future, providing hints of what we might become, offering a vision of what is possible. When the story is over, you want the audience to impatiently rub their hands together and ask how they can get started. Hopefully, the seeds to grow the answers are embedded in the narrative.

Tell Yourself Stories

Since stories are the ways that we best remember the experiences of our lives, they are also the primary means by which we create mental models to explain phenomena and plan for the future.[24] We thus make up stories to account for things we don't understand: "The new product didn't sell as well as we hoped because we didn't invest enough resources into marketing and promotion," or "The CFO didn't provide me with that report I asked for because she's still angry at me for cutting her off in the meeting." These stories provide a semblance of meaning to interactions or events, a sort of working hypothesis.

If leaders wish to become more accomplished at telling persuasive stories to others, the first place to start is with the stories we tell ourselves about the significant moments of our daily lives. In addition to creating a framework or theory, they cement memories that we wish to hold on to and can teach us to compare the internal narrative to what actually may happen in the future. We can imagine, for example, the scenario that we believe will unfold when we introduce a new policy at a staff meeting. In our minds, we go around the room and picture how each person will likely react and what he or she will say. We visualize the interactions, as well as the likely outcomes. Then the truly useful part is to compare the story we created in our heads to what actually occurred. This helps us to better calibrate our ability to anticipate and predict the reactions of others and plan for alternative courses of action.

Whether the goal is to improve responsiveness to others at work, to listen more attentively to family members, or to improve your ability to focus, it is through the simultaneous narration of your life, as you are living it, that those experiences are encoded in such a way that they will remain enduring.[25] In a later chapter, we will discuss more specifically how to deliver the kinds of stories designed to have the most enduring impact on followers.

9

Critical Incidents That Are Often Mishandled

A WIDE VALLEY stretched from the edge of the riverbank to the buttes that framed the limits of the horizon. Thousands of buffalo stood silently, grazing on the rich grass, a single bull standing guard over the herd. The scene looked peaceful, utterly serene.

Hidden among the cottonwoods overlooking the valley was a pack of wolves resting and watching the buffalo that were oblivious to the danger. The alpha of the pack, a huge male, had been sitting almost frozen in the same spot throughout the day, while the others snoozed in the shade or wrestled with one another. Suddenly, the alpha stood on all fours, noticing one of the calves among the herd that had wandered away from a mother's protection. Without uttering a single sound, the wolves stood at attention, following their leader's movements as they crept closer to the herd, waiting for a moment to strike.

The wolves had been spotted, so the herd huddled closer together, at least those that had been alerted by their own leader. By then, the pack was on the move, circling in a coordinated attack that rivaled any military strategy. Although it appeared as if the wolves had rehearsed their movements over and over, they were improvising as the huge animals they sought as prey also had sharp horns that made for an excellent defensive weapon. The alpha quickly evaluated their situation, and with a few yips and howls, sent several of his troops around the side for a pincer action, forcing the helpless calf to break off from the herd. The wolves attacked in concert, cutting off the youngster from the rest, and bringing him down.

The alpha examined the carcass, while the others stood to the side. He would take the first feed, followed afterward by his mate, the alpha female, and then the others. There was a clear and rigid hierarchy of privilege, based on seniority, as one of the pups soon learned when he leaned in to grab a quick bite and found himself unceremoniously knocked aside. This is the way of the world, at least among most living things since the beginning of time. The alpha, the leader, fights for dominance, and once positioned as such, battles any rivals for control. He gets the choicest meals, first dibs on mating with anyone he likes, and is able to reward his closest kin and allies with access to food and resources to cement his status.

Yet if the alpha or leader of most species doesn't literally watch his (or her) back, build solid alliances outside of blood relatives, and learn to make concessions as needed, then competitive battles to dethrone him will become commonplace and exhaust efforts to get things done. In this particular case, another member of the pack, already missing part of his ear from a previous scuffle, has decided he's had enough of leftovers and decides, once again, to challenge the leader. This will not end well for either one of them, or their brood, because the leader seriously miscalculated the stability of his position and the persistence of a competitor.

The Times, They're Indeed Always Changing

It's absolutely staggering to consider how quickly change is occurring in our daily lives, much less within human organizations, at times completely revolutionizing, if not totally dismantling, what we thought were relatively stable conditions and structures that have been consistent for centuries. Consider the tools we use every day to conduct business and accomplish necessary tasks. For hundreds of years, the only "technology" that anyone really needed to master was how to saddle a horse and load a gun. Communication was always face-to-face before the invention of the telegraph and telephone, much less the Internet. Computations were done on one's fingers, or perhaps with paper and quill. But things are evolving so quickly that every year or two there is some new innovation that seems to render what we'd been using or doing previously obsolete. Consider how telephones have evolved during the last century from party lines to dial wall phones, pushbutton devices, original car phones as big as heavy bricks, and now phones (and computers) that fit inside a watch!

Marc Andreessen, one of the founders of Netscape, who watched his own company sink into obsolescence before finding success again investing in other people's new ideas, marvels at how the iPhone changed *everything*. "That iPhone sitting in your pocket," he points out, "is the exact equivalent of a Cray XMP supercomputer from twenty years ago that used to cost ten million dollars."[1] Yet it is just as powerful and can store just as much information as a computer the size of a whole room from a few decades ago. These breakthroughs mean that the pace of change is happening so quickly that leaders are required to recognize and respond to conflicts, as well as opportunities, with the kind of swift, strategic action that boggles the mind. It also means that leaders are under more stress than ever before because of the ever-changing nature of their jobs.

Many leaders actually thrive on crisis and rise to the occasion when presented with game-changing conflicts. Would any of our greatest leaders have ever achieved recognition without facing a major crisis, such as Lincoln during the Civil War or FDR during the Depression? Without crises to handle, a leader is just a "promising custodian of potential."[2]

We have all become addicted to crises in the 24-hour news cycle; it links catastrophes with the leaders who caused—or diverted—them. This has led to a whole herd of counterfeit saviors who are really just "false prophets, the smooth operators, the gangsters, and the demagogues."[3] The public is absolutely infatuated with the *idea* of leadership but then is inevitably disappointed with the actual leaders who can't deliver what was imagined. Sometimes this happens because the leader never intended to follow through on his or her hollow assurances; in other cases, a certain level of stress makes it impossible for the leader to function optimally and arrive at the best possible decisions. It turns out that being able to metabolize stress, and operate under unrelenting pressure, is one of the most important attributes of an effective leader.

Sources of Stress in a Leader's Life

There are different types of stress that leaders experience, each of which has a profoundly different effect on decisions and behavior. Stress can be mild or transient, and occur in relatively benign, controlled circumstances, such as riding a roller coaster, playing a video game, or operating during a relatively minor crisis that is somewhat challenging but not beyond your capabilities. We quite enjoy this kind of stress and are even inclined to pay large sums of money to be stimulated and intensely engaged in activities we find exciting.

However (and you know what's coming next), when stress is chronic, unremittent, all hell breaks loose in the body, especially the brain's ability to make sound decisions. Memory is impaired. Judgment is compromised. Panic sets in. Impulsive and aggressive actions follow, often without concern for their consequences. A vicious cycle emerges in which leaders will try to moderate the continuous suffering that takes a toll on their health, sleep, and well-being.

That's why it's so critical that leaders adopt successful daily strategies for metabolizing the inevitable stressors that come with the job. Some experts talk about the importance of leaders being able to lead themselves first, meaning to establish the kinds of limits and boundaries between work and other aspects of life so each domain can flourish.[4] It's difficult, if not impossible, to develop, articulate, and practice such healthy practices daily when you are constantly in motion. That's where a certain solitude and quiet become important, even among the most gregarious and extroverted leaders.

How does one ever achieve a sense of clarity and relative tranquility in the face of so many demands, crises, and responsibilities? The main problem is rarely a lack of information, but rather a blinding excess of data, input, and opinions. There is a constant barrage of connectivity—texts, emails, calls, video conferences, meetings, consultancies, reports, analyses, all flooding in. Yet until such time that leaders are prepared to take time out from the grueling combat arena and seek some degree of daily solitude and reflection, it is difficult to stay on a stable, solid footing—especially when stress levels are ramped up beyond what is comfortable, or even reasonable.

During times of stress, the body is flooded with hormonal responses that are programmed to respond to *perceived* emergency situations that require instant reactions. Historically, this "fight or flight" response prepares us to either run from potential danger, such as a sabre-tooth tiger in the good ol' Paleolithic days, or else to do battle against a predator or enemy. The body is exquisitely designed to mobilize every possible system that can adapt to a hostile environment. The amygdala in the brain evaluates potential threats and activates other systems that will be called into action. That's why when you feel anxious, you notice all kinds of bodily sensations kick into gear. Breathing becomes more labored, and the heart rate increases to send greater supplies of oxygen that will be needed to fuel the muscular system for flight or fight. Sweat glands kick in to cool off the body. The digestive system shuts down since resources will be needed elsewhere, which is why you may feel a flutter in your stomach under such conditions. Eyes dilate to better perceive danger. And hormones like cortisol flood the system to stimulate emergency responses, but causing side effects when the button is stuck in the "on" position for too long under conditions of chronic stress. Excessive cortisol is associated with all kinds of health issues, such as hypertension, high blood pressure, and even intestinal bleeding and ulcers. The immune system eventually becomes compromised, and a cascade of health problems can result for those with major responsibilities and chronic stress in leadership positions.

Ready for the good news? As we've discussed earlier, the mind has the power to alter the responses of the endocrine system and moderate their chemical overreactions that become toxic over time, especially when people are subjected to continuing, unrelenting pressure. Once you are in the middle of a difficult situation, such as being overwhelmed by an impending deadline, embroiled in conflict or disagreement, confused by the data you are scrutinizing, it helps to apply the self-talk strategies mentioned earlier, reminding yourself that you have a choice as to the optimal way to think about what is happening. It can either feel like a crisis or a challenge, an annoyance or an opportunity, a disaster or a minor setback, an inconvenience or a major pain in the butt. The mind, not the circumstances, dictates the best way to contemplate a stressful encounter. It is also interesting to consider that if you believe the stress you feel is affecting your health and performance, often such is most likely the case, actually increasing the risk of premature death.[5]

Physiologists have discovered that learning meditation-type techniques like deep breathing, mindfulness exercises, and especially self-talk can significantly reduce the stress levels experienced so one is able to function optimally. Moderate degrees of stress can frequently *enhance* performance in many situations, so the goal is not necessarily to eliminate it, but rather to bring stress under manageable limits. When people obsess or perseverate over things they can't control (past mistakes, the weather, economic conditions, others' behavior), they are most vulnerable to the worst effects. Yet when facing an intriguing challenge, stress within reasonable limits mobilizes systems to optimize functioning. That's one reason world-class athletes, musicians, soldiers, and actors actually thrive when they are "on stage" and feeling a bit of anxiety to stoke their capabilities. There's nothing that motivates extraordinary effort more than having a big audience and a prize waiting at the end.

Stress arises from several main sources, the most obvious of which is the work environment. If time pressures and emergencies are frequent occurrences, there is little time to recover and replenish stores of energy. Likewise, if organizational politics become too consuming, or interpersonal conflict is pervasive, the negative energy can invade your consciousness and disrupt sleep and daily functioning. Perhaps more than any other factor, having unsupportive co-workers can result in severely negative emotional reactions, continually feeling evaluated, criticized, and undermined.

In addition to stress triggered by events that occur at work, there are also all kinds of precipitating factors that can take place in our personal lives. Any major life transition (marriage, divorce, relocation, a promotion, the birth of a child, the death of a loved one) can spark extreme adjustment problems. There are also age-related developmental issues, such as milestone birthdays that force us to confront our own mortality.

Saving the best and most important source of stress for last, many struggles don't actually arise from any of the things just mentioned. They are certainly precipitating factors, and it may indeed feel as if they are *causing* the difficulties. However, so much of stress is, in fact, the result of self-induced misery based on the ways in which we choose to think about unfolding events and how we respond.

Adversity Often Leads to Resilience

Omar had been the national sales manager for a large manufacturing operation and his career was flying high. Then a series of downsizing and reorganizing moves within the company left him with only a small portion of his previous responsibilities. At the same time, he had recently been diagnosed with a medical condition that potentially limited his ability to travel frequently. Understandably, he became depressed, but then the disappointment and discouragement started to spin out of control. As he became more morose, he began to withdraw from others, leading to estrangement from many of his co-workers and family members. He began turning more and more often to single malt Scotch to soothe his despair.

Disappointments, tragedies, life crises, even trauma, are not exactly unusual occurrences in people's lives considering that three-quarters of us will experience some severe crisis in our lifetime, whether it is a medical illness, the death of a loved one, or surviving an act of violence, assault, or tragedy.[6] Almost by definition, such experiences catch us off guard and are accompanied by quite strong feelings of anxiety, frustration, and confusion. Like Omar, sometimes serious depression and hopelessness become problems, often managed with forms of self-medication like alcohol, drugs, or other addictions. And yet, such critical incidents also provide incredible opportunities for personal transformation.[7]

It is precisely those episodes that we find most challenging and overwhelming that can often lead to the most significant positive growth. Very few people willingly and enthusiastically make changes in their lives because they *want* to, but rather because they *have* to: It feels as if they have little choice. And what brings people to this transitional state is the acceptance that what they have been doing is no longer working and so they must learn something new in order to survive, much less flourish. It is adversity that provides the most opportunity for growth and development—*if* it is managed effectively.[8]

In the trauma literature, it has been discovered that whereas one-third of individuals who have suffered extreme deprivation, such as surviving natural disasters, battlefields, life-threatening illnesses, or abuse, experience chronic symptoms of posttraumatic stress disorder (PTSD), it is also the case that another one-third recover rather quickly and go on about their lives with few lingering effects. The truly interesting finding, though, is that the remaining one-third of people exposed to terrible situations and life-altering disappointments find ways to use those opportunities for incredible personal benefit and significant growth.[9]

Research has provided us with a fairly thorough blueprint of what can happen when individuals experience what has now been called *posttraumatic growth*. Admiral Jim Stockdale, former president of the Naval War College and awarded the Congressional Medal of Honor for courage, was flying a mission over North Vietnam when he was shot down and imprisoned in the notorious "Hanoi Hilton" for over seven years. Stockdale's narrative about the torture and deprivation he suffered is strikingly similar to that of psychiatrist Viktor Frankl in *Man's Search for Meaning*, writing about how those who survived the Nazi concentration camps seemed to be people who were able to find some purpose in their suffering, even if it was to simply tell the world what had happened.

"I never lost faith in the end of the story," Stockdale remembered, "I never doubted not only that I would get out, but also that I would prevail in the end and turn the experience into the defining event of my life, which, in retrospect, I would not trade."[10] Yet faith alone was not nearly enough to deal with adversity unless it was tempered with a measured, realistic assessment of the situation. He noticed that those prisoners who were unrealistically optimistic and Pollyannaish ("We'll get out of here soon") eventually died of broken hearts because they couldn't recover from the continuous disappointments. "This is a very important lesson," Stockdale recalled. "You must never confuse faith that you will prevail in the end—which you can never afford to lose—with the discipline to confront the most brutal facts of your current reality, whatever they might be."

The Benefits of Traumatic Growth

After surviving a disaster or life tragedy, much less a major disappointment in leadership, there are a number of benefits that some people report as most significant. Perhaps it makes sense that one of the first benefits mentioned is a much greater appreciation for things that might have been taken for granted previously. This includes appreciating friendships and the importance of family support more than ever, but also a greater commitment to engage more attentively in the most ordinary moments of the day.

"After being diagnosed with melanoma, I was a changed man," one department head related to me. He had been all business before his surgeries that, fortunately, were completed in time to save his life. After he was given the all-clear signal and resumed his duties at work, everyone noticed his utter transformation. "I just realized how precious every day of my life is and how much time I frittered away being so concerned with stuff that just didn't matter. People get so bent out of shape about the silliest things—as if the world is going to end because some assignment wasn't completed as quickly as it should, or losing some account." He is quick to point out that although he still does care about such things, which is a requirement of his job, he is now able to keep a more balanced perspective. "Shit happens," he says with a shrug. "You deal with it. Or don't. And then move on."

If he sounds rather cavalier displaying this attitude, he also says his work quality has not suffered even as he has broadened his interests and diversified life priorities. He claims to be happier and more satisfied than ever before and actually enjoys work in ways he hadn't previously. In some ways, he is grateful to the melanoma for getting his attention in a manner that his wife's nagging never could.

There are so many other benefits also reported by those who recover from adversity. In addition to increased appreciation and valuing of relationships, such individuals develop an increased tolerance for discomfort given what they have lived through. It's hard to complain too much about annoying traffic, missed deadlines, or an asshole at work, if you've been through hell and back and lived to tell the story.

It is also common that such posttraumatic growth experiences result in a kind of spiritual renewal or greater interest in the larger questions of life. This leads to deeper questions about the meaning of life, and why some people are spared tragic events while others are subjected to one disaster after another. Survivors of adversity believe they have developed expanded inner resources that allow them to deal with new stressful situations in the future. They feel more self-reliant and better equipped to handle whatever new surprises life has in store for them. Although most people would never have chosen to face difficult situations, they are often appreciative afterward for what they learned about themselves. They also feel immeasurable gratification from the support offered by others, often rededicating a portion of their lives to improving conditions for people who might find themselves in a similar situation of adversity.

How Resilient Would You Be?

Given the point earlier mentioned, that some people fall apart and others rise to the occasion, some variables do exist that best predict how well you might do in difficult circumstances.[11] Of course, readers of a book on leadership are most likely better qualified and positioned to deal with adversity, given that the nature of the work so often involves managing crises. A lot depends, however, on the particular kind and severity of the critical incident. Some people feel strong attachments to their "stuff," their possessions and material comforts, while others may become so overly dependent on particular relationships that devastating reactions result if they suffer loss through rejection, separation, or breakup. Then there are natural disasters from tornadoes, floods, earthquakes, fires, or human-initiated acts of terror or war, as well as accidents, crashes, or assaults—all of which may lead to different degrees of emotional (and physical) injury.

Specific kinds of personality traits predispose people to react to critical incidents in either helpless or empowered ways. Those who are more optimistic and confident, exhibiting what has been called "hardiness," tend to do better in such situations and recover much more quickly. It also helps to have had some prior experience with difficult situations in the past, along with a successful track record of coping. On the other hand, those who were already vulnerable and under stress because of preexisting conditions would likely find it far more challenging to deal with a catastrophe.

What resources and coping mechanisms are available to the leader facing an adverse situation? Depending on your financial resources, access to support and care, chosen forms of self-medication, things will improve quickly or slowly, or not at all. Not surprisingly, those who attempt to manage the situation by further isolating themselves, blaming external factors they can't control, and using excessive drugs or alcohol will have a much harder time adapting and recovering.

A theme that we revisit once again is how the meaning we create from any experience determines, to a great extent, how well we deal with the situation. One of the most popular movements within the field of psychology today looks much more at what is going right in people's lives, instead of focusing on what's gone wrong. Traditionally, when someone seeks help, the first question asked is, "What's your problem?" This would lead to lengthy talks detailing all the complaints, difficulties, and associated conflicts. It is often far more useful to "count one's blessings," so to speak, meaning to keep disappointments and crises in perspective, compared to so many other things in life that are actually going quite well. That's one reason not only why corporations diversify their interests for protection against losses but also why individuals are best advised to do the same. If all you've got is one project, one assignment, one priority, then you become vulnerable to crushing disappointment if circumstances don't pan out as expected.

It helps to be clear about what is most important. This is especially the case when we overreact to circumstances and blow them out of proportion, imagining the worst possible scenarios. This is what leads to feelings of futility and despair. Instead of ruminating about what *could* have been done, or what *should* have been done, it is far more helpful to let go, learn from the mistakes, identify the good stuff that might have resulted (if any), and move on. It is a matter of honoring blessings and gifts that accrue from challenges, rather than just the uncomfortable and undesirable effects.

Posttraumatic growth researchers have summarized all the benefits and gifts that disappointment or trauma can offer and reduced them to several main themes that might alter one's worldview and life's path.[12]

Things change. Once the rug had been pulled out from underneath you—or your house or company literally burns down—you no longer count on everything always remaining the same. Survivors who flourish become far more flexible and accommodating to inevitable changes that occur in every sector, whether it is job responsibilities, health issues, or relationships.

Psychological mindedness. Critical life events throw us into a state of temporary uncertainty, if not chaos. This often leads to deep reflective thought about what happened and why, as well as what can be done to prevent or minimize such situations in the future. Increased self-awareness often results whereby people become far more sophisticated and knowledgeable about their own inner thoughts and feelings, as well as the behavior of others.

Personal empowerment. It is ironic that often through failure, tragedy, or disappointment do we learn the most about our abilities and resilience, our talent for taking things in stride and recovering successfully. Survivors of bad things frequently feel increased confidence afterward, knowing that they can handle situations they may have earlier feared.

I don't mean to sing the praises of adversity without also acknowledging the devastating effects that often result when people feel powerless and lost. Being demoted at work, losing someone or something you love, experiencing a health problem, disaster, or tragedy can certainly compromise someone's life and lead to all kinds of chronic suffering. As you'd expect, some people just surrender to despair, while others go on about their lives and pick up the pieces to rebuild again. It all depends on the ways you choose (and it *is* a choice) to process the experience, just as is the case with the ways that people deal with interpersonal conflicts at work or in their daily lives.

Ignoring Conflicts, Hoping They Will Go Away

Most crises or conflicts do not suddenly appear without warning; there are usually initial signs, subtle (or obvious) symptoms of impending trouble that will likely not go away no matter how much we might wish it so. The difficulty in recognizing and responding to such matters is complicated by often contradictory or confusing signals that can be interpreted in a number of different ways, especially within dysfunctional organizational cultures. The same thing is true with respect to interpersonal conflicts in that they tend to escalate if the participants are reluctant to deal with the underlying issues and simmering resentments.

I suspect you can immediately think of several family members, longtime friends or acquaintances, or co-workers with whom this is the case. You can't seem to spend more than a few minutes in one another's company without some misunderstanding or miscommunication. Once embroiled in chronic conflicts like this, the patterns become so entrenched that they seem impervious to change.

One reason for ongoing impasses is the insistence, on the part of both (or all) parties, to externalize responsibility and blame the other(s) for the difficulty. It initially feels good to absolve oneself of any role in a conflict: It is the *other* person who is being so ornery, unreasonable, rigid, incompetent, or uncooperative. Yet all conflicts—and I do mean every single one—result from an interactive effect whereby each participant in the struggle is both the cause, and effect, of the other's behavior. This is called "circular causality" and is illustrated in situations that you witness frequently within families and at work (if you recognize them).

A supervisor, unaware of how transparent her facial expressions are, inadvertently scowls as she is listening to a subordinate's report. The employee suddenly feels even more defensive and apologetic after seeing what he interprets as a sign of disapproval, but is actually just expressing the supervisor's thoughts with regard to what might have been said beforehand.

The staff member backtracks a little, making excuses for something that the leader neither noticed nor even cares about. The supervisor senses his hesitance and timidity, and so starts pushing for more details that are not available. The subordinate responds to this by becoming more hesitant, feeling both hurt and misunderstood. He is convinced, based on prior interactions, that his boss is a bully, and this experience clearly confirms his assumptions.

The supervisor, on the other hand, has now lost confidence in the quality of this person's work. Now her disdain is real, triggered by what she interprets as a poor-quality performance even though he delivered exactly what had been expected. She shakes her head, dismisses the man, and then complains to others about how incompetent and useless he is.

The subordinate leaves the meeting and immediately huddles with his peers and tells them about his dressing down by the supervisor, and how rude and abusive she was during their conversation. He delivered just what she asked for, and it still wasn't enough. It is *never* enough. He blames her. She blames him. And neither has a clue about how each of them is triggering the other.

This type of misunderstanding and conflict situation is hardly unusual in any human arena. Disputes and disagreements are inevitable with many differences of opinion, especially in fields or industries in which people have rather strong and varied opinions about the best courses of action. Although many leaders dread such challenges, when handled well, they can, in fact, lead to better solutions and even greater trust and cohesion within a team.

On the other hand, we also sometimes have to deal with people who, no matter how accommodating and flexible we might be, nevertheless insist on being as obstructive and annoying as they possibly can. In certain cases, they do this because they are mean, underhanded, and untrustworthy; in other instances, they are just so troubled, they can't help it. Regardless of the reasons why we experience someone as difficult, or find ourselves embroiled in conflict, there are some useful strategies to work through the problem, or at the very least, to insulate its destructive potential on ourselves and others.

Rules of Engagement in Conflict Situations

One of the most admired attributes of great leaders is their ability to remain calm and composed during crises or conflicts. A classic example of this is the frequently told story of Sir Francis Drake, whose game of lawn bowling was interrupted by the invasion of the Spanish Armada appearing along the horizon. He glanced over his shoulder and then announced to his astonished companions, "Time enough to play the game and thrash the Spaniards afterwards." This was seen as evidence of his incredible composure during crises, but it also reflected his knowledge of the seas, realizing there was no way the ships could get close enough to attack until the tides changed and the armada became an actual threat.

Whether facing an enemy approaching the shore, or negotiating a conflict that has become heated, the first and most important task for a leader is to remain cool under fire. And even if you don't feel that way inside because your guts are churning as a result of the perceived attack, it is important to communicate relative composure. We have no way of knowing how Sir Francis Drake really felt as he stood on the beach, looking out at the hundreds of enemy ships lined up along the horizon, but he gave the performance of a lifetime to his troops, reassuring them that he had everything under control.

Within a military setting, the hierarchy of power is both highly structured and clearly demarcated, just as is the case with primates that know exactly where they stand in relation to others within a troop. Such positions of relative power can be sanctioned, such as when a job description provides "legal" authority. This gives police officers the right to order us to stop in our tracks, judges the power to decide guilt or innocence, or leaders the authority they need to make decisions and force others to comply. Power can also be determined by many other factors, such as one's age, socioeconomic status, physical features, or willingness to fight against the status quo.

The most problematic conflict situations tend to be those where someone else holds disproportionate power over others, whether it is real or imagined. For instance, a parent, a former coach or mentor, no longer has any power over us, but it still *feels* as if that person does. We still hear his or her admonishments in our head. We fear his or her scolding and disapproval. We continue to show deference toward those whom we respected—or feared—in the past.

When a child, subordinate, follower, or someone of lower status annoys or upsets someone in authority, it is a rather simple matter—at least on the surface—to shut the person down. On the other hand, if the antagonist is of equal or higher status, conflicts become much more challenging to navigate, as well as to live with internally. When someone *really* gets underneath your skin, or becomes a nemesis, someone you constantly think about in negative ways, there are several rules of engagement that can minimize the deleterious effects. Even if you can't completely alter his or her behavior (which you usually cannot), there are all kinds of things you can do internally to cope more effectively.

Stop Complaining

Gregg Popovich, five-time NBA champion basketball coach, was asked what he looks for when recruiting a player whom he hopes will become a future leader of the team.[13] For Popovich, it's all about character traits, especially someone who appears to take things in stride, rather than complaining constantly about lack of playing time, or that he was unappreciated by his former coach. "I'm not taking that kid," Popovich says, "because he will be a problem one way or another. I know he will be a problem. At some point he'll start to think he's not playing enough minutes, or his parents are going to wonder why he's not playing, or his agent's going to call too much. I don't need that stuff. I've got more important things to do." The coach says he'd much prefer to take a player with less talent but someone who doesn't whine and complain.

Likewise, complaining about a situation, especially one that is actually out of our control, only leads to greater feelings of powerlessness. When things are tough, it may feel initially validating to solicit sympathy, but ultimately such efforts just end up confirming that you are indeed a victim.

Get Support

It's important to reach out for support during times of difficulty, *if* the action is not directed merely to make someone listen to your complaints. We are a tribal species. There were dangerous, hungry predators in our ancient environment, requiring us to stick closely together for collaborative hunting and gathering, protection, and safety. Our nervous systems evolved in such a way to maximize social support as a form of soothing and stress reduction. That is why so many of the methods that people develop for relaxation and recovery alternate between periods of group support with solitude in order to balance the need for validation with being "off stage." There is little doubt that, in most cases when we feel out of sorts, it really helps to spend time with like-minded others who can share the burden, listen compassionately, and provide whatever resources we need to recover.

One key component of the relative value that social support networks can have depends on who exactly is invited into the inner circle. There are both potentially constructive, as well as toxic, social influences that are reflected in the agendas and attitudes of those included. Sometimes friends, family, and co-workers can make things feel far worse by reinforcing feelings of "victimhood" or commiserating in such a way that you feel even more powerless. Sometimes they just offer lousy advice that reflects their own values. And sometimes they hold their own agendas that may conflict with your own and don't at all represent where you would most like to go next.

Do Less, Not More

Conflict situations often feel intractable because the participants are locked into the same behavioral patterns that are clearly not working even though they persist in continuing them. This was mentioned in a previous chapter when discussing the ways that leaders often remain stuck because they are tethered to an agenda that is obsolete and engage in strategies that are obviously falling short.

A boss takes down an employee for coloring outside the lines, so to speak. The employee defends herself, providing a reason to explain why things happened the way they did. The boss becomes more enraged and yells louder, confused and frustrated why the employee is not falling into line with his program. The employee now feels even more threatened and so defends herself ever more vigorously, providing additional reasons for the action. This triggers the boss's anger even more and he yells still louder, backing the employee further into a corner. Before long the interaction spins completely out of control. Both walk away from the encounter feeling angry and holding a grudge. Both seemed incapable, or at least unwilling, to stop what was clearly not advantageous, and instead try an alternative way of relating to each other.

When yelling and attacking don't work very well, this is not a time to yell louder and more aggressively. When providing excuses does not appease the other person, it is not a good idea to offer more of them. Time and time again, you see a parent screaming at a child to stop doing something. Or you will notice someone arguing with a partner, spouse, or friend without noticeable progress, *yet the person continues doing the same thing.* Escalating conflicts consistently produces one of two outcomes, either defiance or surrender, both of which have negative side effects.

As a reminder of what we covered earlier, there are some simple steps to follow in order to untangle and deescalate conflicts: (1) Figure out what you are doing that isn't working; (2) stop those actions immediately; (3) do something else, anything other than what you are already doing that isn't working; (4) start by trying the *opposite* of what you have been doing. For instance, if you tried begging or pleading with the other person to work more collaboratively and that has had little or no effect, then try an alternative approach. Go about your business without considering the other person at all. That might not work either, but at least it frees you up to be more flexible and creative in finding the optimal solution.

Set Limits and Boundaries

There are times when the best we can hope for is damage control. There are some fairly crazy, irrational, unreasonable, mean-spirited people in the world. Some of them end up working with or for you, no matter how careful and selective the hiring process was. Some of them are in your family or live in your neighborhood. These are individuals who are not going to change their behavior no matter what you—or anyone else—does. They derive some benefits from their obstructiveness; it empowers them. They enjoy the wake of chaos they leave in their path.

There are different versions of this kind of person, not all of whom we find equally annoying or difficult. Sometimes we have to deal with those who are passive-aggressive in their behavior, so we never know where things really stand. They will say one thing to us in person, but actively seek or take another course of action when we are not around. They try to mobilize support for their hidden agendas and recruit others to join their revolution. It does no good to confront them because they will deny any ulterior motives. They also have no real incentive to adjust their behavior since it actually works quite well for them.

The opposite of passive-aggressive is just plain aggressive. This is the bully who is verbally abusive, shaming, and intimidating. As long as such individuals are allowed to get away with their behavior, they are also unlikely to change. And for good reason, since this pattern is effective if the goal is dominating others through fear and terror. Attempts may be made to isolate or separate these individuals because they don't tend to play well with others, but sometimes we are simply stuck with them and have to make the best of things. Like each of these examples, the most effective strategy is often to set—and especially enforce—clear boundaries to minimize damage.

Although there are psychological names for people like this—narcissist, borderline, or sociopath—one author of a book about getting along with others at work simply calls them "assholes."[14] They are characterized as aggressive and impatient, yet also oblivious to how they come across to others. And if they do notice, they don't much care. They feel entitled to do whatever they want because they see themselves as special. They are both impatient and unpredictable, except that we can always count on their annoying behavior.

There is a different kind of boundary or limit that needs to be established with another kind of colleague, the person who is clearly clueless, incompetent, or unteachable. Whether you were the one who made the mistake in hiring this clown, or someone else gets the credit, you are still stuck with cleaning up the messes that result from his or her chronic laziness or stupidity. There comes a point when this has got to stop, at least from the perspective of your own involvement in interactions with this individual, which often leave you feeling frustrated and upset. Such individuals must be left to self-destruct on their own, in spite of your best intentions in repeatedly attempting to guide them away from their own worst instincts. There is little chance of "saving" this person, only the reality that he or she will take everyone else down as well.

Finally, there are those who are extremely emotionally unstable. They are impulsive, unpredictable, and volatile. Often they are struggling with serious mental health problems, whether depression, chronic anxiety, or some emotional or personality disorder. They may have attempted to manage their difficulties with forms of self-medication, like drugs or alcohol, leading to even more erratic behavior.

With each of these types, and many others that you could nominate, the clear and best strategy, when all else fails, is simply to minimize the harm when that is indeed a feasible option (sometimes it is not). Another possibility is to consistently enforce critical restrictions, especially considering that you can count on the fact that the person—already out of control—will continue to see what he or she can get away with no matter what you do. The reality is that certain people with whom we must deal are just very toxic, manipulative, and difficult, seeming to thrive on the ways they can get underneath others' skin.

Remember Your Mantras

Within the traditions of meditation, a mantra, or internal chant, is used to focus concentration on a single word or phrase. We use similar techniques in daily life when we remind ourselves of certain things, for instance, "This too will pass," "Take a deep breath," or "This doesn't really matter." These are self-soothing whispers that help us to keep perspective on the little annoyances (or sometimes big crises) that we allow to unnerve us.

It turns out that when actually embroiled in a conflict with someone, this is the optimal strategy for remaining reasonably calm and collected in the moment and to prevent yourself from overreacting. Other examples of mantras or self-managing phrases to repeat to yourself include the following.

Tie-eem. This is actually a real mantra, based on the word "time." It is an example of a single sound (two sounds actually) or word that is used to completely focus all of one's attention on the here and now. Even with years of practice, it is typically challenging to stay in the moment beyond a few seconds before distractions cross one's mind. Each time that happens, you just gently focus back on the mantra. This is very much like a time-out for your brain.

In one hundred years . . . This is a reminder that in time nobody will ever remember what happened, or ever care, no matter how important a critical incident seems in the moment.

What am I missing? Conflicts frequently arise because one or both parties interpret the other's behavior according to their own standards. This, of course, is understandable, because that's what we ordinarily do. Such a limited perspective, however, misses the opportunity for grasping the context of why people act the ways they do, often influenced by their cultural background and personal experiences. Someone can be angry, annoyed, frustrated, or upset with you for an assortment of reasons that may not even occur to you; in some cases, it may not have much to do with you at all.

This isn't about me. Sometimes a conflict arises for reasons that have little to do with your own role in the scenario. This mantra directly contradicts the earlier advice that *every* disagreement is the fault—and responsibility— of everyone involved. Exceptions to every rule exist, and indeed there are times when we tend to overpersonalize what is going on and assume the situation is somehow a reflection of us when it is really about something or someone else.

What am I doing? If you accept that you don't have nearly as much power to change other people as you have to alter aspects of yourself, this reminds you to look closely at your own contributions to a conflict instead of focusing on others. Though such reflection might lead you to take too much responsibility for matters, it can be empowering to realize how much potential control you have over your own reactions to whatever occurs.

He is doing the best he can. We feel most frustrated with others when they don't meet our expectations. In a managerial or leadership role, we have the right and responsibility to make sure that others meet required standards of performance, but conflicts often ensue when leaders attempt to ensure such compliance in other parts of their lives. It isn't surprising that professional leaders are often viewed by friends and family members as control freaks who try to exert their influence in heavy-handed ways when they aren't on the job. It is important, and useful, to recognize that there are times when others are doing the best they can, given the circumstances, their skill set, and readiness level. We will experience greater compassion, patience, and understanding for others when we realize they are doing as much as they can. For now.

I'm getting stronger. If you do believe that adversity can become an important teacher, then remind yourself that you are learning a lot from the chaos and confusion that are unfolding.

Breathe in, breathe out. There is actually a fair bit of research to indicate that taking a deep breath, or counting slowly to ten, when you are upset, angry, or overwhelmed, really does help to calm you down and think more clearly. This is another variation of the mantra theme mentioned previously.

Be. Here. Now. This is the most challenging task of all, given how caught up we get in the numerous little but distracting details that command our attention. All these annoyances and disappointments vanish when the only thing that exists is NOW. Forget the past. The future, too.

Be still, my heart. Your heart is just a muscle, beating once every second. Each of us is entitled to about 3 billion heartbeats if we are lucky, and live to be 80 or so. Right now, since you've been reading these sentences, you've "lost" another few dozen heartbeats, hundreds in the last few minutes, thousands and thousands gone throughout the day. Your life is definitely time-limited, as is your heart that is wearing out. And so all the things you allow to steer you off course, worry you incessantly, speed up your heart rate, take precious moments away from the limited time you have left.

Forgiveness. We spend so much time punishing ourselves for things we regret. We spend even more time being disappointed and angry with others for not living up to our preferences and expectations. Forgiveness is what allows us to put regrets behind and move on. Forgiving ourselves (and others) for perceived transgressions helps us to keep them out of our heads. The only thing worse than having someone treat you unjustly or insensitively is reliving the experience over and over and over again, adding to the initial injury.

Leaders Resolve Conflicts and Critical Incidents

When Genghis Khan arrived in Persia, he first sent emissaries to negotiate with the shah, who responded to the invitation by setting the beards of his two ambassadors on fire. This so enraged Khan that when he showed up with his Mongol army, he decided to wipe out every single inhabitant of the region, killing 300,000 Persians in a single day. Ruling through terror and intimidation (or genocide) is a singularly effective leadership strategy, even if it has certain side effects that will eventually lead to tragic consequences. Yet clearly one approach for handling dissatisfaction, criticism, conflict, or disagreement within a group is to forcefully stamp out all opposition.

Much of what leaders do is provide a moral compass for others within a team or organization, that is, to demonstrate through actions as well as talk the values that are most cherished. More and more often, companies, for instance, are extolling a "corporate conscience," taking a stand on social or political issues. The vast majority believe they have a responsibility to encourage positive changes in the community and world at large. This even impacts the choices that people make regarding where they work and how long they stay at the job.[15]

Conflicts arise in any group when members have competing interests or different perspectives. Since this is inevitable, especially among a collection of rather talented, opinionated individuals, it is perhaps not surprising that leaders spend one-quarter of their time dealing with conflict situations that require some intervention.[16] They have to step in when certain personalities clash, or when others perceive that someone on the team isn't holding up his or her end of the bargain or delivering what was promised. Sometimes it's just a difference in style that leads to problems in that people work to their own rhythms that may not be compatible with others'. Difficulties also arise simply as a result of some miscommunication or misunderstanding. It's safe to say that on any given day, there is somebody at work who is upset or disappointed with someone else, whether justifiable or an exaggerated reaction.

Leaders tend to rely on different styles and strategies to resolve such difficulties, depending on the situation and the particular configuration of trouble. Some conflicts result from competing interests when one or more parties insist that they win the spoils, even if several others might lose benefits, as well as their dignity. Attempting some sort of collaborative effort or compromise resolution is usually preferred, but that requires considerable skill and expertise on the part of the leader, who must then mediate the disputes and negotiate solutions that are acceptable—or at least tolerable—to everyone. There are other circumstances when a reasonable compromise or resolution is not practical, or even possible, requiring some sort of accommodation to preserve harmony. Simply avoiding the conflict altogether can, of course, be dangerous as that generally tends to escalate difficulties over time, especially when strong feelings are involved (which is often the case).

One of the interesting movements within the field of conflict mediation is to redirect efforts away from objectives related to parties winning or losing in a dispute, instead helping them to focus on a deeper understanding of one another's positions. You may have noticed that people sometimes spend an inordinate amount of time, money, energy, and resources arguing about the silliest and most insignificant issues because they are driven, beyond all else, to win the fight at the expense of another person or group. Spouses will spend tens of thousands of dollars in legal fees during a divorce settlement just to secure some household item or concession that is fairly insignificant. Political leaders will sometimes invest extraordinary time and effort in punishing an adversary who was believed to have betrayed them in some minor way. Co-workers will go to battle against others (or the leader) if they feel slighted or disrespected. Just think of the wars that have been fought, with millions of people lost as casualties, because of some misunderstanding or perceived offense. Greece and Bulgaria once declared war on each other after a runaway dog crossed the border and the soldier chasing it was mistakenly shot. Of course, that wasn't the real reason for the conflict, just the excuse.

Before we can ever hope to resolve conflicts, we first need to understand what they are really about and the underlying issues that might be ignored or denied. This takes a certain degree of skill, patience, and insight to help injured parties or disputants not only share their stories, but also truly hear one another. Sometimes the goal of such negotiations is not to resolve the conflict for once and for all, considering that many problems don't, in fact, have a completely satisfying conclusion. Instead, the leader's job is to help people listen to one another in ways they perhaps haven't been able to previously. Even if a total and permanent solution cannot be reached, the parties can at least be helped to hear and respect one another's position, declare a truce, and find ways to work together collaboratively in the future.

Among all the skills that we will explore in connection to leadership, this task of helping others to negotiate settlements, resolve disputes, and deal with critical incidents is the most useful in everyday life. In all the domains of our lives, whether at work, home, or elsewhere, we will sometimes find ourselves embroiled in annoying or upsetting conflicts with others. We will also witness many people constantly at one another's throats: at family gatherings and social events, or on the job. Whereas it does take considerable training and expertise on the part of professional mediators, organizational psychologists, and judges to help people resolve conflicts, leaders can still play an important role in reducing tension within a group or team. Indeed, it isn't really disagreements or different opinions that necessarily lead to problems, but rather a particular work climate that spawns heated conflicts and dysfunctional relationships that are particularly resistant to change.

PART IV

Applications to Daily Life

10

Leadership Within Social, Family, and Community Life

MORE OFTEN THAN NOT, leadership is viewed as some grand steward-ship of an army, political entity, organization, or corporation, a noble effort to change the world in some significant way. This conception is not only discon-certing for most people, much less improbable to achieve, but also shrouded in notions of power, manipulation, and control. Yet leadership can also be viewed as any effort, *any* moment, in which you extend yourself in some way, reaching out to others in need, and somehow make a constructive difference in their lives.

As important as our jobs might be, as ambitious as we might be to achieve recognition, as critical as our work might appear, perhaps the most important leadership of all begins with our own loved ones. It is with our own children, parents, and siblings, our friends and neighbors, that our actions take on the most personal and enduring significance.

It is precisely the experiences we have every day that potentially benefit us in innumerable ways, sparking growth, learning, and personal transforma-tions that enhance our well-being, not just at work but throughout all our interactions. This is what has been called a "growth" rather than "fixed" mind-set of leaders, a condition that totally shapes and guides our ability to perceive and respond to others—and events—in increasingly more effective ways.[1] We have seen how so many of the traits, abilities, and skills of professional lead-ership translate perfectly well to every other domain of life, taking a stand for being helpful and providing guidance wherever and whenever it is most needed.

There is "big" leadership that usually commands all the attention, and then there's "little" leadership that translates into ordinary moments that make a difference. Drew Dudley talks about how we've made leadership into this daunting task, "something bigger than us; something beyond us." It isn't always about changing the world or some great accomplishment; it also means celebrating the "amazing things that hardly anybody can do. . . . We start to devalue the things we can do every day."[2] Dudley defines this as the ways in which we demonstrate leadership simply by making somebody's life better with the words we speak to that person, or through some small act of kindness or generosity. He calls on us to redefine leadership as the ways we use our power, knowledge, and influence to make a difference in all the small, simple acts that matter to others. Although we often assume "big leadership" involves positions of huge responsibility to change the world, or the direction of an organization or company, Dudley insists there is no single world to change, but rather 6 billion different understandings of it, each of which could use some support and guidance along the way.

Congruence and Authenticity in Daily Habits

It has always bothered me within my own specialties of psychotherapy and leadership that some practitioners engage in such hypocrisy, unable or unwilling to practice in their own lives what they preach to others. Certainly you have met helping professionals who are walking paradoxes of the values and lessons that they insist are so important for others, but appear to exempt themselves. Most visible are physicians who don't take care of their own health, clergy caught with their pants down, politicians who engage in corrupt or immoral practices, corporate executives who engage in behavior that is hardly a model for their employees, or teachers who tell students one thing but then do quite another when they believe nobody is watching. Leadership is not just about what we advocate for others, but also how we live those principles in our own daily lives.

The media loves to jump on politicians or ministers who have been caught doing something that is immoral or illegal. Just as potentially detrimental to leaders in *any* context is the perception by their followers that they are inequitable, unjust, or hypocritical, requiring others to follow rules they choose to ignore, engaging in favoritism, or being unable to do what they ask of others. Such behavior is even associated with higher turnover among employees who become dispirited and discouraged by the perceived injustices.[3]

It was once the case that leaders could enjoy a certain amount of secrecy and privacy in their daily lives, but those days are over in this era, with almost every moment of wealthy, privileged, and powerful lives recorded and scrutinized. And there is nothing more detrimental to one's reputation than being captured on an image or video engaging in behavior that directly contradicts one's espoused beliefs that are allegedly so sacred. Most often, this takes the form of celebrities, religious figures, congressmen, or others who are behaving recklessly and thereby diluting their authority and respect among followers.

Leaders are now warned to be more cautious and circumspect than ever because we are forever on stage, always being observed by others with a critical eye. That is only one of the reasons why there is so much literature produced these days offering advice for how to infuse certain skills in everyday life. Check out any of the most popular publications, and you'll see articles that promise simplistic advice with titles like "Things Leaders Say Every Day," as if all you have to do is walk around the office (or your life), pat everyone on the back, and tell them, "You're doing a great job," "I don't know how we would do this without you," "I'm so glad you work for us," and "I've got an important new project for you." Okay, so I agree such affirmations mumbled out loud just *might* communicate that employee work is appreciated, but only if they actually reflect genuine beliefs that are consistently put into action.

Considerably more practical, and likely effective, is another essay on the daily habits of the most successful executives.[4] Most of the 29 suggestions might seem rather pedestrian, but they, in fact, represent an underlying commitment to finding balance and peace in life, especially in relationships that matter the most. Some of these include such daily habits as:

1. Talking to people face-to-face whenever possible, even though it is more inconvenient and time-consuming, because it offers greater intimacy and relational connection that is usually more satisfying (not to mention productive).
2. Instead of just drawing up a "to-do" list, make a "have-done" list to remind yourself what you've accomplished and to review what has yet to get done.
3. Access active empathy by looking at the world through others' eyes and walking in their shoes. This helps us to better understand people's interests, yearnings, motives, and goals, as well as to make sense of their behavior.
4. Focus on the positive whenever possible. Balance challenges, difficulties, rejections, disappointments, and other negative experiences by also looking at the gifts that they might offer.

5. Slow down. *Way* down. Appreciate the joys and beauty of the most ordinary moments instead of always thinking about what comes next, all the things that have yet to be done, all the things you intend to do—as soon as you are done rushing through whatever you are doing right now. Resist distractions and interruptions that interfere with your appreciation for whatever is happening *this* moment.

6. Come to work early, if you must, but don't also stay late. Take time to value the other interests, relationships, and opportunities in life outside of work. Seek and maintain balance *before* things careen out of control.

7. Listen to people, listen *very* carefully, before you speak. It's important for people to feel heard and understood, even if you disagree and ultimately hold the power.

Other optimal daily habits are directly related to self-care and making healthy lifestyle choices. This is not just for our own well-being, but also designed to show others our commitment to these goals, given that they are likely to literally follow our lead. When we take the time to show interest in certain matters, cherish our relationships, and try to be the sort of person in daily life that we wish others would emulate, people take notice in such a way that it influences and affects their own behavior. This is true with respect to our colleagues, subordinates, friends, and family.

When Less Is More

There is often a bias or norm that leaders must learn to counteract in order to negotiate a balance between achievement and life satisfaction, both at work and home. Leaders are usually hired in the first place based on the understanding that their job primarily involves reaching some target goal. A baseball coach is expected to improve the win–loss record of a team. A corporate figure must increase the return on shareholder investment. A sales manager is expected to increase the number of deals closed.

Likewise, there is an assumption within our economic and business climate that no matter how well you are doing, how smoothly things are running, the goal is to expand operations, open more locations, improve profits still further by reducing expenses, and perhaps even initiate a merger or additional acquisition. This is the gold standard by which leaders are often evaluated, almost never taking into consideration such factors as the quality of employee satisfaction or, quite simply, how much fun, enjoyable, satisfying, and meaningful the time spent at work is.

It is quite challenging for rather ambitious, hard-driving individuals to avoid applying a similar standard of "success" to their personal lives in other domains. There is an assumption more is always better—a bigger house, a more expensive wardrobe, a faster, more comfortable car, and other luxuries. Yet there is fairly compelling evidence that few, if any, of these material possessions make any kind of significant difference in improving the actual quality of one's life; in many cases, they lead to further entrapments and obligations.

In so many cases, leaders find themselves overstressed—and often unhappy—when their striving, driving nature pushes them to run their daily lives according to the same demands and expectations that they might meet at work. There are indeed times when doing less, slowing down, actually results in greater appreciation for the simpler things that can provide life's greatest gifts. This is especially the case with the burdens and responsibilities of leadership since the work is never done, there's always one more thing that you can do, and no matter how many hours you work in a day or week, you will *still* not complete all the tasks that seem so urgent.

"I learned long ago," explained the dean of a university college to me, "that it doesn't matter how late I stay in my office, there are still more faculty files to review, more reports to read and write, more communications to read and respond to, more administrative chores that have piled up. I used to think if I worked late into the night, I would some time actually catch up but it never happened. And then a strange thing happened. I started going home at 6 p.m. sharp every day, no matter what was piled on my desk and in my computer inbox."

The university administrator laughs as he tells the story, still amused by his revelation. First of all, he was delighted how much more he actually enjoyed his job now that he carved out time to be home for dinner with his family every night. Second, he liked the message he was sending his staff: while their work was important, so, too, were their outside lives. "But the thing that surprised me most," he said, "is that it didn't seem to matter at all in terms of the work output. Nobody else seemed to care either, or even notice that I had adjusted my schedule."

There are some work settings in which it is absolutely expected and essential that people (especially leaders) demonstrate their commitment to the job by the number of hours they work each week—60, 80, 90 hours or more, as if the quantity is some kind of meaningful measure of a lawyer, medical resident, or leader's performance. In fact, such a lifestyle is unsustainable in the long run, especially if one has an interest and desire to keep one's health, family, and social life intact.

When More Is More

On the other hand, leaders are defined by their passion and commitment to a vision and extraordinarily ambitious goals. It would be virtually impossible for that curiosity and drive not to follow us in many other aspects of our lives, especially considering that they are so often the source of our power, success, and satisfaction. A case could be made, in fact, that successful leaders are simply more engaged, more determined, and more motivated than others—and it thus makes perfect sense that such an attitude would accompany us everywhere we go and affect almost everything we do.

Perhaps the greatest secret to exceptionality in *any* field, whether education, sports, science, literature, or leadership, is what neuropsychologist Angela Duckworth has referred to as "grit," meaning extraordinary stick-to-it-ness and motivation.[5] She had been told most of her early life that she was "just average," reflecting the bias in our culture that supposedly innate ability alone determines success—especially in the area of leadership. Unqualified for a gifted and talented program in her childhood, she nevertheless managed to earn a MacArthur "genius grant" during a distinguished career, an accomplishment she attributes to her dedication and passion rather than talent. Duckworth's research has pointed to the inescapable conclusion that while some degree of "smarts" and aptitude is important in any pursuit, it is really desire and persistence, especially in the face of disappointment, that makes all the difference. Whether speaking about the likes of Warren Buffet or Jeff Bezos in business, or great actors like Will Smith, it isn't talent that matters as much as "a sickening work ethic" in the words of Smith.[6]

The trajectory of my own life has followed such a pattern of being (or feeling) relatively talentless compared to my peers. I barely graduated from high school, earning a C average, and couldn't get into any university. Earlier in life, I had struggled with vision problems, a speech impediment, no particular athletic prowess, and marginal social skills. I have a framed "report card" from preschool on my wall that evaluated my 3-year-old abilities in "table work," "rhythm," and "food habits" as acceptable and rated my "intelligence" as "average." Once I talked my way into a university on probation, it was only to receive grades after the first semester that were still mediocre.

And *then* something changed.

I remember deciding I wanted to be smart, or at least appear that way to others. I was tired of being barely average. I desperately wanted to do something extraordinary with my life. I wanted to be a leader. But what could I possibly offer with my limited abilities and talent? Because of my earlier vision problems, I had never learned basic grammar, algebra, geometry, or any other subject that required being able to see what was written on the blackboard in front of the room. Even with these handicaps, I found (or created) sufficient motivation that first year in college to just flat out work harder than anyone else. I had a lot of catching up to do. When others were out partying and socializing, I was consuming all the books I was supposed to have read earlier.

I have followed this same prescription of passion and grit in so many other areas of life, not only as a psychologist, writer, and leader, but also as a parent, grandparent, spouse, friend, and colleague, prioritizing deep, intimate relationships above most other things. I have never quite met my ideal standard in this regard but I'm still a work in progress. I have also been able to carry this passion and perseverance into recreational and leisure pursuits as a mountaineer and cyclist: I definitely do not have optimal ability or physical prowess in these areas (or most any other activity), but what I do have is exceptional drive and tolerance for pain and discomfort.

The takeaway from these examples is this: Whereas it is certainly important to devote focused energy and commitment to one's role as a leader at work, it is perhaps even more important to do so in the other domains of our lives that involve loved ones and cherished relationships, as well as avocational and recreational interests. I realize, of course, that I'm directly contradicting the points I made earlier in the chapter, on how doing less is more, but when it comes to the things that matter most, holding some of our energies in reserve is worthwhile, so we can fully devote ourselves with passion to those relationships and pursuits that provide the most life satisfaction and pleasure beyond work.

Balancing Work and Family Life

In more than half of all two-parent homes, both partners work—and they are more stressed than ever. Couples are affected in all kinds of ways, including less sleep, less sex, less quality time together. Moreover, many are having a difficult time balancing responsibilities at work with those at home. For women, this is especially the case since they are often saddled with the bulk of child-rearing responsibilities. "You basically just always feel like you're doing a horrible job at everything," a woman executive admitted. "You're not spending as much time with your baby as you want, you're not doing the job you want to be doing at work, you're not seeing your friends [or] hardly ever."[7]

Men, as well, say they feel guilty for not spending enough time with their families. They also feel caught in the middle between never-ending crises at work that must be managed, and the pull toward home from those who want more attention. It is indeed difficult to find a balance. When Speaker of the House of Representatives Paul Ryan was first offered his leadership job in Congress, he balked because he knew it would take so much of his time, compromising his priority as a father to his three young children. He flew home from Washington, D.C., every weekend, but felt as if he was already missing out on so much of his family life. Fortunately for him, Ryan had the leverage to negotiate time that could be devoted to his personal life so that work did not become all-consuming. In spite of best intentions, however, the requirements of holding the second most powerful job in the country no doubt interfered with this laudable goal. The truth is that family members are always more inclined to put up with excuses for not being available than do people at work.

There is another side to this dilemma. Most leaders share the burden of responsibility with their partners or spouses. When you arrive home from a tough day at work, one of your first interactions will often be bringing your partner up to date on what happened, inviting input and suggestions. Our divorce laws seem to recognize the value of "the other" in terms of collective resources since an estate will usually be divided in such a way as to recognize the contributions of a leader's partner or spouse. What this means is that leadership is frequently a team effort, not only with the staff at work, but also loved ones at home.

Many U.S. presidents of this generation seem to echo the cultural shift whereby it is both obvious and legitimate to recruit one's spouse as a valuable partner in leadership. This trend has sparked some resentment in the instance of more actively involved first ladies such as Eleanor Roosevelt and Hillary Clinton, but others such as Rosalynn Carter, Nancy Reagan, Laura Bush, and Michelle Obama have also had considerable influence with their husbands, as well as cultivating their own special projects. Leadership is thus a family enterprise, sometimes to the extent that the next generation is groomed to take over the family business, as happened with the Kennedys, Bushes, or Clintons.

The nature of contemporary marriages or couples is to form a more equal partnership in their relationship and their responsibilities. Many women are now the main breadwinners for their family, and many men prefer to remain at home as caregivers. Daily tasks around the home like cooking, cleaning, shopping, and child care used to fall almost exclusively within the domain of "women's work" but are now more equitably divided (though still not close to being equal). With this renegotiation of relationships, leadership becomes, more than ever, a kind of teamwork regardless of the partner's actual supportive or advisory roles in the background. As much as such a dynamic may solidify greater cohesion and collaboration in the relationship, it also means that work pressures and conflicts are brought home and infused into daily life more than ever. Whatever boundaries once existed between work and family have eroded because of the constant accessibility to information and communications via mobile devices.

Still another variation of the way in which leadership responsibilities have become part of daily life is the example of "power couples," in which each partner brings to the table his or her own responsibilities as a leader. This creates the need for considerable negotiations if the couple is to survive, much less thrive, since sacrifices must inevitably be made as one partner defers to the other. Thus, former cabinet member Elizabeth Dole had to resign her position in the Reagan administration in order to support her husband's political campaign to run for president. In other cases, co-equals in the leadership domain have pooled their different skills to pursue a common mission (Bill and Melinda Gates, Mark Zuckerberg and Priscilla Chan) or otherwise support one another in their own individual missions (Jay-Z and Beyoncé, Alan Greenspan and Andrea Mitchell).

Those couples that have learned to manage their different responsibilities effectively have devised ways to preserve their independence while also working together for mutual support. One's partner becomes a sounding board, a trusted confidante like no other. In the best examples, both partners support each other's visions, not just through words but via actions, like taking turns to give each other access to a new opportunity, or balancing schedules in such a way that both leaders can pursue their ambitions, yet also make it a priority to spend quality time together. This is the new reality: households stocked with very busy family members, each committed to their own ambitions and goals, but also struggling to find their own happiness and satisfaction.

What Contributes Most to So-Called Happiness?

A management professor remembered a time in graduate school when he was studying applied econometrics and made the deliberate decision to forgo his assigned work for the class in order to dedicate time to contemplating what he really wanted most to do with his life to make a difference. While his grades may have suffered a bit because of shifting priorities, years later, he felt no regret about this choice. It may be the case that he was not as strong in regression analysis techniques as he could have been, but he felt quite satisfied with the outcome that resulted from this reflective thought process each day. "I apply the tools of econometrics a few times a year," he reminds himself, "but I apply my knowledge of the purpose of life every day. It's the single most useful thing I've ever done."[8]

During this introspective period, the professor realized that the most important motivator for his career would not be the pursuit of wealth, but rather to find ways that he could continue to learn and grow and feel like he was doing something meaningful with his life. He also found in his own research that the root causes of failed leadership in business were exactly the same as those in one's personal life—a disconnection between espoused values and priorities, versus where time and energy are actually allocated in daily life. People say things all the time about what is most important to them—family, friendships, social engagements, love relationships—but then go ahead and devote most of their time and effort chasing material rewards and recognition in other areas that they actually consider far less important. It is no wonder then that many leaders who appear to already have anything and everything they could ever imagine are still restless, in search of something more to achieve their high standards of satisfaction and happiness.

Among researchers on the subject, "happiness" is now an outdated term. One reason for this is that the relentless pursuit of happiness is what, in part, leads to *un*happiness. Instead, the term "well-being" is thought to be more descriptive and accurate.[9] Regardless of the chosen expression, whether searching for increased happiness, contentment, life satisfaction, or well-being, there are several factors that have been found to be most common—and this is true in most places around the world and during most stages of the lifespan.[10] First and foremost is a feeling of creative achievement and meaningful productivity, whether at work or elsewhere, especially when it is not tempered by constant comparison to others, which can lead to envy and resentments. It is also important to have a *perception* of choices, but not so many that you feel lost and overwhelmed. An optimistic outlook is obviously crucial, but also a willingness to take in stride inevitable periods of sadness or disappointment.

Wealth actually means very little beyond taking care of basic needs and earning a "decent" living (usually defined as making about $60,000 annually, depending on where you live). Surprisingly, earning significantly more than that doesn't make much difference in terms of life satisfaction. Health also doesn't matter much since people are so adaptable that even those who suffer catastrophic injuries often return to their previous "set point" of happiness a few months after recovery.

It turns out that relationships are almost *everything* when it comes to feelings of well-being. Those who feel part of a supportive family (inherited, chosen, or created), who have a handful of close, trusting friends, and who enjoy meaningful work are most satisfied with their lives—and this is true in almost every culture and setting.[11]

When satisfying and supportive relationships just happen to develop while engaged in meaningful work, then that is the perfect formula for life satisfaction—assuming it also is accompanied by feelings of love and support in other aspects of life. Yet, as we've explored previously, it is also entirely possible that some individuals are so focused on their work, and find it so enjoyable and productive, that they don't experience the need for many other outside interests or relationships. They may be labeled as workaholics by others who don't quite understand the singular priority, but that may represent the value judgment of those who believe more diversification and balance are necessary for themselves.

Attitudes toward work are as important as the tasks themselves. Some people have identical jobs yet feel very differently about what they do. During the time when newspapers were routinely delivered to the doorstep of your home, two paperboys, both brothers, described what the job was like for them.[12] The first boy, Cliff, talked about how much fun it was riding his bike down the street before school every day. "You throw the paper off your bicycle and it lands some place in the bushes. It'll hit part of the wall and it'll go booongg! That's pretty fun, because I like to see it go booongg." Cliff enjoyed the solitude in the morning, clearing his head, meeting and talking to neighbors, and delivering what he considers an important service to his community.

Cliff's brother Terry had a very different perspective on the identical job, regarding it as drudgery and one annoyance after another. He vehemently disagreed with that "bull about the kid who's gonna be President and being a newsboy made a President out of him. It taught him how to handle his money and this bull. You know what it did? It taught him how to hate the people in his route. And the printers. And dogs."

Crosby, Stills, and Nash popularized a song long ago with this refrain: "If you can't be with the one you love, then love the one you're with." Although these lyrics might appear to advocate settling for complacency and mediocrity, rather than going after what you really want most, another interpretation is that life is way too short and fragile to spend time at work, or doing anything else, engaged in activities that don't ignite our passion and excitement. Even if you have to awake early in the morning to deliver papers to customers who are less than cordial, the story of Cliff and Terry shows how one's attitude toward the job is everything.

There is always on the horizon a potentially better job, improved situation, or new, exciting challenge, and perhaps someday it will come to fruition, but meanwhile, all we really have, all we will ever really have, is today—with no guarantee that there will even be a tomorrow.

When "Home" and "Office" Become Blurred

As discussed earlier, telecommuting was supposed to make life easier for everyone. It saves time and money, and did I mention it is more convenient? Organizations and businesses initially loved the idea of cutting expenses by reducing office space and the number of salaried employees onsite. And, of course, staff members loved the idea of working from home, being spared the time, expense, and aggravation of commuting. But the reality of the transformation has turned out to be far different than initially expected.

"It's been more difficult than I thought it would be to adjust to my new schedule and work habits now that I'm settled in my newly furnished home office." This national sales manager of a large tech company supervises the workload of hundreds of staff around the world, each in a different time zone. As such, the brain trust of the company decided that it made more sense for her to operate from home, rather than their corporate offices, because so often she had to direct video conferences scheduled in the middle of the night, or early in the morning, if staff were based in India, China, the U.K., or Eastern Europe.

"It was so convenient," she recalled, "just jumping out of bed, putting on a blouse over my nightgown, logging into the conference, and then going back to sleep. I'd be giving instructions or feedback to dozens of different people, all the while I'd be sipping coffee, watching the news with the sound off, and petting my cat sitting on my lap—but out of view."

The delight she experienced didn't last long, however, and she eventually decided to look for another job that might involve more daily support and contact with people. "I found that several days would go by in which I never once left my home. Heck, I'd never even go out shopping because I could get whatever I needed delivered within a few hours. I'd be on duty all day, and all night. But the worst part is how isolated I felt. Talking to people via messages, email, social media, phone and video conferences, just wasn't the same." She reports that although she was incredibly efficient and productive in the use of her time, at least as far as her vice president was concerned, the job had lost its "fun factor." Even worse, her home no longer felt like a sanctuary, but rather became an extension of her harried, stressful work environment.

The new position she found paid less and actually required her to go into the office every day, but she loved it because she felt part of a cohesive team. "There was this one day a few weeks ago," she said with a laugh, "when I had so much stuff to do I decided to stay home so I could focus on things without constant interruptions. But then everyone kept pinging me every few minutes, asking questions, trying to resolve one crisis or another. Finally, I just gave up and went into the office to take care of things."

Although it might sound as if she's recounting this story in annoyance, in fact, she was once again amazed at how much more she could get done with everyone accessible in real time and space. There had been a problem with a customer, and she realized she actually had to sit down and discuss it with different people in order to resolve the difficulty. She met with an analyst to get his input, then visited with the product manager, engineering, tech support, all to coordinate their efforts and talk things through. "When there's so much happening all at once it just doesn't work very well to be in a different place."

When she compares this work environment to that at her previous employer, a huge multinational tech conglomerate, she is constantly surprised by how much more they can accomplish with everyone onsite and available. Recently, she was able to launch a new product in a week whereas it took nine months to do so at her last company, largely because of the staff's distribution all over the world. In addition, she now looks forward to going to the office, just as she does returning home.

Rather than improving the quality of life with family, working from home can indeed create more problems than it solves, leading to increased stress and conflicts. As highlighted in the example just described, people usually end up working longer hours, are almost never off-duty and inaccessible, and feel more isolated than ever before.[13] Even among those who believed working from home would make their family caregiving responsibilities easier, it often made things worse given the blurred boundaries, multiple distractions, and longer hours.

This has led many to wonder whether telecommuting is worthwhile after all. It would seem that one key is actually providing training and collaborative methods to optimize this style of operation; selecting candidates carefully based on factors that best predict success (being single, self-disciplined, a reliable communicator, and highly motivated); and setting clear expectations and performance metrics.[14] Yet the underlying issue that is sometimes exacerbated is that many leaders already work way too hard, often beyond the point where it is productive and healthy.

Working Hard . . . or Way *Too Hard?*

Americans work longer hours than most other developed countries around the world, and it's getting worse, resulting in a clash of competing priorities between work, play, family, community, and other outside interests. Over the last three decades alone, the typical workweek is now 11 hours longer than it used to be. With the ubiquitous presence of mobile devices everywhere we go, there is virtually no downtime at all, extending job responsibilities from the moment you awake to the time you go to sleep at night (with employees sometimes even checking their email in the middle of the night to see if they missed any messages). It is for this reason that 96 percent of all working parents report significant difficulties juggling their jobs with family responsibilities. It is also why the U.S. has the "most family-hostile public policy in the developed world."[15] Compared to other industrialized countries, we boast the least supportive maternity or family leave policies and the most neglectful programs to support sick leave or family emergencies. Needless to say, some aspects of life satisfaction and healthy lifestyles are being increasingly sacrificed in the pursuit of careers.

In the case of leaders, there is even a greater temptation to become seduced by the single-minded devotion to one's job. Leaders who work too hard, or spend excessive hours laboring away, often encounter troubling side effects, regardless of how much they love what they are doing. Certainly, working diligently is lauded and honored in most cultures, especially in America, Korea, and Japan. In fact, the Japanese invented a new word for those who actually die at their desks, *karoshi*, meaning "death from overwork."

There are indeed some organizations and leaders that pressure employees to put their job responsibilities above anything else in their lives, including children, spouse, parents, friends, health issues, community, spiritual or leisure devotions. Employees agree to such indentured servitude because they need the extra income (or think they do) and grow attached to the material benefits. Such "perkaholics" become addicted to the rewards of a bigger office—a reserved parking space, company car, and especially the admiration and approval of the powers that be.

Nevertheless, the reasons for working so hard may sometimes have little to do with professional goals, financial rewards, or personal ambition, and more to do with managing one's emotional difficulties. A recent study found that so-called workaholics, those whose commitment to their jobs sabotages other aspects of their life, often present symptoms of underlying mental disorders.[16] One-third of such leaders are either diagnosed with attention-deficit hyper-activity disorder (ADHD), or meet the criteria for a generalized chronic anx-iety disorder. Another one-quarter of overly engaged leaders can be classified as obsessive-compulsive, with 1 in 10 diagnosed as clinically depressed.

The cause–effect relationship between these conditions, however, isn't clear since it's difficult to determine whether the excessive workload creates the emotional problems, or these personal struggles are what influence certain leaders to "hide" in their jobs. In one sense, such behavior is another form of addiction designed to "self-medicate" from the effects of boredom, distress, lack of intimacy, or dissatisfaction with other aspects of life.

There is a difference between being fully engaged in leadership responsi-bilities versus falling into a workaholic pattern of extreme overinvestment in one's job to the point that negative consequences result. A lot of attention has focused lately on the stratospheric success of workaholic CEOs like Steve Jobs and Tim Cook at Apple, especially after the publication of a series of biog-raphies following Jobs' death describing his creative process. Yet when one entrepreneur and tech CEO delved into the details of Jobs' life and behavior, he became absolutely appalled, realizing how Jobs' priorities and values were so unbalanced and unhealthy. We discussed earlier how hearing or reading stories can be truly transformative and influential in changing the trajectory of one's life course, and indeed, this particular CEO put down his copy of Jobs' biography, after which he decided to sell his company so he could spend more time with his family and reorient his own priorities to focus more on relationships and less on productivity. "If you're going to fail at something," he explained, "fail at building a fucking iPad. Don't fail at building children."[17]

It isn't all doom and gloom, however, for so-called overly engaged leaders (also called "work enthusiasts"). There are, in fact, certain subtypes of proud workaholics, those who consistently work in excess of 60 hours per week, who are still highly functional and adaptive without apparent detrimental effects to their health or relationships.[18] One key appears to be related to how much you actually enjoy what you are doing versus feeling obligated or exter-nally pressured to work excessive hours. Another factor relates to whether the behavior is driven by perfectionistic tendencies and unrealistic standards for oneself and others, which drives everyone else crazy.[19]

As discussed in previous chapters, the ways in which leaders metabolize the pressures they face from overwhelming job responsibilities aren't neces-sarily based on the endless, unrelenting workload itself, but rather the attitude they bring to the situation and what they tell themselves about it. Saying out loud, or to yourself, "I *have* to go to work" feels qualitatively different than "I *want* to go to work." The former implies an obligation, whereas the latter represents a personal choice.

Balance Through Boundaries

There is some evidence that even leaders who work seemingly insane hours, and deal with incredible pressures that even involve continual life-threatening decisions, may still flourish because of the control and power they wield, as well as the success they enjoy. It is both surprising, and counterintuitive, to discover that many such leaders actually have a longer lifespan in spite of the pressure they are under. [20] For instance, most former U.S. presidents live significantly longer than the general population, even though they once held perhaps the most stressful and time-consuming job in the world. Going back to the inception of the nation, every one of the first eight presidents (George Washington through Martin Van Buren) lived to be an average of 80 years old—and this during a time when people were lucky to live to 40![21] Even today, most surviving former presidents live well beyond the average lifespan. It turns out that successful people in general, whether Nobel Prize recipients, corporate executives, or political figures, tend to live longer than those who do not achieve such distinction.[22]

You might find it just as surprising that CEOs of major corporations also report significantly *less* stress than their subordinates, even though they tend to work longer hours and have far greater responsibilities.[23] It would seem, then, that even the weight of one's burdens does not necessarily lead to problems if you have figured out constructive ways to manage the responsibilities. It also helps, naturally, that if you are in a leadership position, you generally have access to better healthcare, resources, diet, and working conditions.

Whether serving a leadership role in politics, corporate or public policy setting, or in a much more modest position with a small project, enterprise, business, or mission, one of the most important skills necessary for continued success—and total well-being—appears to relate to establishing necessary boundaries between work responsibilities and everything else. Those leaders who make themselves available at all times, who constantly interrupt family and social life, who don't consider their friendships a major priority, and who don't take time for exercise, time-outs, breaks, and recreational activities to de-stress, are not going to last very long, both in terms of their jobs and their health.

One executive is smack in the middle of the most exciting, stressful, and overwhelming period in his professional life. Originally trained as a corporate lawyer, he now oversees infrastructure construction projects. Every day, and well into the night and weekends, he fields calls from geologists, engineers, lawyers, lobbyists, governors, members of Congress, community leaders in a half dozen states, plus managing his own staff. He is a busy guy.

As much as he enjoys and loves his work, friendships and family mean a lot more to him. Given his travel schedule, as well as meetings and phone conferences, his life is packed with commitments. So it is all the more surprising that he leaves his phone at home when he goes out to socialize, and keeps the ringer permanently off to avoid interruptions. He has figured out a way to set clear boundaries in his life that don't so much separate work from play, as integrate them in a meaningful way so one does not compromise the other.

There are some who believe that finding work–life balance is a misguided way of thinking about the challenges since "the image of the scale forces you to think in terms of trade-offs instead of possibilities for harmony."[24] Rather than trying to completely separate work life from other interests, a much better alternative is to seek harmony between them.

"I love to take my daughter to the park," the executive related, with a wistful smile, "and do so at least a couple of times a week. When she was first old enough to hop on the swing, I remember looking to my right, and then to my left, and I noticed a carbon copy of the same thing I was doing—a father pushing his child on the swing with one hand, but I also observed that he wasn't paying much attention to what was going on because he was totally focused on his phone. It's as if the guy wasn't really present at all, just satisfied and relieved that he'd manage to distract his child sufficiently so that he could conduct his business uninterrupted. I vowed to myself in that moment to never to be a one-handed swing pusher, that my daughters were far more important than anyone else who could possibly want my attention."

Of course, that declaration sounds good in theory, but it's also unrealistic to expect a busy, responsible executive to put aside work responsibilities just because a family member or friend wants some attention. It's all about the narrative we wish to create about our own life, the role we most wish to play, and the ultimate objectives that are most important to us.

Leaders (Try to) Create Their Own Stories

As discussed in Chapter 8, stories are not just told, but also *lived*. Charismatic leaders, in particular, have been known to go to great lengths to present themselves in the image of how they wish to be known. This is what reflects the personal style of a leader, depending on whether he or she wishes to emphasize a narrative of achievement, self-sacrifice, aristocratic lineage, social status, charm, attractiveness, wit, or power. Jerry Brown, governor of California, projected an image of the ascetic, eschewing luxuries while first serving in office, and then once again when he was mayor of Oakland and favored living in a refurbished warehouse in one of the worst neighborhoods and walking to work each day. Former Secretary of State Henry Kissinger famously traded on his reputation as a lady's man, observing that "power is the greatest aphrodisiac." Donald Trump presented an image of the wildly successful businessman and dealmaker, displaying symbols of his wealth and privilege. Mahatma Gandhi burnished his image as a symbol of rebellion when he jettisoned his Saville Row suits with the simple white robe of a political prisoner, creating a story about the values and priorities that he wanted to disseminate to his followers.[25] Of course, image management is not necessarily congruent with the way leaders actually behave in the real world.

Appearances in daily life are important, so much so that leaders give considerable thought to the "uniforms" they wear in public. Thus, the likes of Fidel Castro, Kim Jong-il, Muammar al-Qaddafi, Adolf Hitler, and other dictators featured military uniforms to spin a story about their ruthless and commanding authority. Political candidates and office holders of every ilk pretend to show interest in activities (going to church, hunting, touring factories or battlefields) that they displayed no particular inclination to visit previously. We frequently see political figures and other leaders with their sleeves rolled up, projecting the image of being a man or woman of the people even though it is fairly obvious that it's all a performance.

Yet in some cases, the story and images are actually consistent with a leader's authentic self. When we saw George Bush riding his mountain bike over hills on his ranch, or Barack Obama playing pickup basketball, or Vladimir Putin riding shirtless on a horse, or Donald Trump playing golf on one of his signature courses, these "stories" worked because they actually seemed consistent with the men's personalities and genuine interests. Great leaders use their strongest attributes, especially those that are truly their own, to magnify the power of their personal stories. Teddy Roosevelt, for example, literally tried to walk his talk: Stories circulated constantly about his remarkable commitment to follow a course of action no matter what obstacles were in his way. This is not a metaphor, by the way, but the actual manner in which he conducted his life on a daily basis, no matter who was watching.

Roosevelt was a big proponent of a popular activity among the upper class at the time called "point-to-point marching"—the idea that you would go for a walk with companions, and to demonstrate your mettle, you would go over, or through, anything in your path without veering off course. So Roosevelt and a few confidantes might discuss some social policy as they walked several miles across Northern Virginia until coming upon an open field with a high thicket blocking the way. Rather than going around the barrier, they would push directly through it even though doing so might result in a number of minor injuries. Given that the White House was essentially built on top of a swamp, there were heavily mosquito-infested ponds on the property and Roosevelt was known to walk right through them, shoulder high in the muck, as he strolled around the property. If he was on his way to a meeting somewhere in the capitol, he would begin a point-to-point march to the location, sometimes knocking on doors and walking through homes, climbing trees, wading through malarial swamps to avoid veering from his path. "He was like that with his policies as well," presidential scholar Steven Parker explained to me. "There was very little that could get in this guy's way in terms of other people's agendas, or the Supreme Court, or opposition that he had in the U.S. Congress, and that's why he kept reusing this 'walk the talk' metaphor, because in real life, he did the same thing."

Parker mentioned another example from the U.S. presidency that illustrates how leaders live their seminal story in daily life. He considers James K. Polk one of the great, unheralded leaders because he was able to deliver exactly what he promised to voters. Rather than proclaiming the ridiculously unrealistic goals that now characterize political campaigns, such as ending poverty, deporting immigrants, eliminating terrorism, building an impenetrable wall around our country, reducing taxes while simultaneously balancing the budget, Polk ran his campaign as he conducted his life—promising only what he was certain he could deliver. He was an expansionist and coveted more territory for the relatively new nation and so focused on one single goal during his administration, which was to bring Texas into the union. This actually set off a complex ripple effect, beginning with the Mexican War, and eventually resulting in expanding the country's holdings, from Chicago to Denver. Once he accomplished this goal, he quit, just as he promised he'd do, not showing much interest in politics ever again.

Leading Every Day

The first thing you'd notice about Deon Joseph is that his arms are bigger than most men's legs. He has a commanding presence, not just from his body sculpted from hours at the gym, and the various implements of law enforcement hanging off his belt, but from the way he walks down the street. Sergeant Joseph is an officer with the Los Angeles Police, based in the Skid Row Station that patrols what may be the most dangerous and chaotic square mile of real estate in the country. There are thousands of people living on the streets, many of them suffering from mental illness, neglect, chronic diseases, and despair. There are also many predators plying their trade on these vulnerable people. It is, in fact, the only place in the world where the Bloods and Crips have negotiated a truce, so they can collaborate in their efforts to keep all the customers addicted to crack cocaine, heroin, and painkillers. They even send "scouts" into the homeless shelters and treatment centers in order to entice recovering residents to reconsider their choice to give up their addictions.

Sergeant Joseph has taken me on walking tours of his beat on several occasions so I could observe him in action. He is the consummate leader in that he views his job as not only to enforce the law but also to keep "his people" safe. And he is quite possessive in the ways he speaks about the residents of Skid Row as his responsibility. He talks about his job patrolling the homeless population as a "calling," a position of leadership that involves a lot more than arresting criminals. He has launched housing projects for those who want to get off the streets. He has started programs for women who have been assaulted and raped.

When asked how he can possibly maintain composure, much less optimism, within such a desperate environment, Joseph just shrugs. He watches carefully for "the little miracles that happen from time to time. I don't have childish optimism that if I give someone a handshake or a hug they are going to turn their life around. I know that the individual I shake hands with is going to one day—or that same day—go around the corner and probably rob somebody. I know that. But if I can continue to be a light in a dark place and not judge them but serve them, they'll come around. Many of the people I've come in contact with have come around."[26] Joseph is greeted in a number of different ways as he makes his rounds. Some people call out to him with raucous greetings, others stop to shake his hand or give him a hug; others yell obscenities and then scuttle away. He just smiles through it all, making a point to engage as many people as he can along the stroll. Yet he also scans windows for snipers. This is indeed a dangerous place, one where human life is sacrificed for the price of a $10 rock of crack, or even a perceived look of disrespect.

Within the span of a half hour, I watched Joseph reassure one woman he would look into her case of assault, break up a dispute between two guys fighting over who "owned" that section of sidewalk, investigate closed tents on the sidewalk that might be hiding a dead body, and then bust a guy for selling beer out of a trash can. But it is his visible presence during his walks that he hopes reassures people that he is there for them, to serve and protect them.

After close to 20 years patrolling these streets, Joseph considers many of the homeless on Skid Row as part of his family. What is truly remarkable is how he manages to balance his compassion and empathy for others with the steely resolve required to deal with some really, really bad individuals who are there to exploit and hurt others. On every block he walks, there is another problem to resolve, a sickly woman teetering on her feet who seems completely lost and disoriented, hostile gang members who challenge his authority, "do-gooders" who show up to distribute food or clothes but soon find themselves in jeopardy.

In each case, and on every block, he knows people are watching his every move. And it is because of this reality that Joseph is so careful about his conduct and interactions with his "followers." This is especially challenging given all the backlash toward police officers for some of the recent unjustified shootings of unarmed Black citizens. But Joseph believes that any of us might end up homeless after a spell of bad breaks, loss of health insurance, and abandonment by others. Or sometimes all it takes is a dose of shame. Joseph sees his job as being not just a representative of law enforcement but also a symbol of order in this environment of complete chaos. He will not be able to save most of the people on the streets, but his goal is to rescue a few every week when the opportunities present themselves. It is what gives him the most satisfaction and his life the greatest meaning. It is also what lies at the heart of any successful stewardship, one in which leaders live in their daily lives the same principles, values, behaviors to which they wish their followers to aspire.

I I

Talking to Larger Groups Without Boring Them to Death

FRANKLIN DELANO ROOSEVELT came to power during an era when the very survival of the nation was at risk. During his time in office, he had to deal with not only the Great Depression and the Second World War, but almost a complete loss of public faith. One-quarter of the population was unemployed. Banks had failed in most states. Breadlines and homeless encampments spouted up across the nation. Riots, strikes, and protests were out of control. The U.S., and perhaps the world, would have been a very different place if an assassin's bullets had been more accurately aimed toward Roosevelt's vehicle just a few weeks before he began his first term in office.

FDR is considered to be perhaps the greatest, most inspiring public speaker and storyteller among presidents, during a time when these skills were so desperately needed. He may have been almost incompetent when it came to organizational skills, leading to chaos and incoherence in his policies and daily administration, but he had an "unequaled capacity to radiate optimism and confidence."[1] It was not only the New Deal that helped get things back toward recovery, but also Roosevelt's ability to sell a new narrative of what could become possible with collective effort.

Roosevelt was not born with this ability to inspire others into action, to move audiences to tears with his call for compassion and mutual support. When his wife Eleanor first heard him rehearsing a speech during the early days of his political career, she was appalled by how boring and listless he sounded. She commented on his distracting mannerisms, the long pauses without end, the slow pace of the rhetoric. Yet FDR recognized that his political future, as well as the welfare of his country, depended on his skills as an orator. In fact, his formal "fireside chats" on the radio became a stabilizing influence throughout his time in office, with him proclaiming, "This nation has a rendezvous with destiny" and "The American people in their righteous might will win through to absolute victory." In so doing, he discovered his greatest leadership tool during a time of overwhelming uncertainty, and learned to hone his storytelling ability as the foundation of his leadership approach.

Inspiring People to Take Action

The point of any talk, speech, or presentation is not merely to inform an audience but to move them emotionally. What most speakers don't seem to understand is that their role is primarily as an entertainer to capture and maintain interest. What we know and understand about persuasion and influence is that they usually do not happen through rational argument, but rather by activating emotional arousal, whether as joy, pride, or even frustration and indignation. You can introduce the most critical ideas or crucial information, but if people are not engaged, not listening, then everything literally falls on deaf ears.

When you consider some of the most persuasive and influential leaders throughout recent history, figures such as Martin Luther King, Winston Churchill, or even evil lunatics like Adolf Hitler, they all found a way to appeal to emotional resonance. In studying the rhetorical styles of U.S. presidents, it's been noted that, once again, Franklin Roosevelt was the consummate professional, not through any specific technique, but rather because of his willingness to adapt his style according to the particular audience.[2] Through practice, as well as constantly seeking to improve his effectiveness, FDR eventually developed his own conversational rhetoric that could either reassure listeners during a chat on the radio, sway big crowds at a rally, or articulate important plans and ideas for media critics.

Abraham Lincoln, as well, devoted a significant part of his life to the singular mission of developing his rhetorical skills, even as a child, by talking to his friends from imaginary pulpits.[3] Even with this constant practice and his legal training, Lincoln was still unable to make much of an impression on crowds, though he excelled at more private conversations. Over time he refined his skills further, working hard to develop his oratory ability, his craft at storytelling, to the point that he eventually mastered debates and speeches. Lincoln is an example of the extent to which effort and commitment to a leadership skill make all the difference, even without natural ability.

We'd have to agree that most lectures, speeches, presentations, and programs are less than inspiring. What if the same principles and skills that are used to engage small groups were also applied to larger audiences? Any talk can be far more influential and effective if it is designed to respond to the needs of those in the room. Regardless of how many people are present, it is important to be able to accurately assess their reactions and make adjustments accordingly. It has always been a bit of a mystery how a speaker, workshop leader, executive, teacher, or professor will stand before a room going on and on, frantically flipping through slides, while it's obvious to everyone else in the room that almost nobody is paying any attention.

Let's face it: Most speeches suck. They're boring. They drone on and on. Many speakers put up endless, tedious slides with corresponding bullet points. Even worse, they turn their backs to the audience and proceed to read the information aloud, as if those present are illiterate. Even professional faculty, who should certainly know better, erroneously believe that an extended lecture can actually teach something meaningful. But that is a mistake because a speech is more accurately described as a form of entertainment before it can have much impact or influence.

Connect with the Audience

I was once scheduled to do a workshop with a group in Sydney, Australia, in the most spectacular setting of the New South Wales Library overlooking the city. While I was waiting to get started, the organizer of the event shared the following story with me: that a colleague who had appeared the previous month engaged in a strange ritual as things were being set up onstage. He took off his shoes and socks and walked around the room, up and down each aisle of seating, at times wiggling his toes in the soft carpet. When he looked up and noticed the organizer staring at him with amusement, he explained that he was "trying to get a feel for the room." After another curious stare, he further elaborated that his ritual helped him feel "grounded" once he began to speak.

I found the story interesting but completely irrelevant as far as I was concerned. I could care less about the setting. In fact, I've delivered talks in some very unusual places—basements, castles, mansions, playgrounds, monasteries, churches, high school auditoriums, village squares, mountaintops. Whereas I'd certainly prefer a luxurious, exotic venue like the one before me in Sydney, the space didn't really mean as much to me as it did to my predecessor. But hearing this story from the organizer changed *everything* for me as a speaker. I realized, in that moment, that although the sense of place wasn't important to me in terms of my talk, I cared deeply about my connection to the people in the room. I'd learned long ago as a therapist that if I feel safe with a group, I'm much more willing to take risks, experiment, be creative, even try things I've never said or done before. When I trust the audience, I am more inclined to jump without a net because I know they will forgive me if things don't work as expected.

It occurred to me that rather than walking around the room to develop a feel for the space, what I really wanted to do was get to know the people in attendance, at least a little bit. So I stood outside the entrance and person-ally greeted each person who showed up, shaking hands, introducing myself, and making some connection. By the time the program began and I looked around the room, I realized that I already "knew" them and they knew me. It was one of my best talks ever because I felt so comfortable with the audience that they no longer seemed like critical strangers, but friends working with me as partners.

The Podium Is a Barrier

Standard operating procedure during any office conference is for the leader to sit behind a desk, a kind of fortification that communicates power and authority—but also creates distance with those in attendance (which may be the goal). Doctors and health professionals do this routinely as well, perhaps as much to insulate themselves from patients' emotions and suffering as for any reason that they need access to information or files on their desk.

When speaking before a large audience, it feels much safer to stand behind a barrier. It is grounding to hold on to something solid and secure. It is com-forting to have access to notes and a stabilized microphone. But such an arrangement also renders the speaker immobile, hiding everything except his or her face and hands. Once you abandon that island, you are adrift, wander-ing the stage, free to roam as the spirit moves you, but also to connect with different parts of the audience. You are now able to act out any points or sto-ries, using gestures, movements, and visual embellishments to illustrate ideas or accentuate drama. I like to wander up and down aisles as I speak, sitting in vacant seats within the audience. I once even started a talk in the *back* of the auditorium, just to shake things up a bit and announce through my behavior to expect the unexpected.

Standing behind a podium is safe, but it is often by challenging audience expectations that we command attention in ways that we otherwise could not: People will then wonder, what will you do or say *next*?

Tell a Story

Once again, we return to the subject of storytelling as the primary means by which to engage audiences. In Chapter 8, we talked about the various functions of stories as employed by those in leadership positions, as well as the kinds of stories that are adapted for particular purposes.

The leader's job often involves convincing people to do things that they would really rather not, or informing them of policies or procedures about which they may not feel much enthusiasm or interest. People are generally resistant to change unless it is absolutely necessary and required. It takes work to change. It takes sustained effort and commitment over time. It is uncomfortable and awkward in the beginning. It requires learning new skills and knowledge, some of which may not be seen as directly relevant or even useful. It means that people are forced to give up something that is already comfortable—even if it isn't all that effective—and to then learn a whole new system that they never asked for in the first place.

One of the customary approaches to initiating changes, whether in an organization or within an individual, is to convince people that it is ultimately in their best interests (and those of the organization) to follow a new strategy or program. This is typically accomplished by presenting objective data, empirical evidence, and persuasive arguments to convince others to proceed along a different, unfamiliar path. Such a presentation might be accompanied by slides and handouts, complete with graphs, tables, statistics, and pie charts showing the predicted trajectory of growth that is supposed to occur if the new plan of action is implemented.

Putting aside for a moment the fact that the audience is usually bored out of their minds, along with their annoyance, disappointment, and fear that these changes will translate into a lot more work, rational arguments may be favored even though they are not all that effective. When is the last time you convinced someone to change his or her religious beliefs or political affiliation? Some beliefs and preferences are so entrenched that it takes considerable pressure to pry them loose. However, the more you pressure people overtly to do something they would rather not do, the more resentment and frustration they might feel. Many leaders just shrug at this reality: After all, that's why they believe they are in charge in the first place—because they supposedly know what is best. There is, however, a subtler way to influence and persuade others, whether at work, at home, or in any other setting, and it often bypasses resistance to changes. It is also far more effective because of its appeal to a number of inherent psychological forces that access and play on emotional arousal.

In the storytelling chapter, I had illustrated how an appeal to emotion was the preferred means by which to persuade an audience to donate money to a charitable cause. The standard way that such presentations usually proceed is to cite data to support the need for action. Let's say, for example, that we want to raise money to support a project to feed malnourished children. We then present our rationale with impressive statistics stating that almost 1 billion people in the world are hungry and don't have enough food to eat, or that half of all children's deaths under the age of 5 may be attributed to malnutrition. Furthermore, it would only take $3 billion to feed all the 66 million children in the world who go to school hungry. That is less than the cost of a single Nimitz-class aircraft carrier in the U.S. fleet, or one-quarter the price of a new nuclear model in development.

These are heartbreaking statistics for sure, and there's no doubt that they would have some effect on the audience, surely persuading them to reach into their pockets or checkbooks. You leave the meeting feeling quite satisfied that you've done your job and begin preparing for the next group. Unfortunately, one of those unforeseeable glitches occurs and the tech staff person can't seem to start up the projector again. He shrugs helplessly. What action do you now take?

It's time for Plan B. You decide to jettison the data and slides altogether and instead tell the stories of three children, from three different parts of the world, all of whom died of starvation and chronic malnutrition. The presentation again seems to go well even though you tried a completely different approach to the subject. This gives you an idea for the final group.

You decide that for this last audience you will just focus on telling a single story about one child who died of chronic malnutrition. Given your limited and focused agenda, you take the time to share details about the child's life, about her family and village. You talk about some of her dreams and aspirations, as well as those of her family. And you talk about how her life could have been saved if only there had been enough money available to supply the family with food, as well as the capacity to grow their own future.

A week later, the staff person in charge of receipts and accounting provides you with a report on the donations that came in from each group you presented to. Which presentation was most effective in raising money?

It turns out that the approach of citing statistics and showing slides with pie charts and data, in terms of its professionalism, was most impressive. Feedback from the participants at this session stated clearly that the presentation was both well organized and beautifully delivered. The interesting thing, however, is that this first program raised the *least* amount of money, and the one that told just a single story about a child who was starving raised the most money. So, how do you account for this difference?

The answer, of course, is related to tugging on heartstrings and evoking high levels of emotional arousal. People may prefer to think of themselves as rational decision makers, but such logical thinking is often tempered by subjective personal feelings that don't necessarily "pollute" analytic processes, but rather augment them with additional input that may, in fact, be a lot more meaningful. The reasons why people donate money to a charity, or purchase a particular product or service, or formulate particular attitudes, are not solely (or even mostly) based on rational choices; they are frequently informed by deep emotional desires. This is clearly the guiding policy of most advertising and marketing campaigns that are designed to appeal more to the heart than the head. The best award-winning commercials ever broadcast on television essentially tell a 60-second story that speaks the language of feelings.

Telling Better Stories

Many companies and organizations are just beginning to understand how important storytelling is to leader effectiveness. Procter & Gamble not only has a "corporate storyteller," whose job is to collect and disseminate stories that enhance the company's image, but it also hired Hollywood directors to teach executives the ins and outs of spinning a good tale.[4] Other companies like Motorola, Kimberly-Clark, and 3M provide workshops for corporate leaders to teach them some of the most important features of a well-told story.[5] In some cases, they are even sent to improvisational theater groups in order to further augment their abilities.

Among all the subjects that leaders are taught in school or seminars, you will rarely encounter a class on storytelling, or even the option to take electives in literature, drama, or debate. That's too bad because you can't just order or direct employees or followers to get with the program, or become more passionate and committed to organization goals—all that would likely happen is that they will fake enthusiasm more convincingly. But it is possible to lead others with a story that inspires them, especially when it is well crafted and contextually appropriate. This means that what is offered actually fits the moment, that it is concise and focused, reasonably coherent. There are other features equally important worth reviewing here.

Before we get started, it is important to remember once again that storytelling is essentially a performance—and that is the first step during preparation and delivery. The style, structure, and script chosen should match the setting and situation. Some stories are told succinctly, sticking with the facts and compressing the details to feature a single theme. Some are drawn-out dramatic reenactments, complete with all the gestures, character voices, and action to bring the story alive. Still others are designed to lower tension in the room and make people laugh, or else to make them feel deeply about some issue. Above all else, the single most important thing to keep in mind is to rely on a style that feels somewhat natural and utilizes your own personal voice. There is nothing more awkward than watching a storyteller try way too hard to pretend to be someone he or she is not.

The First Thing to Ask Yourself:
Why Are You Sharing a Story?

There are several reasons why leaders tell stories—for self-aggrandizement or attention, as a provocation, as a distraction, or (hopefully) to introduce a lesson or theme. When sharing a personal story, it is even more important to carefully consider why you are disclosing the anecdote and whether there might be a less self-indulgent way to get the same point across.

Although people usually tell personal stories from their lives to enhance their standing and reputation, it is far preferable to reveal examples that speak to your imperfections. There is nothing that comes across as more boorish, arrogant, and narcissistic than telling stories about how wonderful or successful you are. Rather than increasing your stature in others' eyes, the result is often to simply create more distance between yourself and others.

If I tell you that even after 40 years of teaching leadership, there are many times that I still have no idea what I'm doing, this could influence your opinion of my credibility in two very different ways. First of all, you could write me off and decide that you aren't interested in hearing from some guy who admits that sometimes he's clueless. Alternatively, this approach could actually *increase* my trustworthiness in your eyes because my confession jibes with your own experience of feeling the same way at times, so you appreciate that validation.

Especially during those instances when you share a story about yourself, there must be a clear message beyond self-congratulations for something you did or said. What is the clear point of the story? You aren't stuck with who you are; you can be someone different, someone better.

Grab Attention. Quickly!

When I was finally able to untwist the rope, I realized that
I had a much more difficult task that lay ahead. That is how
my story begins. . . .

Learning, even listening, can't take place if you are not paying attention. People are now so inundated with stimulation, advertisements, texts, emails, messages, other distractions, that it takes something special—or at least different—to command focused interest. And even when people *seem* to be fully present, they are often secretly thinking about something else.

The best stories signal the brain that something is up, something worth dropping most everything else for in order to make sense of this seductive overture. It can start with something provocative, or something ambiguous and mysterious, like the opening line of the story that begins this section. This is what makes the storytelling experience an active collaboration because the listener has to work to comprehend what is being said—and then what it really means, or rather what it *might* mean.

There are all kinds of standard patterns and templates for the usual expected remarks. The speaker thanks the audience for attending and offers a lame joke that sparks a dutiful, forced laugh. The lights dim and the first slide alights on the screen, sending everyone into a coma.

Once you defy these expectations, the listeners quickly decide it might be worth paying attention, at least for a bit longer. I once dressed up as a homeless person and sat in the middle of the audience until I was introduced, then proceeded to slowly walk up to the stage as I removed my wig and disguise. I didn't do this for fun, but rather to illustrate how often we form impressions of people based on a few physical markers.

Another time I began a talk with a slide containing only two words, "The End," accompanied by the sounds of people clapping wildly. I bowed, thanking the audience and hoping they enjoyed the talk—which hadn't yet started. The people attending naturally looked uneasy and confused, thinking, "What the heck is going on? Is this guy crazy? We just sat down and he says the event is over?"

I then proceeded to ask everyone what they had learned from this talk about creative problem-solving. Once again, confused silence, with everyone looking around at each other, wondering if they were stuck in some time lapse. I persisted once again with my question: "So, what did you learn today that was new for you?"

"That time flies," one voice called out. Everyone laughed.

"Seriously," I repeated, "what are you leaving with today?"

Once the audience realized where this was going, that I was really just asking them about what they hoped to learn, as well as forcing them to consider what they really wanted most, they started announcing their hopes and greatest needs. Given that this was a talk about creative ways to deal with conflicts and difficulties, it was important to set a tone that defied usual expectations and signaled that whatever else followed would be quite different from what they'd heard before.

I'm not suggesting that anyone else use these same strategies as "gimmicks," but rather that whenever we address a group or audience, we give ourselves permission to begin in such a way that everyone's attention and interest are heightened.

Match the Context and Situation

Politicians use basically the same stump speeches at every event, tweaking and adjusting a few nuances to address local issues that might be most relevant to a particular audience. So in Iowa, they talk about corn subsidies; in West Virginia, they address the coal industry. Such an approach may be necessary when the leader is required to talk to different groups every day as part of a campaign for re-election. The best talks, however, appear (or feel) as if they were developed and customized for those present, with the content personalized and the speaker's style adapted to fit those in attendance. It is especially important that the way you begin, with a story, anecdote, or simple introduction, promises content that will be most appealing.

In order to tell good stories, you have to collect them systematically to add to your inventory. You mine them from your own personal experiences. You constantly observe and listen to others, noting interesting dynamics that are worth mentioning sometime in the future. You read voraciously, not just business news, industry publications, newspapers, and magazines, but also fiction and biographies. This allows you to hone in on the lessons learned from others' mistakes and triumphs. The more examples you have in your repertoire, the more likely you can select and customize a story to meld perfectly with the situation.

Most stories ramble on *way* too long. People roll their eyes in exasperation when someone begins with, "Did I ever tell you about that time . . . ?" You can see people becoming restless, disinterested, tuning out, as the leader tells the same exaggerated war stories he has repeated ad nauseam. But the storyteller keeps going—as if it doesn't matter how the listeners are responding; the goal is to finish the story. But audience reaction is *everything*.

It's best to keep stories under just a few minutes. Create the context and setting. Introduce the characters. Describe the conflict. Build the tension. But then get to the point.

On the other hand, sometimes it is more useful to include lots of specific scene-setting details, as well as providing sufficient coloring such that the audience feels as if they are in the middle of the action. "I want to take you on a journey," I began a commencement speech. I had originally been told that I had just six minutes to deliver remarks to the graduates and their families in the audience, but before I began, the organizer whispered in my ear that I could take as much time as I needed, up to a half hour. Rather than panicking because I had prepared something quite different, I relished the opportunity to carry the audience with me on the journey, providing all kinds of vivid descriptions of where we were going, what we were doing, and what we learned as a result. My goal was quite simple: During our time together, I sought to make the audience both laugh and cry.

Stories can also be so contextualized to an audience's interests and specialized knowledge that a leader might introduce the tale in order to explain some arcane point that might have appeal. Such stories might not have a character-driven plot, or much action—at least as defined by the uninitiated—but they still offer useful information. For example, a group of copy machine repair technicians are sitting around shooting the breeze, trading stories about the challenges they've faced during the week, and one of the technicians tells his friends he had to deal with an "E053 error code."[6] Everyone else (but you) nods their head in understanding because obviously this is a problem with the 24-volt interlock. But the speaker acknowledged that he could try to trace the interlock glitch forever and all he'd end up with is an F066 error code, which indicates the true source of malfunction, a shorted out dicorotron.

The technician continues with the story to his rapt audience, all of them curious why the short didn't fry the whole XER board. They all realize, at this point, that there had been a change in circuitry that prevented more extensive damage, but it also created another problem: "Now an E053 error message doesn't give you the true source of the machine's malfunction."

This tale might not seem particularly riveting to you, but the story has been contextualized in such a way that it has maximum relevance and interest to the audience that speaks this language.

Be Dramatic and Expressive

What makes stories captivating and interesting is conflict. There are actually a limited number of plots to all stories ever told around the world, whether in films, plays, novels, fairy tales, tone poems, song lyrics, or an anecdote shared during a public talk or meeting. It has been estimated that seven basic narrative structures exist; they follow a three- or five-act structure, presenting a struggle or conflict with its resolution.[7] There are, of course, variations of these themes, but they fall into several broad categories:

1. *Fighting a monster.* Examples include fairy tales like *Hansel and Gretel*, or films like *Alien, Predator, Dracula, Frankenstein, King Kong*. A leader might tell the story of a ruthless competitor who resorts to unfair labor practices in order to underbid a project.

2. *Rags to riches.* These are stories of redemption, presenting protagonists who are marginalized and then manage to overcome their station in life. Examples include *Cinderella, The Ugly Duckling, David Copperfield, Pretty Woman, Rocky, Shrek*, and *My Fair Lady*. These kinds of talks tend to offer somewhat self-deprecating personal examples in which the leader learned something important as a result of adversity.

3. *The quest.* Ah, the quest. This is a favorite plot of any adventure in which there is a search for some prize, whether that is a physical object like the Holy Grail (*King Arthur, The Odyssey, Raiders of the Lost Ark*) or rescuing someone in distress (*Apocalypse Now, Finding Nemo, Saving Private Ryan*). In the context of a speech, a seemingly impossible goal or difficult reward that can only be achieved through collective effort and desperate action is presented.

4. *Voyage and return.* This also describes a journey, but is just as much about rebirth of the self as a result of the adversity that was faced. *Goldilocks, Gulliver's Travels, Alice in Wonderland, The Wizard of Oz*, and *The Hunger Games* are prime examples. This is a story told when the leader's goal is to command attention through narrative tension and conflict that may parallel the challenges faced by the audience.

5. *Comedy.* This is a staple of so many weekly television shows but also plays (*Taming of the Shrew*) and films (by the Marx Brothers and Monty Python).

Hidden within the entertainment designed to make an audience laugh are also thematic messages that reveal the absurdity of life or the silliness of human behavior. Many speakers like to begin a program by making people laugh at a story that symbolizes the main messages that will follow.

6. *Tragedy*. These are stories that make us cry. They are steeped in emotional resonance and often include themes of character flaws that lead to disaster. They are thus object lessons demonstrating the dangers of self-deceit, greed, and other negative traits. By definition, the stories don't end well, such as *Romeo and Juliet* and *Les Misérables*. For a talk, such stories are selected and told when there is some object lesson that needs to be offered as a warning.

7. *Rebirth*. Although most of the plots mentioned involve some aspect of redemption, others focus more specifically on the powers of transformation, such as illustrated in *Beauty and the Beast*, *A Christmas Carol*, *The Matrix*, or *Dances with Wolves*. When told by a leader, this is a tale of transformation under trial by fire.

In summary, many of the stories shared in a leadership context involve some problem, conflict, or challenge in life or at work that must be faced. A typical scenario involves describing a time in someone's life, including your own, when an impossible situation was faced with courage, perseverance, and resilience. Somehow the protagonist managed to not only survive but also flourish as a result of the hardships that were confronted. The story doesn't need to have a happy ending, but it should reveal a relevant message that can be applied to the current situation.

Be Dramatic to Make the Action Come Alive

You are trying to create an alternative world, one that the listener can inhabit along with the protagonists. You are seeking a balance to provide enough detail to make the context and setting seem real and present, but not so much that there isn't room for the listener to actively fill in the open spaces. It may seem as if we are "giving" others a story we found or created, but instead we are actually providing a stimulus that allows others to take the narrative and run with it. Each person hears something different.

That is one reason why editors and professional storytellers realize that it is far better to "show" action, rather than merely "tell" what is happening. We want others to use their own imagination and active involvement in the story, instead of merely being passive recipients.

The more dramatic and evocative the way the message is delivered, the more likely it will land solidly. It's just so difficult to break through the barriers of boredom, predictability, distractibility, and fatigue—especially after people have been sitting still for more than a few minutes. Their attention hovers just about as long as they can get away with it, before lapsing into fantasy, planning their next moves, reviewing past actions, sneakily (or not so quietly) checking and sending messages, whispering to someone sitting nearby. Everyone is so inundated with stuff being offered to/thrown at/pushed toward/forced onto them, that once the lights go out and the slides appear on screen, they lapse into an apparent coma.

So, how does one break through such barriers of predictability and utter hopelessness?

By doing the unexpected. By using your voice, body, movements, your whole being, to convey such extraordinary passion and drama that the audience must attend fully for fear that it might miss what comes next (or the spectacle of complete implosion).

I was recently making this very point to an audience while talking about the power of storytelling. I could visibly see that I'd gone on too long without a break. Some people were starting to nod off; others were glancing longingly at their watches or phones. I knew I needed to ramp up the drama so we could end on a memorable note. There's considerable research suggesting that what bookends a speech (or any experience) tends to be the way it is remembered (the so-called primacy/recency effects), rather than the stuff in the middle. It was already apparent I'd lost my audience midstream, but there was still time for a comeback.

I had a few final messages to impart relating to the importance of providing relatively ambiguous imagery that will allow listeners to do the work, creating their own meaning from a story. I also wanted to emphasize how important it is to give oneself permission to be dramatic, just as would an actor or musician on stage (and life is a stage after all).

I mentioned in Chapter 8 one of my go-to stories, about frogs searching for a new homeland. Two scouts become trapped in a hole and can't get out no matter how hard they try. As I explained earlier, the story was never intended to have a precise message or lesson, at least in terms of the way I prefer to include it. My only intention in this case was to provide an engaging narrative that was ambiguous enough that the audience would try to draw some meaning from it. But that's still not the reason I'm revisiting the story here. It was how I told the tale that is relevant: I became a lunatic. I jumped around like a frog, making croaking sounds. I leaped out of an imaginary hole and landed on my back, with my legs kicking in the air. I must have looked insane. And I'm not necessarily recommending that anyone else try this at home (or at work). But I could hear the audience laughing uproariously. Nobody was looking at their watch or phone any longer: Everyone was riveted by whatever crazy thing I might do next. There was little doubt in my mind that as the lights came back on and I walked offstage, the people in attendance would remember that performance for a long time. I hoped they might also recall a few of the critical themes that I considered so important for them to make a difference in the lives of their followers.

Access All the Senses

As mentioned, your goal is to place the listener *in* the story. One way to increase that likelihood is to engage as many senses as possible, including sound, smell, sight, touch. Just saying certain words aloud, like "coffee" or "rancid garbage," automatically lights up the olfactory part of the brain, almost as if you were actually smelling those aromas. The more you can do to bring listeners *inside* the story, the more potential impact it can wield.

You don't have to be a novelist or playwright to try your hand at activating sensory arousal in a story. You just give yourself permission to set a mood and context, as if you were trying to re-create the moment. Imagine, for example, that you begin by describing the physical environment in which the story takes place: *The conference room's wall of North-facing windows presented a spectacular view of the city at night. The lights in the neighboring skyscrapers' windows looked like huge, towering giants with twinkling eyes. Although the polished mahogany table could easily sit a few dozen people, there were only four of us in the room.*

Next you describe the inner state of the protagonist. *It was eerily quiet in the building this late at night; even the air conditioning had stopped running. I could feel my heart pounding in my chest and swear I could actually hear the steady duh-dum echo in my ears. I wiped the palms of my hand on my pants so that by the time they were folded on top of the table, I appeared composed and ready for whatever came next.*

Most stories include not only a protagonist, the hero(ine) of the tale, but also antagonists who join in the conflict that is highlighted. *The three people sitting on the other end of the table looked indistinguishable to me, dressed alike in their dark suits, rep ties, and $100 haircuts. Even though it had already been a long, grueling day, they all looked like they had time to freshen up before the meeting, as if they were savoring what would come next.*

It is important to introduce the tension and conflict as soon as possible to hook the listeners and keep them interested enough in what will follow. In this case, the story introduces a bit of mystery, implying that there is some conflict coming next between the characters challenging one another on opposite sides of the table. It is at this point that listeners would hopefully be using their own imagination to picture the scene and predict what might unfold.

I've heard quite a few leaders define themselves, what they do, and how they do it, in somewhat limited ways. "That's just not who I am," or "I don't do that sort of thing." In other words, they see themselves as following a comfortable script, sticking with what is familiar and already part of their repertoire. I am suggesting, however, that all of us could give ourselves permission to be more expressive and dramatic in our communications when the situation calls for it. Once again, if the goal is to persuade, influence, and impact people, the most effective way to do that is by first capturing their attention and then providing some kind of novel stimulus in the form of content or delivery.

Reveal the "Truth"

Peter Guber, filmmaker as well as CEO of both Mandalay Entertainment and the Golden State Warriors basketball team, is ideally positioned to understand the power of telling a great story. After leading Sony Pictures with its successful run of hits during the 1980s, Guber launched his own new company. He has produced some spectacular stories, such as *Rain Man, Batman, The Color Purple*, and *This Boy's Life*. He also teaches leadership through storytelling at UCLA.

Guber has long been fascinated by why some films do so well at the box office, while others are complete flops. After all these years in the storytelling business, he still wonders about the features of a well-told story that don't merely entertain but move people deeply in such a way that they learn something about the way the world works—and about themselves. He has settled on four kinds of truth that are uncovered in good stories.[8]

The first kind of truth is what Guber refers to as authenticity and congruence. Leaders must be able to embed their deepest values in a story in which they come across as genuine, honest, and sincere. When a political figure nowadays begins a story with the statement, "I was recently talking to Sergeant Braveheart who, although he lost his legs fighting for his country. . . ." That's about the time we start to roll our eyes because this sort of device is so overused and obviously manipulative. Guber mentions an alternative example that embodies the truth to which he is referring. Jim Sinegal, former CEO of Costco, revealed to his employees that whereas they had an opportunity to mark up the price of a pair of jeans an extra 30 percent because of a wholesale deal that Costco had just negotiated with the manufacturer, they instead passed along the extra savings to their faithful customers. The story reveals that the company's priority is not just to make a profit but also to show commitment to those who have been loyal to them.

A second kind of truth involves delivering what was implicitly promised in the story, that it's worthwhile to spend valuable time listening to the tale because its end will reveal the prize. There's nothing more frustrating than listening to some windbag go on and on about some incident or event and then wonder at the end of it, "So, why are you telling us this?" A story represents a contract between the teller/author and the listener/reader whereby we must deliver what we pledged.

Truth in storytelling is also about the veracity of the narrative. Sure, there are always embellishments and exaggerations, just as certain features are left out, but the essence of the story must be truthful in the sense that it reveals the most cherished values of the organization's purpose and mission.

Guber believes that the authenticity—and ultimate effectiveness—of a story are directly related to our ability to elicit a strong emotional reaction in the audience, but to do so in a way that calls them to take constructive action. It isn't enough to be merely entertained or informed unless listeners feel increased motivation to tackle a challenge that has proven difficult.

Include a Surprise

The nervous system kicks most strongly in gear when encountering some novel stimulus. We have evolved in such a way as to mistrust strangers who might do us harm, or to feel apprehension in unfamiliar terrain. Whenever we encounter something we have never experienced before, there is a rush of adrenaline to prepare for the possible "fight or flight reflex" to ensure survival. The startle reflex and endocrine system are all part of both the fear and fascination we feel toward something that shocks us. Peekaboo is one of the first games that infants learn to play, to their endless delight, because in their undeveloped brains when you cover your face, you actually seem to disappear.

Hormonal releases that accompany surprises are associated with enhanced memory of those experiences. You may not remember, for instance, what you had for lunch last Wednesday, or what songs you listened to on the way to work, or the name of that guy in the mail room, or even where you put the file you are looking for, but you sure as heck can recall those times when you were shocked out of your mind or caught by surprise.

Consider some of the most memorable films that still haunt you. All led you in one direction, then wham, hit you with an unexpected plot twist that left you reeling and challenged your perceptions and assumptions. It isn't necessary to include a shocking ending to your story, but it is useful to play a little with audience expectations. For instance, in the earlier example of sitting at the conference table, you may have formed a number of hypotheses with regard to what is going to happen next—that the participants are about to fire the protagonist, or perhaps they are negotiating a business merger, but what if instead they were there for an entirely unrelated reason that you never considered? What if your initial assumption was wrong and the lone man at the end of the table feeling apprehensive is actually there to consider hiring one of the three perfectly coifed jobseekers at the other end? This turns around the scenario and now makes the listener readjust his or her thinking as the rest of the story plays out.

Engage Curiosity

All learning is an active process. Stories should have an element of mystery and uncertainty about them. Rather than filling in all the gaps, you want listeners to do half the work since they are your "collaborators" in the process. When you read a book, you use your imagination to picture the ways that characters might look. You make up backstories for them. This is an interactive process so, as much as possible, you want others to become active participants in the storytelling experience.

In many cultures in Africa, storytelling is a performance art and the audience is expected to participate in the event through their responses, questions, laughter, and verbal encouragement. Members of the audience have roles to play as the story unfolds, expected to help guide the process as collaborators.

Invite Wonder and Meaning-Making

Most of all when presenting to an audience, or talking to a group, you want people asking themselves, "What does this have to do with *me*?" You are partners in the process, since people come up with all kinds of personal interpretations and derived meanings. Great stories are never told the same way, but rather are constantly adjusted and adapted according to audience responses. If you see a look of puzzlement, you provide more clarity in the details. If you observe people becoming restless and disengaged, you speed things up and insert more flamboyant drama. If you notice the audience is not laughing when you hoped they would, you change the tone to reflect their mood. Such corrective actions sound rather obvious, but so often speakers and presenters fail to make these sorts of adjustments, sticking with their rehearsed script, programmed slides, and canned story.

Great storytellers often pause for dramatic effect, but also to allow listeners to respond out loud or in the private dialogue of their own minds. They stop at points and ask for a response, "So, can you guess what happened next?" You want listeners not just to know, but to *feel* what the characters in the story are going through—their confusion or uncertainty or fear.

If you are sufficiently persuaded to develop your own storytelling abilities in order to empower your own influence as a leader, as well as to control the central narrative of your accomplishments and reputation, I've included a fairly comprehensive list of additional resources you might consult.[9] The idea is that we are all born with the capacity to tell a story: Even a 2-year-old can already experiment with the basics of sequencing events, setting the action in time and place, and providing a somewhat intelligible narrative. However, one of the most consistently compelling ways to move an audience and provide a blueprint for leadership priorities is through the skill of becoming an accomplished storytelling artist, one who employs dramatic enactments to inspire an audience.

12
———————

It's Not Just About What You Do, *but Who You* Are

SO OFTEN, the impressions of leaders are based on the illusion of self-promotion and image management, rather than actual assessment of measurable outcomes. Some people talk a good game but don't actually deliver much in the way of improving things, either in terms of results, or even enjoyable engagement in the process. There are certain public figures who seem to be admired more for their self-marketing than for anything significant they've ever accomplished.

Being productive can be defined in so many different ways other than just getting tasks done. Are they done well? How were personnel maximized? What did it cost in terms of resources? And what about the process for everyone involved: Was it satisfying and enjoyable? Are we all better off as a result of whatever was accomplished?

Truly exceptional leaders may work harder, or longer hours, than anyone else, but such efforts tend to be carefully targeted. They know how to make certain choices in particular ways that lead to collaboration among followers and create a sense of community that promotes support. They have figured out ways to help others feel in control and motivate themselves, which leads to greater output, as well as greater satisfaction, not only with their work but also in everyday life.[1] This is more important than ever considering that just a few decades ago, 90 percent of American workers reported directly to a supervisor and now half of the workforce will soon be independent contractors, freelancers, or contractual employees who make their own decisions related to how they operate.

Leaders have been required to adapt to this changing context, functioning less often as absolute authority figures and more frequently in a collaborative, supportive role. While such a leadership position is certainly a privilege, it is also a tremendous burden. As we have examined throughout this journey together, leadership in everyday life is not just about *doing* (skills) or *having* (abilities) but about *being*—the ways we live our most cherished values and rely on a more ethical center that emphasizes to a greater extent a sense of trust, integrity, honesty, humility, compassion, and essential kindness.[2]

The Price Paid for Leadership

Leaders are usually well compensated for their effort, and the reasons for this have as much to do with the additional expenditure of time and energy as they do with their expertise. They tend to experience more stress and shoulder tremendous responsibility for the welfare of others; the really good ones have figured out ways to metabolize that pressure in constructive ways. I mentioned previously, for instance, that even though presidents of the United States put up with all kinds of crises, sleep deprivation, constant demands for their time, unrelenting concern about the status of the Free World, those who have served the highest office actually live significantly longer than the general population.[3] This corresponds to similar data about those who win Nobel Prizes or Academy Awards,[4] casting doubt on the supposedly corrosive health effects of chronic stress. It would seem, then, that the high status, prestige, and recognition that accompany leadership can have a moderating impact on the frustrations and burdens that come with the job.

Nevertheless, leaders are, in a sense, always on duty, always thinking, processing, planning for the next steps. Their privacy is compromised, yet they hold the secrets of everyone else. They are constantly on guard, circumspect about what they say, careful what they do, because people read all kinds of things into the most insignificant behavior. Everyone wants something from a leader—validation, approval, mentoring, guidance, a promotion or raise—resulting in constant questioning about others' intentions and motives. At times, leaders see people at their worst and then are required to do something about these breaches of conduct. And then there are the temptations to become corrupted by power and take themselves so seriously that they imagine they really are more important than everyone else.

Taking One for the Team

Leaders are respected and found most inspiring and influential when they are perceived to make personal sacrifices for the common good. Ideally, such devotion and commitment are strategically measured, rather than simply correlated with the number of hours they've clocked. The former CEO of Yahoo, Marissa Mayer, believed that working 130 hours a week was the clearest sign of ultimate success in that it demonstrated commitment to the cause. She believed this was only possible when a leader was absolutely strategic: functioning on a few hours' sleep each night and only slipping off to the bathroom when it was really necessary. Although Yahoo ultimately failed to remain viable as an independent company in spite of all her hard work, Mayer still insisted that the best way to predict success was to make one's job all-consuming. "Perhaps too much hard work got in the way of enlightened strategic thinking," observed one critic who questioned the wisdom of leading such a one-dimensional life.[5]

What appears to matter most isn't how many hours leaders actually work, but rather whether there seems to be congruence between what they say versus what they are prepared to do themselves. When Staff Sergeant Clinton Romesha found himself and his platoon trapped at a firebase in Afghanistan, surrounded and outnumbered by the Taliban, who had a number of strategic advantages (like the high ground), it looked as if they would all perish. Romesha, who would later be awarded the Congressional Medal of Honor for his courage leading a counterattack in such a hopeless situation, believed that although his assigned job was to remain in the headquarters directing actions, he needed to rally his troops through action, rather than verbal orders. He remarked that the best leaders in such critical situations at the level of an infantry unit understand action carries a lot more weight than words. "In that moment, I could not have asked these men to participate in a counterattack unless I demonstrated that I was willing to take part in it myself and run the show." Against the orders of his superior officer, he grabbed a rifle and equipment and prepared to launch his own reckless mission to try and defend the base against such hopeless odds, knowing that nobody would follow him unless he was the first one out the door. "We're taking this bitch back," he announced to the soldiers who were listlessly hunkered down to avoid incoming fire. "I need a group of volunteers. Who's with me?"[6]

This is not just an example of bravery, but rather of understanding adaptation and flexibility during the ever-changing nature of battle, whether in combat, commerce, or interpersonal struggles. After all, Nike founder Phil Knight once commented on the competitive nature of business as "just war without the bullets."[7]

Circumstances change rather quickly during crises and lousy leaders fail to adjust effectively, persisting in what has worked for them in the past. Yet environmental, cultural, economic, and marketing forces are constantly evolving, requiring immediate and dramatic shifts in the ways we go about our business most effectively.

Most leaders fail to realize that people work not just for money, status, and resources, not only to feel productive and achievement-driven, but also for their own well-being that is often fed by close caring relationships.

Certainly, exceptional leaders take one for their team by conveying to others that they work hard, putting in the required hours to get the job done, but also by modeling balance and self-care in their lifestyle. It isn't just a matter of becoming the kind of leader who rallies his or her troops by being the first one out the door, but also showing others who you really are by what you do every day.

Self-Interest Versus Serving Others

As has been mentioned earlier, military leaders, business executives, and more recently, sports figures, coaches, and certain elected politicians are portrayed as heroic figures who single-handedly deliver results through the sheer force of their personalities. Imagine Teddy Roosevelt leading a charge, George Patton chomping on a cigar as he orders soldiers into battle, or Tom Brady throwing the winning touchdown and then being carried off the field in glory. Likewise, business leaders have become celebrities in their own right, becoming household names as a result of their success accumulating (or holding on to) family wealth. Without a doubt, success making money, building a business, negotiating deals, winning battles, or earning tangible rewards contributes to a big ego and feelings of self-satisfaction. As we've observed, they are also associated with bold actions, notoriety, driving ambition, and rampant narcissism. Earlier I discussed how this is, in fact, a mixed blessing since those who are overly concerned about their own self-interests can be quite effective in attaining and maintaining power, counteracting perceived threats, intimidating rivals, and gaining attention for preferred outcomes even if there are some notable side effects alienating others and isolating themselves from meaningful relationships.[8]

As we've also discussed, the dark side of such narcissistic leaders is that they tend to be bullies and more than a little crazy. We certainly witness this with some individuals in public office who are spectacularly unqualified except for a huge dose of hubris. They thrive on attention, no matter what the cost, and leave a wake of abuse in their path. The good news is that, eventually, most of them end up self-destructing precisely because they are immune to self-reflection and feedback.

Narcissism may be useful in the self-promotion of leaders and their agendas, but it is also accompanied by a certain level of immorality—skirting rules, unethical behavior, exploitation of others, and abuse of power. I've mentioned how such leaders tend toward overconfidence, overestimate their abilities, steal others' ideas and make them their own, and rarely feel any guilt or remorse over such behavior.[9] They also respond to any provocation or criticism with harsh retribution because any such contrary opinions represent a perceived threat to their authority. Perhaps most disturbing of all, even though they are in a position that is supposed to take care of others' welfare, they almost always consider their own needs first. That is one reason why narcissistic characteristics may help people to achieve positions of prominence but, once installed there, they don't necessarily perform very well because of their obsessive self-involvement and constant need for approval.[10]

Of course, some people, maybe even most people in leadership positions, really *are* extraordinary in some ways. They have talents and skills that make them ideally suited for doing wonderful things. But when such individuals believe that their specialness elevates them above others, as well as entitles them to do whatever they want, whenever they want, many others suffer in their wake. Well-regarded leaders earn their sterling reputations not from self-promotion, but rather from the appreciation of followers who see the clear benefits of operating within their orbit. In addition, the best examples are among those who actually put themselves last instead of first.

We may sometimes forget that people work not just for money, status, and resources, not only to feel productive and achievement-driven, but also for their own well-being that is often fed by close caring relationships. This may sometimes become a difficult challenge for leaders, given the perceived (or actual) worlds within which they live and flourish. Since leaders tend to be wealthier and enjoy more resources than others within their realm, they frequently occupy a privileged space that is quite a distance from their followers'. As we've seen, this can lead to a sense of entitlement that is, at the very least, off-putting.

It is ironic that often those who have the least are inclined to be among those who are most big-hearted. In studies of so-called prosocial or generous behavior, researchers found that those on the lower socioeconomic spectrum are actually far more generous, sensitive, and caring toward others. In addition, privileged, wealthy leaders are far more inclined to be selfish and unethical in their behavior, to cheat and take advantage of others who don't enjoy the same opportunities.[11]

Mirroring the world of commerce, the game of Monopoly is usually based on some degree of skill, but also a lot of luck depending on the roll of the dice. But when players are randomly assigned the role of "disadvantaged" versus "wealthy" in terms of the amount of money they are given to start the game, and the one or two die they are allowed to use during their respective turns, the privileged player was more inclined to gloat and engage in selfish actions, also feeling that it was superior skill and judgment that led to his or her success, rather than "inheriting" wealth and privileges.[12] This is a cautionary tale for anyone in a position of power who would succumb to the temptations of corruption and a sense of entitlement.

Hypocrisy

We no longer even question the disconnect between what many leaders advocate as core values versus what they actually do in their own lives. Homophobic politicians are caught having gay sex in men's bathrooms. Anti-immigration foes hire undocumented workers. Religious figures preach moral responsibility and are literally caught with their pants down. Politicians running for office spout personal accountability all the while acting irresponsibly and deceptively in their own lives. CEOs order belt-tightening policies while giving themselves a bonus. In one especially devastating case, the CEO of British Petroleum heralded the company's commitment to social responsibility and environmental protection. Yet at the same time he was announcing its "Beyond Petroleum" campaign, he simultaneously launched major cost-cutting measures throughout the company that resulted in safety shortcuts eventually leading to two different catastrophic oil spills. Even that wasn't enough for his dismissal until attention was also drawn to scandals in his personal life. Because of the spectacular level of deceit and hypocrisy (also referred to as "word–deed misalignment"), he was given a special award by Greenpeace for "imitating an environmentalist."

People expect a level of competence in their leaders, but also a degree of congruence. There is nothing that dooms a leader more quickly than the perception of living by a double standard.[13] There have been quite a number of prominent preachers who have been defrocked in recent years because of their indiscretions that went against their moral preaching. At one time, Jim Bakker was head of a church that boasted over 2,000 employees and reached 10 million homes around the world. Most of the money he collected somehow disappeared and he ended up in prison for fraud. Jimmy Swaggart was a competitor of Bakker and appeared on CNN to announce that his wayward colleague was a "cancer in the body of Christ." Alas, Swaggart himself was later cast aside when it was found that he liked to frequent the company of prostitutes.

I don't mean to pick only on religious leaders, but because their talk is so passionately critical and judgmental toward others who don't follow their path, it is especially disconcerting when they are discovered to be as human and flawed as everyone else. It also seems ludicrous that leaders in the public eye act so surprised when they are caught reaching into the cookie jar or someone else's pants.

Being More Authentic and Congruent

The major theme of this book is that we have not only an opportunity to practice in our everyday lives what we preach to others but also a mandate to do so. This means that our training and experience particularly prepare us to make a difference in others' lives in whatever setting we find ourselves, whether at work, home, social engagements, or community events. We live our most cherished values of integrity and compassion. We become models for others to emulate, not just because of our lofty positions but because of our daily actions. In addition, leaders have a responsibility, perhaps above all else, to mentor their apprentices in the tradition that has existed for thousands of years.

Whether as a blacksmith, artist, hunter, tradesman, or village elder, the principal job of a master was to pass on the traditions and collective knowledge to the next generation. This process occurred as much through observational learning as any formal apprenticeship, in much the same manner that often takes place in professional coaching today. Bill Walsh, the legendary coach of Stanford University and the San Francisco 49ers, mentored so many other successful coaches in his "family tree," including some of the most effective leaders in the sport. When Walsh's disciples talk about his leadership, it isn't just about his creative mind and encyclopedic knowledge of the game, but also the personal manner in which he taught and mentored others.

There are certainly critics of the so-called authentic leadership movement, as exemplified by the likes of Bill Walsh and others. This alternative viewpoint represents a fairly strong indictment of the idea that we should all be true to ourselves, claiming that "being authentic is pretty much the opposite of what leaders do." The argument goes: Rather than being true to oneself, leaders must be true to what others need and want from them most.[14]

After all, leaders sometimes lie. They regularly engage in subterfuge, manipulation, duplicity, and misdirection. They tell people what they want to hear. They are ultimately performers, if not actors, who play a role that is staged for a critical audience. In any field, the best performers are those who have learned to disguise their intentions and hide their genuine feelings. Just as athletes teach themselves to "play through pain" and hide their injuries from competitors, so, too, must leaders learn to control their impulses, moderate their emotions, stifle their authentic selves, and appear impervious to any crisis or conflict that comes their way.

So, What Is Exemplary Leadership?

Nancy has worked for one of the largest tech companies in the world. Twice actually, because she left in frustration a few years ago when the culture of the company created and maintained by the CEO was hardly conducive to a healthy lifestyle. She was enticed back to her job a short time later when the firm made an offer she couldn't refuse, but abandoned ship once again when the stress became untenable.

Nancy took a cut in pay, gave up a number of perks and a lot of status, all to go to work for a much smaller entity run by a man she greatly admires. "He's such a good person," she says, shaking her head in wonderment, as if it seems impossible that someone could be both brilliant and nice. "He's smart and analytical, which I like, but he also cares deeply about people. He trusts me and defers to me, doesn't try to control or micromanage what I do." Yet she also mentioned that he will step in when needed, but without being intrusive or overcontrolling. "Here I'd been thinking I was going to retire from the industry and now I've never enjoyed my work more than I do now, mostly because he is such an inspiring and supportive leader."

It's really quite simple: Extraordinary leaders exemplify the qualities they wish to instill in others. They are the walking embodiment of their core values, not just when at the office, but in the other dimensions of their lives. They are not only interested in achievement, productivity, and profit margins, but also display genuine caring for others. They are able to create and enforce a culture of psychological safety within their domain, a place where it is possible to not only speak one's mind and heart freely, but to do so without fear of ridicule or personal criticism. Leaders are able to do this not by fiat or directive but through all the ways they model such behavior. In their interactions with others, they demonstrate deep listening and exquisite interpersonal sensitivity. When there is tension or disagreement in the room, these feelings are readily acknowledged and worked through, rather than simply ignored and swept under the table. Consistently, these are the teams that operate most effectively, produce the best-quality work, and do so with shared passion and excitement.[15]

Based on a study of extraordinary leaders in a variety of fields, such as Mahatma Gandhi, General George Marshall, Martin Luther King, and other transformational figures, psychologist Howard Gardner concluded that the following themes appeared most evident in their lives.[16] I have integrated those findings with what I discovered during my own research over the past few years, talking to exemplary leaders in education, business, sports, advocacy, and community engagement.

1. There was a willingness during leaders' early life to confront perceived injustices, even a rebelliousness toward other authority figures who were not regarded as fair. In other words, a moral compass was calibrated during leaders' formative years that served as a guide for what were perceived as righteous actions.

2. Great leaders often experienced parental loss during their childhood, such as the death or absence of a father or mother figure. This seemed to promote greater independence and self-sufficiency, as well as high levels of resilience and resourcefulness that allowed these individuals to recover quickly from disappointment or rejection and continue to move forward.

3. There was definitely a feeling of entitlement and specialness among this group, that they were destined to achieve something significant, fueling their ambition and drive and further immunizing them against discouragement in the face of initial failures.

4. Even though these leaders had no problem speaking their mind in forceful and persuasive ways, they also learned patience with respect to the optimal timing for such revelations. They were clearly fearless risk-takers, but they were also able to balance their initiative and aggression with the need for calculated timing.

5. Obviously, these leaders were competitive to a certain point, driven to attain positions of power and control, but what distinguishes the truly great ones is that this motive was primarily driven to pursue some greater good, rather than a self-serving objective.

6. Great leaders work incredibly hard to become accomplished in the skills they believe matter most. They acquire the knowledge and experience

that best equip them to make a difference within their chosen domain. They were proactive in recruiting mentors who were in the best position to teach and guide them. In many cases, it took at least a decade before they felt ready to assume a position of leadership.

7. They are seen as "attractive" by followers. That is perhaps one reason why leaders tend to be taller and more physically imposing than the general population, although attractiveness can be conveyed in a number of different ways other than physical attributes, such as personality traits, behavioral patterns, or even symbols of success. Eleanor Roosevelt, Mahatma Gandhi, Winston Churchill, or Charles de Gaulle were hardly physically attractive figures, so they relied on other attributes to endear themselves to their followers.

8. Flexibility is clearly a key factor, especially considering how likely, if not inevitable, it will be to experience failure at some point. Name a great leader and somewhere in his or her background are catastrophic disappointment and discouragement. Politicians usually run for office several times before they are eventually successful. Those who do attain their goals learn to become adaptable. If it isn't within their power to change certain circumstances, then they make the best of whatever opportunities they already have.

9. Speaking of attitude, exceptional leaders maintain a positive outlook, even in the face of apparent disappointments and failure. They are able to look at the "gifts" offered by almost any situation and find the opportunities they present to take things to another level. They are seen as optimistic and hopeful, within realistic parameters.

10. Exemplary leaders view their primary role as a "servant" of their followers, rather than the other way around. They are exquisitely attuned to the moods, interests, and needs of those within their care, and responsive to those preferences and desires. They are often reflective and analytic about their own behavior, as well as that of others, constantly discovering new ways to be more responsive and effective in their actions. They were also more inclined to see the "big picture," rather than getting caught up in all the distracting and nonessential details.

11. Great leaders are able to present an inspiring story to followers and constituents that is reassuring, inspiring, and emphasizes decisive action. Especially during times of crisis or fear, the public doesn't care much about the details; they just want reassurance. That is one reason why political candidates can enjoy so much popularity in the polls by offering absolutely nothing in the way of a plan except a catchy slogan like "Make America

great again!" Followers love a good "identity story," one that reveals some heroic actions on the part of their leaders, such as overcoming adversity or achieving distinction in athletics or the battlefield. Ideally, this is a story that allows others to identify with the struggles and provides hope for the future: "If she can do this, maybe I can too."

Most relevant to one of the themes of this book is that these exceptional leaders are committed to applying their relational skills to those within their own personal orbit, especially with family, neighbors, and members of the community.[17]

Live Your Story

It isn't enough to have an inclusive, persuasive leader and organizational identity unless it is wide-ranging enough that *everyone* can feel a part of the narrative. Second, it is crucial that the leader *embodies* the dominant story, appearing in daily interactions as trustworthy, caring, and accessible to followers.

In a survey of healthy, sustainable work practices that include physical, emotional, mental, and spiritual daily habits, only 25 percent of those surveyed reported that their leaders lived their story and practiced what they preached to others.[18] Given that among primates, an alpha male or female is observed by followers constantly during the day, averaging two or three times *each minute*, modeling desirable behavior would appear to be crucial. Indeed, among those workers whose leaders did walk their talk, they were twice as likely to be fully engaged in their efforts, and significantly more likely to enjoy their jobs and remain with the organization. In addition, they were 72 percent more likely to practice good health habits to take care of themselves, resulting in fewer addictions, bad tendencies, and missed days at work.

Tom Kolditz, former head of leadership at West Point and an expert on "extremis" leadership (when your life literally depends on it), related a story he had heard when conducting research for his book on the subject that exemplifies this commitment.[19] When I asked him about the ways in which extraordinary leaders in the military walk their talk to inspire loyalty, he dismissed the myth that soldiers just follow orders. He cited statistics recorded during the Vietnam War in which there had been 788 "assaults with explosive devices" against U.S. officers *by their own men* as a way to demonstrate their unwillingness to follow them into battle because of perceived incompetence. These "fraggings" don't even include the number of lieutenants who were shot in the back as "friendly fire."

Kolditz makes the point that personal credibility, integrity, and competence are absolutely essential for enlisted personnel to follow their officers into life-threatening situations. They will risk a court martial and be sent back to headquarters (warm meals and hot showers!), rather than follow an untrustworthy leader into battle—or worse yet, venture into a dangerous predicament while the leader remains safely behind. "So," I asked him, "what then determines whether soldiers *will* follow orders that they don't understand or agree with?"

Kolditz smiled. "I'm glad you asked!" He then related a story he'd heard during his research; it was about a classic leader completely in touch with his rifle squad. The Marine unit had been deployed to Iraq during the Gulf War and had advanced so far behind enemy lines that they were completely cut off from all resupply. Their ammunition and food were almost running out, limiting the nine marines to the same number of meal packages (MREs) that had to last four more days. Each "meal ready to eat" included some crackers, cheese, bread, and a few other snacks designed to feed one person with one meal. Yet they had to share this food among *all* of them to last 20 times longer. Ordinarily, a leader might select the most desirable item for himself (cake or peanut butter) since, after all, he has to be able to operate at peak functioning to save his men. But in this case, the corporal in charge earned the respect and loyalty of his men by dividing the food items equally among his squad, saving only the nondairy creamer for himself each day.

After Kolditz interviewed the corporal, he was so moved by the story that he asked what he could do for him. Perhaps put in a recommendation for a citation to the Pentagon? The corporal emphatically shook his head back and forth. No, all he wanted was clean socks for his men. Forever after, Kolditz's own vision of leadership, now as director of a leadership institute that prepares students for positions of responsibility, was informed by what he refers to as one of his own heroes, "Corporal Creamer."

What Kolditz discovered in his research has been confirmed by others within the military context, especially with regard to challenging some of the fundamental assumptions of leadership as presented in the *Army Field Manual.* The emphasis throughout the regulations is on a dozen personality characteristics that may, or may not, have empirical support beyond common sense and personal experiences. Yet there are a few of these qualities that do indeed have a huge impact, most notably a leader's levels of ethical reasoning, resilience and hardiness in the face of stressful situations, emotional intelligence, and relationship skills. What has often been ignored, though, is the social context of an officer or leader's decisions and actions.[20]

The *Army Field Manual* is quite clear, emphasizing that "what leaders do emerges from who they are," supporting the argument that our way of being is just as important as anything else we say and do. Yet exceptional leaders, in the military or elsewhere, also have a command of the "social context" of their unit and organization, especially with regard to group identity. It is this ability to recognize and understand the ways in which followers view themselves, individually (via empathy) and collectively (via social awareness), that permits the leader to be seen as "one of us," rather than a privileged outsider. It is quite clear that when soldiers view their officers as a champion of common values, they are more likely to approve of the policies and decisions made.

Lessons from the Masters

A colleague and I investigated what distinguishes average practitioners of psychotherapy from those who have achieved eminence in their field.[21] Whereas this is a highly specialized form of leadership since it ordinarily takes place in one-to-one settings, or sometimes with whole families present, it nevertheless highlights some key principles that are just as applicable to organizational or social settings.

We couldn't rely on self-identified experts in the field, or even necessarily trust such individuals' reputation in the community, since these pathways might not necessarily reflect true exceptionalism in action as much as the myths and stories circulated that may not be accurate. The "illusory superiority" effect, mentioned in Chapter 4, describes the phenomenon of tending to overestimate our own abilities when compared to others. Almost everyone thinks they are "above average" in basic life skills, whether it involves leadership potential or anything else. We also learned in our study that therapists and other leaders are frequently clueless about what they do that has the most impact. You will recall that they repeatedly talk about their diagnostic skills and brilliant interventions when, in fact, their clients mention feeling heard and understood as the leaders' most valuable accomplishment.

We found patterns that define mastery in therapeutic practice that parallel those identified in exemplary leadership. Adding to the dozen or so factors described earlier, great practitioners know things that others do not. They have specialized expertise that allows them to see patterns and "deep structures" that may escape the uninitiated. They demonstrate a high degree of flexibility and adaptability, which has already been mentioned. This allows them to recover quickly from miscalculations, especially if sufficient trust has been created in relationships with followers or clients.

There are also some interesting features that really don't mean very much in predicting excellence. With respect to therapeutic practice, as an example, it doesn't seem to matter what degrees clinicians have, their particular theoretical orientation, their licensure, or even their preferred strategies. This finding is consistent with much of the literature on leadership as well: In spite of the fascination and interest in the latest miraculous, foolproof techniques, they appear to matter much less than the leader's perceived strength of character and expertise.

Master leaders and therapists flat out work harder than their more average brethren. Malcolm Gladwell popularized the so-called 10,000-hour rule, the concept that exceptional athletes, musicians, and professionals in any field practice their skills over and over again until they master them at the highest possible level.[22] But what is interesting is that they tend to practice the things they do not do well, rather than those that already feel comfortable. Thus every off-season, an exceptional athlete will identify weaknesses in reading zone defenses (football), or hitting 3-point shots from the weak side corner (basketball), or hitting to the opposite field (baseball) in order to improve significantly. Gladwell was particularly struck by the example of the Beatles, explaining how it was no coincidence that they managed to take the musical world by storm. During their early formative days, they spent up to 12 hours on stage, seven days per week, performing all kinds of genres in their repertoire. Few musicians before them, or since then, have worked so hard, for so long, to achieve such greatness. They just flat out wanted excellence in their work so badly that they were willing to make the necessary commitment and personal sacrifices to see that happen. The same could be said for the likes of Tom Brady (football) or LeBron James (basketball), whose work ethics led their teams to championships.

Exceptional leaders and therapists don't rely on "standard" strategies just because they are familiar and comfortable, but rather contextualize their behavior to fit the situation, problem, environment, and audience. Followers need different things at different times and nobody wants to feel as if they are just a cog in a wheel. In order to become optimally responsive, they are able and willing to collect accurate assessments of how their actions have been interpreted and received, rather than relying solely on their own biased self-perceptions. It often seems incredible how blind various celebrities, athletes, and leaders are to the impact of their behavior. They may find the dominant story circulating about them is not reflective of the way they'd like to be viewed, but they are powerless to alter that narrative until such time that they are willing to craft a different set of responses.

I have a few more things to mention again that can be extrapolated to leadership contexts. It has been estimated that the majority of positive outcomes in therapy may be attributed to the quality of the relationship that develops in the encounter. When followers feel there is a solid alliance, they are more likely to feel satisfied with the experience, even during those times when they were unable to meet identified goals. Leaders (and therapists) are given much more latitude when trust is featured in the relationship.

One of the favorite things that excellent therapists do is offer alternative interpretations of the problem presented. I described this in Chapter 5 as "reframing," and it involves looking at an issue from a perspective that makes it more easily resolved. People feel discouragement and frustration when they see their problems as intractable.

"I wish I could take on this responsibility," a staff member responds to an offer, "but I've just never been good at that sort of thing." Of course, that may very well have been true in the past, but that doesn't necessarily mean it always has to remain that way.

"You mean to say," the leader responds, "that in order to do this job, you'd need some additional training and support in order to improve the skills you consider so important to accomplish the tasks. That's why I picked you in the first place—because of your honest assessments of situations and your willingness to do what must be done." Now, of course, that is not at all what the person meant to say, but his or her reluctance was reframed as a learning and growth opportunity. Therapists engage in this practice all the time when clients feel hopeless and stymied about some life situation.

Most of all, what we learned from our study of master therapists is that it wasn't their techniques, skills, methods, approaches, even their vast knowledge, that truly distinguished them as exceptional practitioners of their profession. Rather, it was a "way of being" when they were present with those they were helping, as well as in the larger world. Their sense of passion and curiosity, their love of adventure, created a parallel process in the relationships with those they were helping, a phenomenon that led to their own continued growth and learning. They felt it was not only an opportunity, but absolutely a requirement, to be the kind of person that they wished others to be.

Leadership Modeling

Mahatma Gandhi was certainly one of the more influential and persuasive leaders of the 20th century, wrestling his country away from the control of Great Britain through the sheer power of his determination and persuasive abilities. Yet one of the qualities most admirable about Gandhi's leadership style was the way he tried so hard to follow his own principles in his daily life.

I interviewed his grandson Arun Gandhi, who shared a story about his own early life growing up during the Apartheid in South Africa. Arun had been a rather angry and belligerent adolescent, his rage stoked further by his father's imprisonment for opposing the racist government policies. His mother could do nothing to control his behavior and so shipped him off to his grandfather in India.

This occurred during a critical period, when Gandhi was in the final stages of negotiating with Britain's home secretary for his nation's independence, yet his first and most important priority was to help his grandson give up his anger. Their time together thus became a war of wills, in which Arun continuously tested his grandfather's patience, being obstructive, annoying, at times even disrupting his high-level meetings. During one such summit, Arun rushed into the room to interrupt the proceedings and Mahatma only smiled indulgently and held his grandson's head to his chest to calm him down.

Unfortunately, Gandhi was murdered before he could complete his work teaching compassion and forgiveness to his grandson, but the lessons still stuck, so much so that Arun eventually devoted his life and career to promoting peace and nonviolence. This, of course, is only one of the many stories about the ways that the great leader tried to practice what he preached. When a man grabbed onto him as he was once boarding a train, Gandhi turned to hear him beg for a message to guide his life. Gandhi nodded, jotted a few words on a piece of paper, folded it and handed it to him. Once the train departed, the man found inscribed on the piece of paper, "My life is my message."

This theme has been repeated so often in Gandhi stories (or legends). Perhaps my all-time favorite, most clearly related to leadership in everyday life, involved a mother who made the long, difficult pilgrimage to consult with Gandhi during the height of his fame—perhaps even when Arun was living with him.

"My son," she explained, "he is not healthy. He eats too much sugar in his food. I keep telling him that this is not a good thing, that it is bad for his health, but he never listens. You must tell him to stop eating so many sweets."

Gandhi smiled at the woman, but shook his head. "I'm sorry," he said in a quiet voice, "but I cannot tell him that. But if you bring him back to me in a few weeks I will have a talk with him."

"But we have traveled so far to see you. Can you not speak to him now?"

Gandhi once again shook his head. "Perhaps I will see you both in a few weeks."

The mother and boy returned later and Gandhi agreed to meet with them as he had promised. He knelt down to look directly in the boy's eyes. "Listen to me carefully. You should not eat so much sugar. It is not good for you."

The boy was, of course, mesmerized by this famous man who spoke to him with such intensity and caring. All the boy could think to do was nod his head and promise he would follow this directive.

The mother, however, was quite confused. "Why did you make us travel so far again? Why couldn't you just tell him this the last time I brought him to see you?"

Gandhi nodded his head and smiled at her apologetically. "Well, Mother, two weeks ago I was still eating a lot of sugar myself."

Behavioral scientists have long recognized what Gandhi understood intuitively, that one of the most powerful ways to influence and inspire others isn't through our proclamations, directives, and advice, but through the ways we live our own lives. Human beings develop and grow primarily through observational learning: We watch others carefully and internalize those behaviors that appear to be most effective. Children, from their earliest years, imitate the actions of adults in all kinds of ways, including language acquisition, social behavior, and beliefs about the world. Young children can be observed literally trying on the shoes of their parents, or engaging in other fantasy play that imitates everything they have observed throughout the day.

Likewise, a case can be made that the most inspirational leadership derives not just from decisions that are made behind closed doors, from specialized expertise that permits deep understanding of complex patterns, but also from carefully observing our choices and actions in daily life. "What you *are*," offered poet Ralph Waldo Emerson, "speaks so loudly I cannot hear what you say."

Extraordinary leaders, whether involved in corporate, religious, educational, athletic, charitable, military, community, or social contexts, model for their followers precisely those behaviors that they consider most important. Whether a point guard, quarterback, CEO, commander, supervisor, minister, or host, our lifestyle choices related to health considerations (diet, exercise, stress management, leisure pursuits, scheduling, family, friendships) impact and influence the behavior of others. When followers see their leaders making certain choices related to their quality of life, there are contagious effects that can also lead to unintended consequences, for better or worse. A leader who works insane hours and puts everything else in his or her life on hold in pursuit of the collective goals may be admired and respected for this level of dedication, but such actions also convey a message to followers about what is expected from them. This may lead to increased productivity in the short run but at a cost of literally running everyone ragged.

That is one reason why it is considered so important for military leaders (at least those in the battlefield) to achieve their own high level of physical fitness as a message to their troops. In his research on leadership in high-risk, dangerous situations, Tom Kolditz generalizes some of the principles he learned from teaching and talking to elite warriors.[23] Functionality is the key to leadership in any context or situation, which means being able to handle the strains and demands of whatever might be required. Specifically, he believes that leaders must work just as hard on their physical conditioning as they do on their annual reports; to do otherwise could be catastrophic for the organization in a multitude of ways. He cites the example of a former CEO of McDonald's who died suddenly at the age of 64, sending the company's stock plummeting afterward.

This is very good news in terms of the power of mutual influence. If people are watching us with a critical eye, observing carefully what they like and dislike most about our conduct, then leadership is not only a matter of making good and wise decisions, as well as implementing plans of action. It is about creating an organizational culture that empowers people, that supports them in their work, but also in the pursuit of healthy choices.

How This Book Has Changed Me

Every research project I've undertaken has been fueled as much by personal curiosity and confusion as any academic desire. As you will remember from the introduction, this book is no exception given my level of dismay and frustration at how poorly those in leadership positions seem to apply what they are supposed to know and understand to their work and everyday life.

There are few things that seem worse than feeling—or being seen—as a hypocrite. During the time I've been engaged in the investigation of leadership, I couldn't help but begin to notice some ways that I have changed as a result—and I hope the same is true for you as well. This wasn't a deliberate or conscious effort on my part, but rather just a greater awareness that I am responding differently in certain situations. I smile more at strangers—and not just token smiles but genuine expressions of delight. When I encounter someone in the world who is unusually nice or competent, I no longer just acknowledge this to myself. I also now make an effort to share the observation out loud with that person. Even more so, I take the time to write to his or her supervisor to share the story of such an individual's excellence.

Alas, one thing that hasn't yet changed as much as I would like is my patience and tolerance of those whom I believe are shortchanging others and themselves. There is a lot of mediocrity in the world, a lot of folks who merely go through the motions of doing their jobs—and could care less what any of us really think about that. I try to tell myself this is a choice that some people make, one we may not prefer, but others are entitled to live according to their own minimal standards. Of course, if the slacker should happen to report to us, then we have other options regarding what we are willing to tolerate.

As I walk through the world, I am far more conscious and mindful about the role I have chosen to serve. After all, that's what leaders do: We *serve* others. We are indeed servants who have been chosen or delegated to help others.

All of us are certainly held accountable for the results we produce—or fail to—but work and daily life are also about the unfolding process that we experience. This leads to a number of important questions so often ignored if they don't lead directly to increased productivity or a bottom line. These are the questions, however, that best predict work satisfaction and personal well-being.

- Are you having fun?
- Are you learning something new?
- Are you stimulated and excited?
- Are you engaging deeply in intimate connections with others?
- Are you *really* making a difference?

In spite of the choices that many people make, and the priorities they seem to give the most attention, life is not really about our accomplishments or accumulated wealth and recognition; it is about living fully with passion and love for what you do, and with whom you choose to spend the precious moments you have left.

As we bring our journey to an end, I am reminded once again that one reason why there are so many books about leadership is because people are so hungry for templates they can follow in simple steps to become a "superboss," "virtuous leader," "transformative leader," and all the other names for exemplary stewardship. In fact, there is no Holy Grail, no discernible formula, that works for everyone in any context or organization. There are no easy rules and effortless program, in spite of all the book titles proclaiming it so.

We circle back to the main theme of this book—that it isn't only what we tell followers, or what we *do* as leaders, that makes a difference, but also *who we are*. We know clearly from a variety of sources that the best leaders set the highest standards of excellence for followers, but also for themselves. They rule not by threats and intimidation, but rather by the ways they live their lives on a daily basis. They work incredibly hard, even compulsively, but they also seek balance—and encourage others to follow their lead.

Not only is it desirable that leaders take better care of themselves and become more skilled at dealing with their own negative emotions, it is imperative that we do so. Leadership is one of the few professions in which everything you learn to be a leader makes you a better person. And if that isn't attractive enough, everything you learn as a person—every experience, conversation, book you read, film you watch, life crisis, personal triumph or disappointment—helps you to become a better leader. You learn compassion and empathy not from a class, seminar, or a book, but from all your life experiences.

Notes

PREFACE

1. Hogan, J., Hogan, R., & Kaiser, R. B. (2010). Management derailment. *American Psychological Association Handbook of Industrial and Psychology, 3*, 555–575.
2. Torres, R. (2013, October). What it takes to be a great leader. *TED Talks*. Retrieved from https://www.ted.com/talks/roselinde_torres_what_it_takes_to_be_a_great_leader/transcript?language=en
3. Martin, A. (2006). *Everyday leadership*. Greensboro, NC: Center for Creative Leadership.

CHAPTER I

1. Duhigg, C. (2016). *Smarter, faster, better: The secrets of being productive in life and business*. New York: Random House; Gwynne, P. (2012). Group intelligence, team-work, and productivity. *Research Technology Management, 55*(2), 7.
2. Geimer, J. L. (2015). Meetings at work: Perceived effectiveness and recommended improvements. *Journal of Business Research, 68*(9), 2015–2026.
3. Tredgold, G. (2015, July 11). How my wife calling me out taught me about leadership. *The Good Men Project*. Retrieved from http://goodmenproject.com/featured-content/how-my-wife-calling-me-out-taught-me-about-leadership-kcon/
4. Friedman, S. D. (2006). Learning to lead in all domains of life. *American Behavioral Scientist, 49*(9), 1270–1297.
5. Rhode, D. L., & Packel, A. K. (2011). *Leadership: Law, policy, and management*. New York: Wolters Kluwer.
6. Padilla, A. (2013). *Leadership: Leaders, followers, environments*. New York: Wiley. See p. 3.
7. Bennis, W. (1959). Leadership theory and administrative behavior. *Administrative Science Quarterly, 4*, 259–260.

8. Hogan, R., & Kaiser, R. B. (2005). What we know about leadership. *Review of General Psychology, 9*(2), 169–180.

9. Hogan & Kasier (2005), p. 174.

10. Hogan & Kaiser (2005), p. 171.

11. Higgs, M. (2009). The good, the bad, and the ugly: Leadership and narcissism. *Journal of Change Management, 9*(2), 165–178.

12. Hogan, R. (2006). *Personality and the fate of organizations*. Hillsdale, NJ: Lawrence Erlbaum.

13. Solomon, L. (2015, June 24). *Harvard Business Review*. Retrieved from https://hbr.org/2015/06/the-top-complaints-from-employees-about-their-leaders

14. Nyberg, A., et al. (2009). Managerial leadership an ischaemic heart disease among employees: The Swedish WOLF study. *Journal of Occupational and Environmental Medicine, 66*, 640.

15. Sapolsky, R. M. (2017) *Behave: The biology of humans at our best and worst*. New York: Penguin.

16. Kottler, J. A. (2014). *Change: What really leads to personal transformation*. New York: Oxford University Press; Kottler, J. A., & Balkin, R. (2017). *Relationships in counseling and the counselor's life*. Alexandria, VA: American Counseling Association; Norcross, J. C. (Ed.). (2011). *Psychotherapy relationships that work* (2nd ed.). New York: Oxford University Press; Knox, R., & Cooper, M. (2015). *The therapeutic relationship in counseling and psychotherapy*. London: SAGE; Charura, D., & Paul, S. (Eds.). (2014). *The therapeutic relationship handbook: Theory and practice*. Berkshire, UK: Open University Press.

17. Kottler & Balkin (2017).

18. Eguchi, H., Wada, K., & Smith, D. R. (2016). Recognition, compensation, and prevention of Karoshi, or death due to overwork. *Journal of Occupational and Environmental Medicine, 58*(8), 313–314.

19. Maestripieri, D. (2012). *Games primates play*. New York: Basic Books.

20. Conniff, R. (2005). *The ape in the corner office*. New York: Three Rivers Press.

21. Catmull, E. (2014). *Creativity, Inc: Overcoming the unseen forces that stand in the way of true inspiration*. New York: Random House.

22. Stephens-Davidowitz, S. (2015, March 21). Just how nepotistic are we? *The New York Times*. Retrieved from http://www.nytimes.com/2015/03/22/opinion/sunday/seth-stephens-davidowitz-just-how-nepotistic-are-we.html

23. Lipman-Blumen, J. (1996). *Connective leadership*. New York: Oxford University Press.

CHAPTER 2

1. Pfeffer, J. (2015). *Leadership bs*. New York: HarperCollins.

2. Campbell, A., & Park, R. (2004, July–August). Stop kissing frogs. *Harvard Business Review*, 27–28.

3. Grint, K. (2013). *The arts of leadership*. New York: Oxford University Press.
4. Kellerman, B. (2012). *The end of leadership*. New York: HarperCollins. See p. 1.
5. Pfeffer (2015).
6. Rothman, J. (2016, February 29). Shut up and sit down: Why the leadership industry rules. *The New Yorker*, 64–69.
7. Denning, S. (2011). *The leader's guide to storytelling*. New York: Wiley.
8. Nicholson, N. (2012). The evolution of business and management. In S. C. Roberts (Ed.), *Applied Evolutionary Psychology* (pp. 16–35). New York: Oxford University Press.
9. Kets de Vries, M. F., & Miller, D. (2009). Narcissism and leadership: An object relations perspective. *Human Relations, 38*, 583–601.
10. Miller, G. F. (2000). Aesthetic fitness: How sexual selection shaped virtuosity as a fitness indicator and aesthetic preference as mate choice criteria. *Bulletin of Psychology and the Arts, 2*, 20–25.
11. Iredale, W., & van Vugt, M. (2012). Altruism as showing off: A signaling perspective on promoting green behavior and acts of kindness. In S. C. Roberts (Ed.), *Applied Evolutionary Psychology* (pp. 173–185). New York: Oxford University Press.
12. Beersma, B., & Van Kleef, G. A. (2011). How the grapevine keeps you in line: Gossip increases contributions to the group. *Social Psychological and Personality Science, 2*(6), 642–649; Beersma, B., & Van Kleef, G. A. (2012). Why people gossip: An empirical analysis of social motives, antecedents, and consequences. *Journal of Applied Social Psychology, 42*(11), 2640–2670.
13. Woods, S. (2016, April). Bill Walton. *Men's Journal*, p. 90.
14. Padilla, A. (2013). *Leadership: Leaders, followers, environments*. New York: Wiley.
15. van Vugt, M., & Ronay, R. (2014). The evolutionary psychology of leadership: Theory, review, and roadmap. *Organizational Psychology Review, 4*(1), 74–95.
16. Courtiol, A., and colleagues. (2012). Natural and sexual selection in a monogamous historical human population. *Proceedings of the National Academy of Sciences, 109*(21), 8044–8049.
17. Junger, S. (2016). *Tribe: On homecoming and belonging*. New York: Twelve; Hidika, B. H. (2012). Depression as a disease of modernity: Explanations for increasing prevalence. *Journal of Affective Disorders, 140*(3), 205–214.
18. Arvey, R. D., Wang, N., Song, Z., & Li, W. (2014). The biology of leadership. In D. V. Day (Ed.), *The Oxford Handbook of Leadership and Organizations* (pp. 73–90). New York: Oxford University Press.
19. Blaker, N. M., Rompa, I., Dessing, I. H., Vriend, A. F., Herschberg, C., & van Vugt, M. (2013). The height leadership advantage in men and women: Testing some evolutionary psychology predictions. *Group Processes and Intergroup Relations, 16*, 17–27.
20. Buunk, A. P., & Dijkstra, P. (2012). The evolution of business and management. In S. C. Roberts (Ed.), *Applied Evolutionary Psychology* (pp. 36–51). New York: Oxford University Press.

21. Prime, J. L., Carter, N. M., & Welbourne, T. M. (2009). Women "take care," men "take charge": Managers' stereotypic perceptions of women and men leaders. *Psychologist-Manager Journal, 12*, 25–49.

22. Siegel, B. (1996). Crying in the stairwells: How should we grieve for our dying patients? *Journal of the American Medical Association, 272*, 659.

23. Nicholson (2012), p. 30.

24. Von Hippel, W., & Trivers, R. (2011). The evolution and psychology of self-deception. *Behavioral and Brain Sciences, 34*, 1–16.

25. McGregor, J. (2016, April 10). Amazon CEO Jeff Bezos shares thoughts on corporate culture, decision-making and failure. *Los Angeles Times*. Retrieved from http://www.latimes.com/business/la-fi-0410-on-leadership-bezos-20160410-story.html

26. Guiso, L., Sapienza, P., & Zingales, L. (2015). The value of corporate culture. *Journal of Financial Economics, 117*, 60–76.

27. Quoted in Guiso, Sapienza, & Singales (2015), p. 60.

28. Logan, D., & King, J. (2011). *Tribal leadership*. New York: Harper Business.

29. Barrett, E., & Martin, P. (2014). *Extreme: Why some people thrive at the limits*. New York: Oxford University Press.

30. Palinkas, L. A., et al. (2004). Cross-cultural differences in psychological adaptation to isolated and confined environments. *Aviation, Space, and Environmental Medicine, 75*, 973–980.

31. Kottler, J., & Marriner, M. (2006). *Changing people's lives while transforming your own*. New York: Wiley. See p. 210.

32. Kottler & Marriner (2006), p. 211.

33. Baron, J. N., & Hannan, M. T. (2002). Organizational blueprints for success in high-tech startups: Lessons from the Stanford Project on emerging companies. *California Review of Management, 44*(3), 8–36.

34. Shaw, R. B. (2014). *Leadership blindspots*. San Francisco: Jossey-Bass.

35. Pienaar, C. (2009). The role of self-deception in leadership effectiveness: A theoretical overview. *South African Journal of Psychology, 39*(1), 133–141. Burke, R. J. (2006). Why leaders fail: Exploring the dark side. *International Journal of Manpower, 27*, 91–100.

36. Kaplan, R. (2010). What to ask the person in the mirror. In *On Managing Yourself* (pp. 147–167). Boston: Harvard Business Review Press.

37. Kaplan, R., & Kaiser, R. (2009). Stop overdoing your strengths. *Harvard Business Review, 87*(2), 100–103.

38. Kerfoot, K. M. (2009). The neuropsychology of good leaders making dumb mistakes. *Nursing Economics, 27*(2), 134–135.

39. Haselton, M. G., & Nettle, D. (2006). The paranoid optimist: An integrative evolutionary model of cognitive biases. *Personality and Social Psychology Review, 10*, 47–66.

40. van Vugt, M., & Ronay, R. (2014). The evolutionary psychology of leadership: Theory, review, and roadmap. *Organizational Psychology Review, 4*(1), 74–95.

41. Hunter, S. T., Tate, B. W., Dziewceszynski, J. L., & Bedell-Avers, K. E. (2011). Leaders make mistakes: A multilevel consideration of why. *The Leadership Quarterly, 22*(2), 239–258.
42. Groopman, J. (2008). *How doctors think.* Boston: Houghton Mifflin.
43. Rothman, J. (2016, February 29). Shut up and sit down: Why the leadership industry rules. *The New Yorker,* 64–69.

CHAPTER 3

1. Przybyliski, A., & Weinstein, N. (2012). Can you connect with me now? How the presence of mobile communication technology influences face-to-face conversation quality. *Journal of Social and Personal Relationships, 30*(3), 237–246; Misra, S., Lulu, C., Genevie, J., & Yuan, M. (2016). The iPhone effect: The quality of in-person social interactions in the presence of mobile devices. *Environment and Behavior, 48*(2), 275–298.
2. Turkle, S. (2015). *Reclaiming conversation: The power of talk in a digital age.* New York: Penguin. See p. 21.
3. Levine, L. E., Waite, B. M., & Bowman, L. L. (2012). Mobile media use, multitasking, and distractibility. *International Journal of Cyber Behavior, Psychology and Learning, 2*(3), 15–29; Carrier, L., Rosen, L., Cheever, N., & Lim, A. (2015). Causes, effects, and practicalities of everyday multitasking. *Developmental Review, 35,* 64–78.
4. Krishnan, A., Kurtzberg, T. R., & Naquin, C. E. (2014, April). The curse of the smartphone: Electronic multitasking in negotiations. *Negotiation Journal, 30*(2), 191–208.
5. Uhls, Y. T., Michikyan, M., & Morris, J. (2014). Five days at outdoor education camp without screens improves preteens' skills with nonverbal emotional cues. *Computers in Human Behavior, 39,* 387–392.
6. Waber, B. N., Olguin, D. O., Kim, T., & Pentland, A. (2010). Productivity through coffee breaks: Social networks by changing break structure. *Social Science Research Network.* Retrieved from http://papers.ssrn.com/sol3/papers.cfm?abstract_id=1586375
7. Wilkie, D. (2015). Has the telecommuting bubble burst? *Society for Human Resource Management, 60*(5).
8. Dahlstrom, T. R. (2013). Telecommuting and leadership style. *Public Personnel Management, 42*(3), 438–451.
9. Pearlson, K., & Saunders, C. (2001). There's no place like home: Managing telecommuting paradoxes. *Academy of Management Executive, 15,* 117–128.
10. This example is described in Turkle (2015), pp. 270–271.
11. Snyder, K. (2012, Spring). Enhancing telework: A guide to virtual leadership. *The Public Manager,* 11–14.
12. Tobia, P. M., & Becker, M. C. (1990). Making the most of meeting time. *Training and Development Journal, 44,* 34–38.

13. Luong, A., & Rogelberg, S. G. (2005). Meetings and more meetings: The relationship between meeting load and daily well-being of employees. *Group Dynamics: Theory, Research, and Practice, 9*(1), 58–67.

14. Gouveia, A. (2013). Wasting time at work survey. *Salary.com*. Retrieved from http://www.salary.com/2013-wasting-time-at-work-survey/slide/13/

15. Jay, A. (1976). How to run a meeting. *Harvard Business Review*. Retrieved from https://hbr.org/1976/03/how-to-run-a-meeting

16. Morieux, Y. (2011, September). Smart rules: Six ways to get people to solve problems without you. *Harvard Business Review*, 78–81.

17. Luong, A., & Rogelberg, S. (2015). Meetings and more meetings: The relationship between meeting load and the daily well-being of employees. *Group Dynamics: Theory, Research, and Practice, 9*(1), 58–67; Lehmann-Willenbrock, N., Allen, J. A., & Belyeu, D. (2016). Our love/hate relationship with meetings. *Management Research Review, 39*(10), 1293–1312.

18. Allen, J. A., & Rogelberg, S. G. (2013). Manager-led group meetings: A context for promoting employee engagement. *Group and Organization Management, 38*(5), 534–569.

19. Seidler, A., et al. (2014). The role of psychosocial working conditions on burnout and its core component emotional exhaustion: A systematic review. *Journal of Occupational Medicine and Toxicology, 9*(10), 1–13.

20. Blanda, S. (2015). How to run your meetings like Apple and Google. Retrieved from http://99u.com/articles/7220/how-to-run-your-meetings-like-apple-and-google

21. Wainright, C. (2014, June 12). You're going to waste 31 hours in meeting this month. *Hubspot*. Retrieved from http://blog.hubspot.com/marketing/time-wasted-meetings-data

22. Edmondson, A. C., Higgins, M., Singer, S., & Weinder, J. (2016). Understanding psychological safety in health care and education organizations: A comparative perspective. *Research in Human Development, 13*(1), 65–83.

23. Duhigg, C. (2016). *Smarter, faster, better: The secrets of being productive in life and business*. New York: Random House.

24. Levine, L. E., Waite, B. M., & Bowman, L. L. (2012). Mobile media use, multitasking and distractibility. *International Journal of Cyber Behavior, Psychology and Learning, 2*(3), 15–29.

25. Carrier, L. M., Rosen, L. D., Cheever, N. A., & Lim, A. F. (2015). Causes, effects, and practicalities of everyday multitasking. *Developmental Review, 35*, 64–78.

26. Yu, A. (2014, March 16). Physicists, generals, and CEOs agree: Ditch the Powerpoint. *NPR*. Retrieved from http://www.npr.org/sections/alltechconsidered/2014/03/16/288796805/physicists-generals-and-ceos-agree-ditch-the-powerpoint

27. Kottler, J. A., & Englar-Carlson, M. (2015). *Learning Group Leadership* (2nd ed.). Thousand Oaks, CA: SAGE.

28. Reynolds, G. (2012). *Presentation Zen*. Berkeley, CA: New Riders.

29. Rogelberg, S. G., Allen, J. A., Shanock, L., Scott, C., & Shuffler, M. (2010). Employee satisfaction with meetings: A contemporary facet of job satisfaction. *Human Resource Management, 49*(2), 149–172.

CHAPTER 4

1. Griffith, J., Connelly, S., Thiel, C., & Johnson, G. (2015). How outstanding leaders lead with affect: An examination of charismatic, ideological, and pragmatic leaders. *The Leadership Quarterly, 26*, 502–517.
2. Mukunda, G. (2012). *Indispensable: When leaders really matter.* Boston: Harvard Business School.
3. Quinn, R. E., and collaborators. (2015). *Becoming a master manager* (6th ed.). New York: Wiley.
4. Csikszentmihalyi, M. (1990). *Flow: The psychology of optimal experience.* New York: Harper.
5. Zaccaro, S. J., Kemp, C., & Bader, P. (2004). Leader traits and attributes. In J. Antonakis, A. Cianciolo, & R. Steinberg (Eds.), *The Nature of Leadership* (pp. 101–124). Thousand Oaks, CA: SAGE.
6. Popper, M., Amit, K., Gal, R., Mishkal-Sinai, M., & Lisak, A. (2004). The capacity to lead: Major psychological differences between leaders and nonleaders. *Military Psychology, 16*(4), 245–263.
7. Judge, T. A., Piccolo, R. F., & Kosalka, T. (2009). The bright and dark side of leader traits: A review and theoretical extension of the leader trait paradigm. *Leadership Quarterly, 20*, 855–875.
8. Rothman, J. (2016, February 29). Shut up and sit down: Why the leadership industry rules. *The New Yorker*, p. 67.
9. Hogan, R., & Kaiser, R. B. (2005). What we know about leadership. *Review of General Psychology, 9*(2), 169–180.
10. Kaplan, R. E., & Kaiser, R. B. (2003). Developing versatile leadership. *MIT Sloan Management Review, 44*(4), 19–26.
11. Rubenzer, S. J., & Faschingbauer, T. R. (2004). *Personality, character, and leadership in the White House.* Washington, DC: Potomac Press.
12. Greenstein, F. I. (2009). *Presidential difference: Leadership style from FDR to Barack Obama* (3rd ed.). Princeton, NJ: Princeton University Press.
13. Cutler, A. (2014). *Leadership psychology: How the best leaders inspire their people.* London: Kogan Page.
14. Simonton, D. K. (1987). *Why presidents succeed: A political psychology of leadership.* New Haven, CT: Yale University Press; Spiegel, A. (2012, October 23). Charming, cold: Does presidential personality matter? *NPR*. Retrieved from http://www. npr .org/2012/10/23/163487916/charming-cold-does-presidential-personality-matter
15. Claxton, G., Owen, D., & Sadler-Smith, E. (2015). Hubris in leadership: A peril of unbridled intuition. *Leadership, 11*(1), 57–78.

16. Sapolsky, R. (2017). *Behavior: The biology of humans at our best and worst.* New York: Penguin; Wright, N. D., Bahrami, B., Johnson, J., Di Malta, G., Rees, G., Frith, C. D., & Dolan, R. J. (2012). Testosterone disrupts human collaboration by increasing egocentric choices. *Proceedings of the Royal Society: Biology, 279,* 1736.

17. Dowd, M. (2017, July 29). President Trump's really weak week. *The New York Times.* Retrieved from https://www.nytimes.com/2017/07/29/opinion/sunday/president-trumps-really-weak-week.html

18. Kruglanski, A. W. (2013). *The psychology of closed mindedness.* New York: Psychology Press.

19. Duhigg, C. (2016). *Smarter, faster, better: The secrets of being productive in life and business.* New York: Random House. See p. 109.

20. Keohane, N. O. (2010). *Thinking about leadership.* Princeton, NJ: Princeton University Press.

21. Deal, J. J. (2013, September 12). Welcome to the 72-hour work week. *Harvard Business Review.* Retrieved from https://hbr.org/2013/09/welcome-to-the-72-hour-work-we/

22. Nisen, M. (2013, April 4). Top CEOs work crazy hours even on normal days. *Business Insider.* Retrieved from http://www.businessinsider.com/top-ceo-schedules-2013-4

23. Tough, P. (2012). *How children succeed.* New York: Houghton Mifflin. Baer, D. (2015, April 30). The personality trait that predicts success. *Business Insider.* Retrieved from http://www.businessinsider.com/personality-conscientiousness-and-success-2015-3

24. Friedman, H. S., & Martin, L. (2011). *The longevity project.* New York: Penguin.

CHAPTER 5

1. Barling, J. (2014). *The science of leadership.* New York: Oxford University Press.

2. Mawritz, M. B., Mayer, D. M., Hoobler, J. M., Wayne, S. J., & Marinova, S. V. (2012). A trickle-down model of abusive supervision. *Personnel Psychology, 65,* 325–357; Carlson, D. S., Ferguson, M., Perrewe, P. L., & Whitten, D. (2011). The fallout from abusive supervision: An examination of subordinates and their partners. *Personnel Psychology, 64,* 937–961.

3. Hoobler, J. M., & Brass, D. J. (2006). Abusive supervision and family undermining as displaced aggression. *Journal of Applied Psychology, 91,* 1125–1133.

4. Sapolsky, R. (2017). *Behave: The biology of humans at our best and worst.* New York: Penguin.

5. Williams, R. (2015). The rise of toxic leadership and toxic workplaces. *Psychology Today.* Retrieved from https://www.psychologytoday.com/blog/wired-success/201601/the-rise-toxic-leadership-and-toxic-workplaces

6. Hogan, R., & Kaiser, R. B. (2005). What we know about leadership. *Review of General Psychology, 9*(2), 169–180.

7. Pfeffer, J. (2015). *Leadership bs: Fixing workplaces and careers one truth at a time.* New York: Harper.

8. Kellerman, B. (2004). *Bad leadership.* Boston: Harvard Business School.

9. Bentz, V. J. (1985). Research findings from personality assessment of executives. In J. H. Bernardin & D. A. Bownas (Eds.), *Personality assessment in organizations* (pp. 82–144). New York: Praeger.

10. Arbinger Institute. (2002). Leadership and self-deception. San Francisco: Berrett-Koehler.

11. Sutton, R. (2007). *The no asshole rule: Building a civilized workforce and surviving one that isn't.* New York: Warner.

12. Higgs, M. (2009). The good, the bad, and the ugly: Leadership and narcissism. *Journal of Change Management, 9*(2), 165–178.

13. Benson, M. J., & Hogan, R. S. (2008). How dark side leadership personality destroys trust and degrades organizational effectiveness. *Organizations and People, 15*(3), 10–18.

14. Raskin, R., & Terry, H. (1988). A principal components analysis of the Narcissistic Personality Inventory and further evidence of its construct validity. *Journal of Personality and Social Psychology, 54*, 890–902.

15. Ronningstom, E. F. (2005). *Identifying and understanding the narcissistic personality.* New York: Oxford University Press.

16. Chatterjee, A., & Hambrick, D. C. (2007). It's all about me: Narcissistic, confidence, and risk attitude. *Administrative Science Quarterly, 52*, 351–386.

17. Owens, B. P., Wallace, A. S., & Waldman, D. A. (2015). Leader narcissism and follower outcomes: The counterbalancing effect of leader humility. *Journal of Applied Psychology, 100*(4), 1203–1213.

18. Schlender, B., & Tetzeli, R. (2015). *Becoming Steve Jobs.* New York: Crown.

19. Kaiser, R., & Hogan, J. (2011). Personality, leader behavior, and overdoing it. *Consulting Psychology Journal: Practice and Research, 63*, 219–242.

20. Shamir, B., Dayan-Horesh, H., & Adler, D. (2005). Leading by biography: Towards a life-story approach to the study of leadership. *Leadership, 1*(1), 13–29; Liu, H. (2010). When leaders fail: A typology of failures and framing strategies. *Management Communication Quarterly, 24*(2), 232–259.

21. Goffee, R., & Jones, G. (2001). Why should anyone be led by you? *Harvard Business Review, 78*(5), 62–70.

22. Groopman, J. (2008). *How doctors think.* Boston: Houghton Mifflin.

23. Kottler, J., & Blau, D. (1989). *The imperfect therapist: Learning from failure in therapeutic practice.* San Francisco: Jossey-Bass; Kottler, J. A., & Carlson, J. (2002). *Bad therapy: Master therapists share their worst failures.* New York: Brunner/Routledge.

24. Firestein, S. (2016). *Failure: Why science is so successful.* New York: Oxford University Press.

25. Firestein (2016).

26. Mukherjee, S. (2010). *The emperor of all maladies*. New York: Scribner.
27. Gavrilov, L., & Gavrilova, N. (2002). Evolutionary theories of aging and longevity. *Scientific World Journal, 2,* 339–356; Gawande, A. (2014). *Being mortal*. New York: Henry Holt.
28. von Hippel, W., & Trivers, R. (2011). The evolution and psychology of self-deception. *Behavioral and Brain Sciences, 34,* 1–56; Bond, C. F., Jr., & DePaulo, B. M. (2006). Accuracy of deception judgments. *Personality and Social Psychology Review, 10,* 214–234.
29. Kusy, M., & Essex, L. (2007, Spring). Recovering from leadership mistakes. *Leader to Leader,* 14–19.
30. Barling (2014), p. 309.
31. Lien, T. (2017, April 12). United CEO apologizes, promises changes and reimbursements after passenger dragged off plane. *Los Angeles Times*. Retrieved from http://www.latimes.com/business/technology/la-fi-united-apology-20170412-story.html
32. Liu (2010), p. 249.
33. Kusy, M., & Essex, L. (2007, Spring). Recovering from leadership mistakes. *Leader to Leader,* 14–19.

CHAPTER 6

1. Grint, K. (2010). *Leadership: A very short introduction*. New York: Oxford University Press. See p. 12.
2. Parker, Geoffrey (2005). *Life of Nelson*. Cambridge, UK: Cambridge University Press.
3. McDonald, S. P. (2013, January). Empirically based leadership. *Military Review,* 2–10.
4. Kottler, J. A., & Balkin, R. (2017). *Relationships in counseling and everyday life*. Alexandria, VA: American Counseling Association.
5. DeCellesa, K. A., & Norton, M. I. (2016). Physical and situational inequality on airplanes predicts air rage. *PNAS, 113,* 5588; Adler, N., Epel, E. S., Castellazzo, G., & Ickovics, J. R. (2000, November). Relationship of subjective and objective social status with psychological and physiological functioning. *Health Psychology 19*(6), 586–592.
6. Goleman, D., Boyatzis, R. E., & McKee, A. (2006). Primal leadership. In *On Managing Yourself* (pp. 169–170). Boston: Harvard Business Review Press.
7. Thomas, L. (1978). *The lives of a cell*. New York: Penguin.
8. Gottman, J., & Silver, N. (2012). *What makes love last?* New York: Simon & Schuster.
9. Kottler, J. A. (1996). *The language of tears*. San Francisco: Jossey-Bass.
10. Swanson, A. (2015, June 4). The number of Fortune 500 companies led by women is at an all-time high: 5 percent. *Washington Post*. Retrieved from https://www.washingtonpost.com/news/wonk/wp/2015/06/04/the-number-of-fortune-500-companies-led-by-women-is-at-an-all-time-high-5-percent/
11. Azar, B. (2000). A new stress paradigm for women. *Monitor on Psychology, 31*(7), 42.

12. Junger, S. (2016). *Tribe: On homecoming and belonging.* New York: Twelve.

13. Denning, S. (2011). *The leader's guide to storytelling.* New York: Wiley.

14. Kottler, J. A., & Englar-Carlson, M. (2015). *Learning group leadership* (2nd ed.). Thousand Oaks, CA: SAGE.

15. Goodwin, D. (2005). *Team of rivals: The political genius of Abraham Lincoln.* New York: Simon & Schuster.

16. Gabriel, Y. (1997). Meeting God: When organizational members come face to face with the supreme leader. *Human Relations, 50,* 315–342.

17. van Vugt, M., & Ahuja, A. (2011). *Naturally selected: The evolutionary science of leadership.* New York: HarperCollins.

18. Lipman-Blumen, J. (1996). *Connective leadership.* New York: Oxford University Press.

19. Described in Lipman-Blumen (1996), pp. 214–217.

20. Lipman-Blumen (1996), p. 222.

CHAPTER 7

1. Zaccaro, S. J. (2014). Leadership memes: From ancient history and literature to twenty-first century theory and research. In D. Day (Ed.), *The Oxford Handbook of Leadership and Organizations* (pp. 13–39). New York: Oxford University Press.

2. Mumford, M. D., et al. (2017). Cognitive skills and leadership performance: The nine critical skills. *The Leadership Quarterly, 28,* 24–39.

3. Bisoux, T. (2002, September/October). The mind of a leader. *BizEd,* pp. 26–31.

4. Hogan, R., & Kaiser, R. B. (2005). What we know about leadership. *Review of General Psychology, 9*(2), 169–180.

5. Hoffman, D. D. (2012). The construction of visual reality. In J. Blom & I. Sommer (Eds.), *Hallucinations* (pp. 7–16). New York: Springer.

6. Anderson, W. T. (1990). *Reality isn't what it used to be.* New York: HarperCollins.

7. Kouzes, J. M., & Posner., B. Z. (2012). *The leadership challenge* (5th ed.). San Francisco: Jossey-Bass; Dirks, K. T., & Ferrin, D. L. (2002). Trust in leadership: Meta-analytic findings and implications for research and practice. *Journal of Applied Psychology, 87,* 611–628; Peterson, C., & Seligman, M. E. P. (2004). *Character strengths and virtues.* Washington, DC: American Psychological Association.

8. Junger, S. (2016). *Tribe: On homecoming and belonging.* New York: Twelve.

9. Junger (2016).

10. Adkins, A. (2015, January 28). Majority of U.S. employees not engaged despite gains in 2014. *Gallup Poll.* Retrieved from http://www.gallup.com/poll/181289/majority-employees-not-engaged-despite-gains-2014.aspx

11. Ariely, D. (2016). *Payoff: The hidden logic that shapes our motivations* (p. 27). New York: Simon & Schuster.

12. Ladley, D., Wilkinson, I., & Young, L. (2015). The impact of individual versus group rewards on work group performance and cooperation: A computational social science approach. *Journal of Business Review, 68*(11), 2412–2425;

Nohria, N., Groysberg, B., & Lee, L. (2008, July/August). Employee motivation: A powerful new model. *Harvard Business Review.* Retrieved from https://hbr .org/2008/07/employee-motivation-a-powerful-new-model; Williams, R. (2015, November 28). Why financial incentives don't improve performance. *Psychology Today.* Retrieved from https://www.psychologytoday.com/blog/wired-success/ 201511/why-financial-incentives-don-t-improve-performance; Pink, D. H. (2011). *Drive: The surprising truth about what motivates us.* New York: Riverhead.

13. Short, D. (2016, October 21). Happiness revisited: A household income of 75K? *Advisor Perspectives.* Retrieved from https://www.advisorperspectives.com/dshort/ commentaries/2016/10/21/happiness-revisited-a-household-income -of-75k#ixzz37eM5xPxF

14. Ariely (2016).

15. Sapolsky, R. (2017). *Behave: The biology of humans at our best and worst.* New York: Penguin.

16. Dweck, C. (2012). *Mindset: How you can fulfill your potential.* London: Constable and Robinson.

17. Day, D. V. (2012). The nature of leadership development. In D. V. Day and J. Antonakis (Eds.), *The Nature of Leadership* (2nd ed., pp. 108–140). Thousand Oaks, CA: SAGE.

18. Owen, J. (2014). *The leadership skills handbook: 50 essential skills you need to be a leader.* London: Kogan Page.

19. Martin, A. (2006). *Everyday leadership.* Greensboro, NC: Center for Creative Leadership.

20. DeChurch, L. A., & Mesmer-Magnus, J. R. (2010). The cognitive underpinnings of effective teamwork: A meta-analysis. *Journal of Applied Psychology, 95,* 32–53; Kozlowski, S. W., & Ilgen, D. R. (2006). Enhancing the effectiveness of work groups and teams. *Psychological Science in the Public Interest, 7,* 77–124.

21. Barrett, E., & Martin, P. (2014). *Extreme: Why some people thrive at the limits.* New York: Oxford University Press.

22. Safari, S., & Kottler, J. A. (2017). *Follow my footsteps: A journey of adventure, disaster, and redemption inspired by the plight of at-risk girls.* New York: CreateSpace.

23. Sitkin, S. B., and colleagues (2011). The paradox of stretch goals: Organizations in pursuit of the seemingly impossible. *Academy of Management Review, 36*(3), 544–566.

24. Kellerman, B. (2012). *The end of leadership.* New York: HarperCollins.

25. Makridakis, S., Hogarth, R. M., & Gaba, A. (2009). Forecasting and uncertainty in the economic and business world. *International Journal of Forecasting, 25,* 794–812.

26. Taleb, N. N. (2007). *The black swan: The impact of the highly improbable.* New York: Random House.

27. Bazerman, M. H., & Watkins, M. D. (2008). *Predictable surprises: The disasters you should have seen coming and how to prevent them.* Boston: Harvard Business

School; Petty, M. (2012). The dark side of leadership: Catastrophic failure. *Strategic Leadership Review*, *1*(1), 20–29.

28. Examples of their writing include: Ellis, A., & Harper, R. (1973). *A new guide to rational living*. New York: Citadel; Beck, A. (1979). *Cognitive therapy and the emotional disorders*. New York: Plume.

CHAPTER 8

1. Sparrowe, R. T. (2005). Authentic leadership and the narrative self. *Leadership Quarterly*, *16*, 419–439; Bolden, R., Hawkins, B., Gosling, J., & Taylor, S. (2013). *Exploring leadership: Individual, organizational, and societal perspectives*. New York: Oxford University Press.

2. Frieberg, K., & Frieberg, J. (1996). *Nuts! Southwest Airlines recipe for business and personal success*. New York: Broadway.

3. Gostick, A., & Elton, C. (2009). *The carrot principle*. New York: Free Press.

4. Marciano, P. (2010). *Carrots and sticks don't work*. New York: McGraw-Hill.

5. Quoted in Gardner, H. (2011). *Leading minds: An anatomy of leadership*. New York: Basic Books. See pp. 91–92.

6. Lionhardt, D., & Thompson, S. (2017, July 21). Trump lies. *The New York Times*. Retrieved from https://www.nytimes.com/interactive/2017/06/23/opinion/trumps-lies.html?mcubz=1; Stolberg, S. (2017, August 7). Many politicians lie. But Trump has elevated the art of fabrication. *The New York Times*. Retrieved from https://www.nytimes.com/2017/08/07/us/politics/lies-trump-obama-mislead.html?mcubz=1

7. Martin, A. (2006). *Everyday leadership*. Greensboro, NC: Center for Creative Leadership.

8. Eilenberg, J. J. (2017, September). Kids these days: It's time to stereotype a new generation. *Wired*, p. 26.

9. McCormick, R. (2016, June 2). Odds are we're living in a simulation, says Elon Musk. *The Verge*. Retrieved from http://www.theverge.com/2016/6/2/11837874/elon-musk-says-odds-living-in-simulation

10. Kelly, S., White, M. I., Rooksby, J., & Rouncefield, M. (2005). Storytelling and design: The problem with leadership. Paper presented at New Directions in the Learning and Skills Sector Conference, Lancaster, UK.

11. Griffith, J., Connelly, S., Thiel, C., & Johnson, G. (2015). How outstanding leaders lead with affect: An examination of charismatic, ideological, and pragmatic leaders. *Leadership Quarterly*, *26*, 502–517.

12. Monarth, H. (2014, March 11). The irresistible power of storytelling as a strategic business tool. *Harvard Business Review*. Retrieved from http://www.cobblearning.net/kellmarketing/files/2015/10/The-Irresistible-Power-of-Storytelling-as-a-Strategic-Business-Tool-29p4dfh.pdf

13. Schlender, B., & Tetzeli, R. (2015). *Becoming Steve Jobs*. New York: Crown.

14. Hirai, M., & Clum, G. A. (2006). A meta-analytic study of self-help interventions for anxiety problems. *Behavior Therapy, 37*, 99–111.

15. Appel, M. (2008). Fictional narratives cultivate just-world beliefs. *Journal of Communication, 58*, 62–83; Appel, M., & Richter, T. (2007). Persuasive effects of fictional narratives increase over time. *Media Psychology, 10*, 113–134; Burns, S. T. (2008). Utilizing fictional stories when counseling adults. *Journal of Creativity in Mental Health, 3*, 441–454; Paul, A. M. (2012, March 17). Your brain on fiction. *The New York Times.* Retrieved from http://www.nytimes.com/2012/03/18/ opinion/sunday/the-neuroscience-of-your-brain-on-fiction.html; Zipes, J. (2006). *Why fairy tales stick.* New York: Routledge.

16. Iacoboni, M. (2008). *Mirroring people: The new science of how we connect with others.* New York: Farrar, Straus & Giroux; Hess, M. (2012). Mirror neurons, the development of empathy and digital storytelling. *Religious Education, 107*(4), 401–414; Rizzolatti, G., & Craighero, L. (2004). The mirror-neuron system. *Annual Review of Neuroscience, 27*, 169–192.

17. Zak, P. J. (2015, February). Why inspiring stories make us react: The neuroscience of narrative. *Cerebrum*, pp. 1–13.

18. Quesenberry, M., & Coolsen, M. (2014). What makes a Super Bowl ad super? *Journal of Marketing Theory and Practice, 22*(4), 437–454.

19. Gottschall, J. (2012). *The storytelling animal: How stories make us human.* New York: Houghton Mifflin; Kottler, J. A. (2014). *Stories we've heard, stories we've told: Life-changing narratives in therapy and everyday life.* New York: Oxford University Press.

20. Treasure, J. (2013). How to speak so that people want to listen. *TED Talk.* Retrieved from https://www.ted.com/talks/julian_treasure_how_to_speak_so _that_ people_want_to_listen?language=en

21. Useful resources include: Anderson, C. (2016). *TED talks: The official TED guide to public speaking.* New York: Houghton Mifflin; Kottler (2014); Gallo, C. (2015). *Talk like TED: 9 public speaking secrets from the world's top minds.* New York: St. Martin's Press; Gottschall (2012); Spaulding, A. E. (2011). *The art of storytelling: Telling truths through telling stories.* Lanham, MA: Scarecrow Press; Duarte, N. (2010). *Resonate: Present visual stories that transform audiences.* New York: Wiley; Knaflic, C. N. (2016). *Storytelling with data: A data visualization guide for business professionals.* New York: Wiley; Karia, A. (2015). *TED Talks storytelling: 23 storytelling techniques from the best TED talks.* New York: CreateSpace; Zipes (2006); Alexander, B. (2011). *The new digital storytelling: Creating narratives with new media.* Santa Barbara, CA: Praeger; Gallo, C. (2016). *The storyteller's secret.* New York: St. Martin's Press.

22. Denning, S. (2011). *The leader's guide to storytelling.* New York: Wiley.

23. Campbell, J. (1949). *The hero with a thousand faces.* Princeton, NJ: Princeton University Press.

24. Johnson-Laird, P. N. (2006). *How we reason.* New York: Oxford University Press.

25. Duhigg, C. (2016). *Smarter, faster, better: The secrets of being productive in life and business*. New York: Random House. See p. 92.

CHAPTER 9

1. Schlender, B., & Tetzeli, R. (2015). *Becoming Steve Jobs*. New York: Crown. See p. 365.
2. Rothman, J. (2016, February 29). Shut up and sit down: Why the leadership industry rules. *The New Yorker*, pp. 64–69.
3. Samet, E. D. (Ed.). *Leadership: Essential writings by our greatest thinkers*. New York: W. W. Norton.
4. Kethledge, R. M., & Erwin, M. S. (2017). *Lead yourself first*. New York: Bloomsbury.
5. Keller, A., Litzelman, K., Wisk, L. E., Maddox, T., Cheng, E. R., Creswell, P. D., & Witt, W. P. (2012). Does the perception that stress affects health matter? The association with health and mortality. *Health Psychology, 31*(5), 677–684.
6. Rollins, J. (2012, February). The transformative power of trauma. *Counseling Today*, pp. 40–43.
7. Heatherton, T. F., & Nichols, P. A. (1994). Personal accounts of successful versus failed attempts at life change. *Personality and Social Psychology Bulletin, 20*, 664–675.
8. Lyubomirsky, S. (2013). *The myths of happiness*. New York: Penguin; Seery, M. D., Holman, E. A., & Silver, R. C. (2010). Whatever does not kill us: Cumulative lifetime adversity, vulnerability, and resilience. *Journal of Personality and Social Psychology, 99*, 1025–1041.
9. Joseph, S. (2011). *What doesn't kill us: The new psychology of posttraumatic growth*. New York: Basic Books; Kottler, J. A. (2014). *Change: What leads to personal transformation*. New York: Oxford University Press; Rendon, J. (2015). *Upside: The new science of posttraumatic growth*. New York: Touchstone.
10. Collins, J. (2001). *From good to great*. New York: Harper Business.
11. Hefferon, K., Grealy, M., & Mutrie, N. (2009). Post-traumatic growth and life threatening physical illness: A systematic review of the qualitative literature. *British Journal of Health Psychology, 14*, 343–378; Park, C. L., & Calhoun, L. G. (Eds.). (1998). *Posttraumatic growth: Positive changes in the aftermath of crisis*. Mahwah, NJ: Lawrence Erlbaum; Tedeschi, R. G., & McNally, R. J. (2011). Can we facilitate posttraumatic growth in combat veterans? *American Psychologist, 66*(1), 19–24; Joseph, S., Linley, P. A., & Harris, G. J. (2005). Understanding positive change following trauma and adversity: Structural clarification. *Journal of Loss and Trauma, 10*, 83–96.
12. Joseph (2011); Rendon (2015); Feldman, D. B., & Kravetz, L. D. (2014). *Supersurvivors: The surprising link between suffering and success*. New York: HarperCollins; Tedeschi, R. G., & Moore, B. A. (2015). *The post-traumatic growth workbook*. Oakland, CA: New Harbinger.

13. Finkel, J. (2015, October). Forces of character. *HoopsHype*. Retrieved from http://hoopshype.com/2015/10/13/forces-of-character-a-conversation-with-gregg-popovich/

14. McCammon, R. (2015). *Works well with others*. New York: Dutton.

15. Steinmetz, K. (2016, April 11). Why more companies are coming out of the political closet. *TIME Magazine*, pp. 19–20.

16. Kohlrieser, G. (2007, June). Six essential skills for managing conflict. *Perspectives for Managers*, *149*. Retrieved from http://www.imd.org/research/publications/upload/PFM149_LR_Kohlrieser.pdf

CHAPTER 10

1. Buchanan, A., & Kern, M. L. (2017). The benefit mindset: The psychology of contribution and everyday leadership. *International Journal of Wellbeing*, *7*(1), 1–11.

2. Dudley, D. (2012). Everyday leadership. *TED Talk*. Retrieved from https://www.ted.com/talks/drew_dudley_everyday_leadership

3. Greenbaum, R. L., Mawritz, M. B., & Piccolo, R. F. (2015). When leaders fail to "walk their talk." *Journal of Management*, *41*(3), 929–956.

4. Desmarais, C. (2016, January 28). 29 daily habits of incredibly successful executives. *Inc.* Retrieved from http://www.inc.com/christina-desmarais/29-daily-habits-of-incredibly-successful-executives.html

5. Duckworth, A. (2016). *Grit: The power of passion and perseverance*. New York: Simon & Schuster.

6. Grant, M. (2009). Will Smith interview: Will power. *Readers Digest*. Retrieved from http://www.rd.com/advice/relationships/will-smith-interview/

7. Miller, C. C. (2015, November 4). Stressed, tired, rushed: A portrait of the modern family. *The New York Times*. Retrieved from https://www.nytimes.com/2015/11/05/upshot/stressed-tired-rushed-a-portrait-of-the-modern-family.html?mcubz=1

8. Christensen, C. M. (2010). How will you measure your life? In *On Managing Yourself* (p. 5). Boston: Harvard Business School.

9. Mauss, I. B., Tamir, M., Anderson, C. L., & Savino, N. S. (2011). Can seeking happiness make people unhappy? Paradoxical effects of valuing happiness. *Emotion*, *11*(4), 807–815.

10. Nettle, D. (2005). *Happiness: The science behind your smile*. New York: Oxford University Press; Graham, C. (2009). *Happiness around the world: The paradox of happy peasants and miserable millionaires*. New York: Oxford University Press; Seligman, M. (2011). *Flourish: A visionary new understanding of happiness and well-being*. New York: Free Press; Diener, E., & Biswas-Diener, R. (2008). *Happiness: Unlocking the mysteries of psychological wealth*. Malden, MA: Blackwell; Lyubomirsky, S. (2013). *The myths of happiness: What should make you happy doesn't, what shouldn't make you happy, but does*. New York: Penguin.

11. Diener & Biswas-Diener (2008); Diener, E., Oishi, S., & Lucas, R. E. (2015). National accounts of subjective well-being. *American Psychologist, 70*(3), 234–242.

12. Terkel, S. (1972). *Working.* New York: Avon. See p. 161.

13. Noonan, M. C., & Glass, J. L. (2012, June). The hard truth about telecommuting. *Monthly Labor Review*, pp. 38–45.

14. Wilkie, D. (2015). Has the telecommuting bubble burst? *Society for Human Resource Management, 60*(5).

15. Williams, J. C., & Boushey, H. (2010). *The three faces of work-family conflict.* Berkeley, CA: Center for American Progress.

16. Orosz, G., Dombi, E., Andreassen, C. S., Griffiths, M. D., & Demetrovics, Z. (2015, December). Analyzing models of work addiction: Single factor and bi-factor models of the Bergin Work Addiction Scale. *International Journal of Mental Health Addiction, 14*(5), 1–10.

17. Austen, B. (2012, July 23). The story of Steve Jobs: An inspiration or a cautionary tale? *Wired.* Retrieved from http://www.wired.com/business/2012/07/ff _stevejobs/all/

18. Malinowska, D., & Tokarz, A. (2014). The structure of workaholism and types of workaholic. *Polish Psychological Bulletin, 45*(2), 211–222.

19. Douglas, E. J., & Morris, R. J. (2006). Workaholic, or just hard worker? *Career Development International, 11*(5), 394–417.

20. Friedman, A. S., & Martin, L. R. (2012). *The longevity project.* New York: Plume.

21. Goldbaum, G. (2012). Accelerated aging of U.S. presidents. *Journal of the American Medical Association, 307*(12), 1254.

22. Friedman & Martin (2012).

23. Sherman, G. D., Lee, J. J., Cuddy, A. J., Renshon, J., Oveis, C., Gross, J. J., & Lerner, J. S. (2012, October). Leadership is associated with lower levels of stress. *Proceedings of the National Academy of Sciences, 109*(44), 17903–17907.

24. Friedman, S. D. (2014). *Leading the life you want: Skills for integrating work and life.* Boston: Harvard Business Review.

25. Many of these examples are mentioned in Lipman-Blumen, J. (1996). *Connective leadership.* New York: Oxford University Press.

26. Arnold, S. R. (2015, March 5). Officer Deon Joseph on the heartbreaking job of policing Skid Row. *Los Angeles Magazine.* Retrieved from http://www.lamag.com/ citythinkblog/officer-deon-joseph-heartbreaking-job-policing-skid-row/#sthash .hSt8WRp4.dpuf

CHAPTER 11

1. Greenstein, F. I. (2009). *Presidential difference: Leadership style from FDR to Barack Obama* (3rd ed.). Princeton, NJ: Princeton University Press.

2. Greenstein (2009).

3. Goodwin, D. K. (2005). *Team of rivals: The political genius of Abraham Lincoln.* New York: Simon & Schuster.

4. Smith, P. (2012). *Lead with a story: A guide to crafting business narratives that captivate, convince, and inspire.* New York: American Management Association.

5. Schawbel, D. (2012, August 13). How to use storytelling as a leadership tool. *Forbes.* Retrieved from https://www.forbes.com/sites/danschawbel/2012/08/13/how-to-use-storytelling-as-a-leadership-tool/#65cfd7aa5e8e

6. Orr, J. (1990). *Talking about machines.* Ithaca, NY: Cornell University Press.

7. Booker, C. (2004). *The seven basic plots: Why we tell stories.* London: Continuum.

8. Guber, P. (2007, December). The four truths of the storyteller. *Harvard Business Review.*

9. Beersma, B., & Van Kleef, G. A. (2012). Why people gossip: An empirical analysis of social motives, antecedents, and consequences. *Journal of Applied Social Psychology, 42*(11), 2640–2670; Booker (2004); Dietz, K., & Silverman, L. (2013). *Business storytelling for dummies.* New York: Wiley; Forman, J. (2013). *Storytelling in business.* Stanford, CA: Stanford University Press; Gottschall, J. (2012). *The storytelling animal: How stories make us human.* New York: Houghton Mifflin; Hsu, J. (2008). The secrets of storytelling: Our love for telling tales reveals the workings of the mind. *Scientific American Mind, 19*(4), 46–51; Kottler, J. A. (2014). *Stories We've Heard, Stories We've Told: Life-Changing Narratives in Therapy and Everyday Life.* New York: Oxford University Press; Knaflic, C. (2013). *Storytelling with data.* New York: Wiley; Maguire, J. (1998). *The power of personal storytelling: Spinning tales to connect with others.* New York: Jeremy Tarcher; McKee, R. (2003, June). Storytelling that moves people. *Harvard Business Review,* 51–55; Mehl-Madrona, L. (2010). *Healing the mind through the power of story.* Rochester, VT: Bear and Company; Simmons, A. (2006). *The story factor: Inspiration, influence, and persuasion through the art of storytelling.* New York: Basic Books; Spaulding, A. E. (2011). *The art of storytelling: Telling truths through telling stories.* Lanham, MA: Scarecrow Press; Yashinsky, D. (2004). *Suddenly they heard footsteps: Storytelling for the twenty-first century.* Jackson: University Press of Mississippi; Zipes, J. (2006). *Why fairy tales stick.* New York: Routledge; Dolan, G., & Naidu, Y. (2013). *Hooked: How leaders connect, engage, and inspire with storytelling.* New York: Wiley; Anderson, C. (2016). *TED talks: The official TED guide to public speaking.* New York: Houghton Mifflin; Borje, D. M., Roslie, G. A., & Saylors, J. (2015). Using storytelling theatrics for leadership training. *Advances in Developing Human Resources, 17*(3), 348–362.

CHAPTER 12

1. Duhigg, C. (2016). *Smarter, faster, better: The secrets of being productive in life and business.* New York: Random House.

2. Fry, L., & Kroger, M. (2009). Towards a theory of being-centered leadership: Multiple levels of being as context for effective leadership. *Human Relations, 62*(11), 1667–1696.

3. Olshansky, J. (2011). Aging of U.S. presidents. *Journal of the American Medical Association, 306*(21), 2328–2329.

4. Szalavitz, M. (2011, December 7). Why American presidents (and some Oscar winners) live longer. *TIME Magazine*. Retrieved from http://healthland.time.com/2011/12/07/why-american-presidents-and-some-oscar-winners-live-longer/

5. Matyszczyk, C. (2016, August 4). Marissa Mayer says the secret of success is working 130 hours a week. *CNET*. Retrieved from http://www.cnet.com/news/marissa-mayer-says-the-secret-of-success-is-working-130-hours-a-week/

6. Romesha, C. (2016). *Red platoon*. New York: Penguin.

7. Woods, S. (2016, September). The last word: Phil Knight. *Esquire*, p. 98.

8. Higgs, M. (2009). The good, the bad, and the ugly: Leadership and narcissism. *Journal of Change Management, 9*(2), 165–178.

9. Campbell, W. K., Goodie, A. S., & Foster, J. D. (2004). Narcissism, confidence, and risk attitude. *Journal of Behavioral Decision Making, 17*, 297–311.

10. Grijalva, E., Harms, P. D., Newman, D. A., Gaddis, B. H., & Fraley, R. C. (2015). Narcissism and leadership: A meta-analytic review of linear and nonlinear relationships. *Personnel Psychology, 68*, 1–47.

11. Piff, P. K. (2013). Wealth and inflated self: Class, entitlement, and narcissism. *Personality and Social Psychology Bulletin, 40*(1), 34–43; Piff, P. K., & Robinson, A. R. (2017). Social class and prosocial behavior: Current evidence, caveats, and questions. *Current Opinion in Psychology, 18*, 6–10.

12. Piff, P. (2013). Does money make you mean? *TED Talk*. Retrieved from https://www.ted.com/talks/paul_piff_does_money_make_you_mean

13. Greenbaum, R. L., Mawritz, M. B., & Piccolo, R. F. (2015). When leaders fail to "walk the talk": Supervisor undermining perceptions of leader hypocrisy. *Journal of Management, 41*(3), 921–956.

14. Pfeffer, J. (2015). *Leadership bs: Fixing workplaces and careers one truth at a time*. New York: Harper. See p. 87.

15. Edmondson, A. C., Higgins, M., Singer, S., & Weinder, J. (2016). Understanding psychological safety in health care and education organizations: A comparative perspective. *Research in Human Development, 13*(1), 65–83.

16. Gardner, H. (2011). *Leading minds: An anatomy of leadership*. New York: Basic Books.

17. Gardner (2011), p. 271.

18. Schwartz, T. (2014, July 11). What happens when leaders walk their talk? *Huffington Post*. Retrieved from http://www.huffingtonpost.com/tony-schwartz/what-happens-when-leaders_b_5578212.html

19. Kolditz, T. A. (2006). *In extremis leadership: Leading as if your life depends on it*. San Francisco: Jossey-Bass.

20. McDonald, S. P. (2013, January). Empirically based leadership. *Military Review*, 2–10.

21. Kottler, J. A., & Carlson, J. (2015). *On being a master therapist: Practicing what we preach*. New York: Wiley.

22. Gladwell, M. (2008). *The outliers: The story of success*. New York: Hatchette Books.

23. Kolditz (2006).

Select Bibliography

Anderson, C. (2016). *TED talks: The official TED guide to public speaking.* New York: Houghton Mifflin.

Anderson, W. T. (1990). *Reality isn't what it used to be.* New York: HarperCollins.

Ariely, D. (2016). *Payoff: The hidden logic that shapes our motivations.* New York: Simon & Schuster.

Armitage, A. (2015). The dark side: The poetics of toxic leadership. *Advances in Developing Human Resources, 17*(3), 376–390.

Ashby, M. D., & Miles, S. A. (Eds.). (2002). *Leaders talk leadership: Top executives speak their minds.* New York: Oxford University Press.

Athanasopoulou, A., & Dopson, S. (2015). *Developing leaders by executive coaching: Practice and evidence.* New York: Oxford University Press.

Barling, J. (2014). *The science of leadership.* New York: Oxford University Press.

Barrett, E., & Martin, P. (2014). *Extreme: Why some people thrive at the limits.* New York: Oxford University Press.

Bazerman, M. H., & Watkins, M. D. (2008). *Predictable surprises: The disasters you should have seen coming and how to prevent them.* Boston: Harvard Business School.

Benson, M. J., & Hogan, R. S. (2008). How dark side leadership personality destroys trust and degrades organizational effectiveness. *Organizations and People, 15*(3), 10–18.

Bisoux, T. (2002, September/October). The mind of a leader. *BizEd*, pp. 26–31.

Blaker, N. M., Rompa, I., Dessing, I. H., Vriend, A. F., Herschberg, C., & van Vugt, M. (2013). The height leadership advantage in men and women: Testing some evolutionary psychology predictions. *Group Processes and Intergroup Relations, 16*, 17–27.

Bolden, R., Hawkins, B., Gosling, J., & Taylor, S. (2013). *Exploring leadership: Individual, organizational, and societal perspectives.* New York: Oxford University Press.

Britt, T. W., & Jex, S. M. (2015). *Thriving under stress: Harnessing demands in the workplace.* New York: Oxford University Press.

Buunk, A. P., & Dijkstra, P. (2012). The evolution of business and management. In S. C. Roberts (Ed.), *Applied Evolutionary Psychology* (pp. 36–51). New York: Oxford University Press.

Campbell, W. K., Goodie, A. S., & Foster, J. D. (2004). Narcissism, confidence, and risk attitude. *Journal of Behavioral Decision Making, 17*, 297–311.

Carlson, D. S., Ferguson, M., Perrewe, P. L, & Whitten, D. (2011). The fallout from abusive supervision: An examination of subordinates and their partners. *Personnel Psychology, 64*, 937–961.

Carrier, L. M., Rosen, L. D., Cheever, N. A., & Lim, A. F. (2015). Causes, effects, and practicalities of everyday multitasking. *Developmental Review, 35*, 64–78.

Catmull, E. (2014). *Creativity, Inc: Overcoming the unseen forces that stand in the way of true inspiration*. New York: Random House.

Chatterjee, A., & Hambrick, D. C. (2007). It's all about me: Narcissistic, confidence, and risk attitude. *Administrative Science Quarterly, 52*, 351–386.

Claxton, G., Owen, D., & Sadler-Smith, E. (2015). Hubris in leadership: A peril of unbridled intuition. *Leadership, 11*(1), 57–78.

Clifton, J. (2014). Small stories, positioning, and the discursive construction of leader identity in business meetings. *Leadership, 10*(1), 99–117.

Collins, J. (2001). *From good to great*. New York: HarperCollins.

Conniff, R. (2005). *The ape in the corner office*. New York: Three Rivers Press.

Craughwell, T. J. (2008). *Failures of presidents*. Beverly, MA: Fair Winds Press.

Cuddy, A. (2016). *Presence: Bringing your boldest self to your biggest challenges*. New York: Little, Brown.

Cutler, A. (2014). *Leadership psychology: How the best leaders inspire their people*. London: Kogan Page.

Daskal, L. (2015, June 22). 10 seconds to take your leadership from good to great. *Inc.* Retrieved from http://www.inc.com/lolly-daskal/10-seconds-to-take-your-leadership-from-good-to-great.html

Day, D. V. (Ed.). (2014). *The Oxford handbook of leadership and organizations*. New York: Oxford University Press.

Day, D. V., & Antonakis, J. (Eds.). (2012). *The nature of leadership* (2nd ed.). Thousand Oaks, CA: SAGE.

De Meuse, K. P., Dai, G., & Wu, J. (2011). Leadership skills across organizational levels: A close examination. *The Psychologist-Manager Journal, 14*, 120–139.

DeChurch, L. A., & Mesmer-Magnus, J. R. (2010). The cognitive underpinnings of effective teamwork: A meta-analysis. *Journal of Applied Psychology, 95*, 32–53.

Denning, S. (2011). *The leader's guide to storytelling*. New York: Wiley.

Dolan, G., & Naidu, Y. (2013). *Hooked: How leaders connect, engage, and inspire with storytelling*. New York: Wiley.

Dotlich, D. L, & Cairo, P. C. (2003). *Why CEOs fail*. New York: Wiley.

Dweck, C. (2012). *Mindset: How you can fulfill your potential*. London: Constable and Robinson.

Duhigg, C. (2016). *Smarter, faster, better: The secrets of being productive in life and business*. New York: Random House.

Finkelstein, S. (2016). *Superbosses: How exceptional leaders master the flow of talent*. New York: Portfolio.

Finkelstein, S., Hambrick, D. C., & Cannella, A. A. (2009). *Strategic leadership: Theory and research on executives, top management teams, and boards*. New York: Oxford University Press.

Finzel, H. (2007). *The top ten mistakes leaders make*. Colorado Springs: David C. Cook.

Firestein, S. (2016). *Failure: Why science is so successful*. New York: Oxford University Press.

Friedman, S. D. (2006). Learning to lead in all domains of life. *American Behavioral Scientist, 49*(9), 1270–1297.

Friedman, S. D. (2014). *Leading the life you want: Skills for integrating work and life*. Boston: Harvard Business Review.

Fryer, M. (2012). *Ethics and organizational leadership: Developing a normative model*. New York: Oxford University Press.

Gabel, S. (2013). Psychotherapy and relationship-based change: It's about leadership. *Journal of Psychotherapy Integration, 23*(4), 345–358.

Gabriel, Y. (2015). The caring leader: What followers expect of their leaders and why. *Leadership, 11*(3), 316–334.

Gallagher, D., & Costal, J. (2012). *The self-aware leader*. Alexandria, VA: American Society for Training and Development.

Gallo, C. (2016). *The storyteller's secret*. New York: St. Martin's Press.

Gardner, H. (2011). *Leading minds: An anatomy of leadership*. New York: Basic Books.

Gawande, A. (2014). *Being mortal*. New York: Henry Holt.

Geimer, J. L., Leach, D., DeSimone, J. A., Rogelberg, S. G., & Warr, P. B. (2015). Meetings at work: Perceived effectiveness and recommended improvements. *Journal of Business Research, 68*, 2015–2026.

Ginia, A., & Green, R. M. (2013). *10 virtues of outstanding leaders*. New York: Wiley.

Goffee, R., & Jones, G. (2001). Why should anyone be led by you? *Harvard Business Review, 78*(5), 62–70.

Goleman, D., Boyatzis, R., & McKee, A. (2002). *Primal leadership*. Boston: Harvard Business School Press.

Goodall, A. H., Kahn, L. M., & Oswald, A. J. (2011). Why do leaders matter? A study of expert knowledge in a superstar setting. *Journal of Economic Behavior and Organization, 77*, 265–284.

Gostick, A., & Elton, C. (2009). *The carrot principle*. New York: Free Press.

Greenbaum, R. L., Mawritz, M. B., & Piccolo, R. F. (2015). When leaders fail to "walk the talk": Supervisor undermining perceptions of leader hypocrisy. *Journal of Management, 41*(3), 921–956.

Greenstein, F. I. (2009). *Presidential difference: Leadership style from FDR to Barack Obama* (3rd ed.). Princeton, NJ: Princeton University Press.

Griffith, J., Connelly, S., Thiel, C., & Johnson, G. (2015). How outstanding leaders lead with affect: An examination of charismatic, ideological, and pragmatic leaders. *The Leadership Quarterly, 26*, 502–517.

Grijalva, E., Harms, P. D., Newman, D. A., Gaddis, B. H., & Fraley, R. C. (2015). Narcissism and leadership: A meta-analytic review of linear and nonlinear relationships. *Personnel Psychology, 68*, 1–47.

Grint, K. (2010). *Leadership: A very short introduction.* New York: Oxford University Press.

Grint, K. (2013). *The arts of leadership.* New York: Oxford University Press.

Groopman, J. (2008). *How doctors think.* Boston: Houghton Mifflin.

Guiso, L., Sapienza, P., & Zingales, L. (2015). The value of corporate culture. *Journal of Financial Economics, 117*, 60–76.

Gwynne, P. (2012). Group intelligence, teamwork, and productivity. *Research Technology Management, 55*(2), 7.

Higgs, M. (2009). The good, the bad, and the ugly: Leadership and narcissism. *Journal of Change Management, 9*(2), 165–178.

Hogan, J., Hogan, R., & Kaiser, R. B. (2010). Management derailment. *American Psychological Association Handbook of Industrial and Psychology, 3*, 555–575.

Hogan, R. (2006). *Personality and the fate of organizations.* Hillsdale, NJ: Lawrence Erlbaum.

Hogan, R., & Kaiser, R. B. (2005). What we know about leadership. *Review of General Psychology, 9*(2), 169–180.

Howell, J. P. (2013). *Snapshots of great leadership.* New York: Routledge.

Hunter, S. T., Tate, B. W., Dziewceszynski, J. L., & Bedell-Avers, K. E. (2011). Leaders make mistakes: A multilevel consideration of why. *The Leadership Quarterly, 22*(2), 239–258.

Jha, S., & Jha, S. (2015). Leader as anti-hero: Decoding nuances of dysfunctional leadership. *Journal of Management and Public Policy, 6*(2), 21–28.

Johansen, B. (2012). *Leaders make the future.* San Francisco: Berrett-Koehler.

Johnson, W. B., Skinner, C. J., & Kaslow, N. J. (2014). Relational mentoring in clinical supervision: The transformational supervisor. *Journal of Clinical Psychology: In Session, 70*(1), 1073–1081.

Joseph, S. (2011). *What doesn't kill us: The new psychology of posttraumatic growth.* New York: Basic Books.

Judge, T. A., Piccolo, R. F., & Kosalka, T. (2009). The bright and dark side of leader traits: A review and theoretical extension of the leader trait paradigm. *The Leadership Quarterly, 20*, 855–875.

Junger, S. (2016). *Tribe: On homecoming and belonging.* New York: Twelve.

Kaiser, R., LeBreton, J. M., & Hogan, J. (2015). The dark side of personality and extreme leader behavior. *Applied Psychology, 64*(1), 55–92.

Kellerman, B. (2004). *Bad leadership.* Boston: Harvard Business School Press.

Kellerman, B. (2012). *The end of leadership.* New York: HarperCollins.

Kelly, S., White, M. I., Rooksby, J., & Rouncefield, M. (2005). Storytelling and design: The problem of leadership. In *Rethinking leadership: New directions in the learning and skills sector.* Lancaster, UK: Lancaster University Press.

Keohane, N. O. (2010). *Thinking about leadership*. Princeton, NJ: Princeton University Press.

Kerfoot, K. M. (2009). The neuropsychology of good leaders making dumb mistakes. *Nursing Economics, 27*(2), 134–135.

Kethledge, R. M., & Erwin, M. S. (2017). *Lead yourself first*. New York: Bloomsbury.

Kets de Vries, M. F., & Miller, D. (2009). Narcissism and leadership: An object relations perspective. *Human Relations, 38*, 583–601.

Kilburg, R. R. (2012). *Virtuous leaders*. Washington, DC: American Psychological Association.

Kolditz, T. A. (2006). *In extremis leadership: Leading as if your life depends on it*. San Francisco: Jossey-Bass.

Kottler, J. A. (2014). *Change: What leads to personal transformation*. New York: Oxford University Press.

Kottler, J. A. (2017). *On being a therapist*. New York: Oxford University Press.

Kottler, J. A., & Balkin, R. (2017). *Relationships in counseling and the counselor's life*. Alexandria, VA: American Counseling Association.

Kottler, J. A., & Blau, D. (1989). *The imperfect therapist: Learning from failure in therapeutic practice*. San Francisco: Jossey-Bass.

Kottler, J. A., & Carlson, J. (2002). *Bad therapy: Master therapists share their worst failures*. New York: Brunner/Routledge.

Kottler, J. A., & Carlson, J. (2009). *Creative breakthroughs in therapy: Tales of transformation and astonishment*. New York: Wiley.

Kottler, J. A., & Carlson, J. (2015). *On being a master therapist: Practicing what we preach*. New York: Wiley.

Kottler, J. A., & Englar-Carlson, M. (2015). *Learning group leadership* (2nd ed.). Thousand Oaks, CA: SAGE.

Kouzes, J. M., & Posner., B. Z. (2012). *The leadership challenge* (5th ed.). San Francisco: Jossey-Bass.

Kozlowski, S. W., & Ilgen, D. R. (2006). Enhancing the effectiveness of work groups and teams. *Psychological Science in the Public Interest, 7*, 77–124.

Kusy, M., & Essex, L. (2007, Spring). Recovering from leadership mistakes. *Leader to Leader*, pp. 14–19.

Levine, L. E., Waite, B. M., & Bowman, L. L. (2012). Mobile media use, multitasking and distractibility. *International Journal of Cyber Behavior, Psychology and Learning, 2*(3), 15–29.

Lilienfeld, S. O., & Watts, A. L. (2015, September 4). The narcissist in chief. *The New York Times*. Retrieved from https://www.nytimes.com/2015/09/06/opinion/the-narcissist-in-chief.html?mcubz=1

Lipman-Blumen, J. (1996). *Connective leadership*. New York: Oxford University Press.

Lipman-Blumen, J. (2005). *The allure of toxic leaders*. New York: Oxford University Press.

Lipman-Blumen, J. (2005). Toxic leadership: When grand illusions masquerade as noble visions. *Leader to Leader, 36*, 29–36.

Liu, H. (2010). When leaders fail: A typology of failures and framing strategies. *Management Communication Quarterly, 24*(2), 232–259.

Logan, D., & King, J. (2011). *Tribal leadership*. New York: Harper Business.

Luong, A., & Rogelberg, S. G. (2005). Meetings and more meetings: The relationship between meeting load and daily well-being of employees. *Group Dynamics: Theory, Research, and Practice, 9*(1), 58–67.

Maestripieri, D. (2012). *Games primates play*. New York: Basic Books.

Malinowska, D., & Tokarz, A. (2014). The structure of workaholism and types of workaholic. *Polish Psychological Bulletin, 45*(2), 211–222.

Marciano, P. (2010). *Carrots and sticks don't work*. New York: McGraw-Hill.

Martin, A. (2006). *Everyday leadership*. Greensboro, NC: Center for Creative Leadership.

Martinko, J. J., Harvey, P., Sikora, D., & Douglas, S. C. (2011). Perceptions of abusive supervision: The role of subordinates' attribution styles. *Leadership Quarterly, 22,* 751–764.

Mawritz, M. B., Mayer, D. M., Hoobler, J. M., Wayne, S. J., & Marinova, S. V. (2012). A trickle-down model of abusive supervision. *Personnel Psychology, 65,* 325–357.

McDonald, S. P. (2013, January). Empirically based leadership. *Military Review,* pp. 2–10.

Moccia, S. (2012). Leadership that gets results: Lessons from Don Quixote. *Review of Business, 33*(11), 5–18.

Mukunda, G. (2012). *Indispensable: When leaders really matter*. Boston: Harvard Business School.

Mukherjee, S. (2010). *The emperor of all maladies*. New York: Scribner.

Mulhern, D. G. (2007). *Everyday leadership*. Ann Arbor: University of Michigan Press.

Nicholson, N. (2012). The evolution of business and management. In S. C. Roberts (Ed.), *Applied Evolutionary Psychology* (pp. 16–35). New York: Oxford University Press.

Nye, J. S. (2008). *The powers to lead*. New York: Oxford University Press.

Orosz, G., Dombi, E., Andreassen, C. S., Griffiths, M. D., & Demetrovics, Z. (2015, December). Analyzing models of work addiction: Single factor and bi-factor models of the Bergin Work Addiction Scale. *International Journal of Mental Health Addiction,* 1–10.

Owen, D., & Davidson, J. (2009). Hubris syndrome: An acquired personality disorder? A study of U.S. presidents and UK prime ministers over the last 100 years. *Brain, 132,* 1396–1406.

Owen, J. (2014). *The leadership skills handbook: 50 essential skills you need to be a leader*. London: Kogan Page.

Owens, B. P., Wallace, A. S., & Waldman, D. A. (2015). Leader narcissism and follower outcomes: The counterbalancing effect of leader humility. *Journal of Applied Psychology, 100*(4), 1203–1213.

Padilla, A. (2013). *Leadership: Leaders, followers, environments*. New York: Wiley.

Palinkas, L. A., et al. (2004). Cross-cultural differences in psychological adaptation to isolated and confined environments. *Aviation, Space, and Environmental Medicine, 75*, 973–980.

Pater, R. (2014, June). Overcoming the top 10 leadership mistakes. *Professional Safety*, pp. 30–32.

Petty, M. (2012). The dark side of leadership: Catastrophic failure. *Strategic Leadership Review, 1*(1), 20–29.

Pfeffer, J. (2015). *Leadership bs: Fixing workplaces and careers one truth at a time.* New York: HarperCollins.

Pienaar, C. (2009). The role of self-deception in leadership effectiveness: A theoretical overview. *South African Journal of Psychology, 39*(1), 133–141.

Pink, D. H. (2011). *Drive: The surprising truth about what motivates us.* New York: Riverhead.

Popper, M. (2004). Leadership as relationship. *Journal for the Theory of Social Behavior, 34*, 119–125.

Popper, M., Amit, K., Gal, R., Mishkal-Sinai, M., & Lisak, A. (2004). The capacity to lead: Major psychological differences between leaders and nonleaders. *Military Psychology, 16*(4), 245–263.

Quinn, R. E., and collaborators. (2015). *Becoming a master manager* (6th ed.). New York: Wiley.

Raskin, R., & Terry, H. (1988). A principal components analysis of the Narcissistic Personality Inventory and further evidence of its construct validity. *Journal of Personality and Social Psychology, 54*, 890–902.

Reed, G. E. (2010, November–December). Toxic leadership: Part deux. *Military Review*, pp. 58–64.

Rego, A., Cunha, M. P., & Clegg, S. (2012). *The virtues of leadership.* New York: Oxford University Press.

Rendon, J. (2015). *Upside: The new science of posttraumatic growth.* New York: Touchstone.

Rogelberg, S. G., Allen, J. A., Shanock, L., Scott, C., & Shuffler, M. (2010). Employee satisfaction with meetings: A contemporary facet of job satisfaction. *Human Resource Management, 49*(2), 149–172.

Ronningstom, E. F. (2005). *Identifying and understanding the narcissistic personality.* New York: Oxford University Press.

Rothman, J. (2016, February 29). Shut up and sit down: Why the leadership industry rules. *The New Yorker*, pp. 64–69.

Rubenzer, S. J., & Faschingbauer, T. R. (2004). *Personality, character, and leadership in the White House.* Washington, DC: Potomac Press.

Rucki, A. (2014, October 7). Average smartphone user checks device 221 times a day, according to research. *London Evening Standard*. Retrieved from http://www.standard.co.uk/news/techandgadgets/average-smartphone-user-checks-device-221-times-a-day-according-to-research-9780810.html

Samet, E. D. (Ed.) (2015). *Leadership: Essential writings by our greatest thinkers.* New York: W. W. Norton.

Sapolsky, R. M. (2017) *Behave: The biology of humans at our best and worst.* New York: Penguin.

Schilling, J., & Schyns, B. (2014). The causes and consequences of bad leadership. *Zeitschrift fur Psychologie, 222*(4), 187–189.

Schlender, B., & Tetzeli, R. (2015). *Becoming Steve Jobs.* New York: Crown.

Schyns, B., & Hansbrough, T. (2008). Why the brewery ran out of beer: The attribution of mistakes in a leadership context. *Social Psychology, 39*(3), 197–203.

Schyns, B., & Hansbrough, T. (Eds.). (2010). *When leadership goes wrong.* Charlotte, NC: Information Age Publishing.

Shamir, B., Dayan-Horesh, H., & Adler, D. (2005). Leading by biography: Towards a life-story approach to the study of leadership. *Leadership, 1*(1), 13–29.

Shaw, R. B. (2014). *Leadership blindspots.* San Francisco: Jossey-Bass.

Simonton, D. K. (1987). *Why presidents succeed: A political psychology of leadership.* New Haven, CT: Yale University Press.

Sinek, S. (2014). *Leaders eat last.* New York: Penguin.

Smith, P. (2012). *Lead with a story: A guide to crafting business narratives that captivate, convince, and inspire.* New York: American Management Association.

Spiegel, A. (2012, October 23). Charming, cold: Does presidential personality matter? *NPR.* Retrieved from http://www.npr.org/2012/10/23/163487916/charming-cold-does-presidential-personality-matter

Sutton, R. (2007). *The no asshole rule: Building a civilized workforce and surviving one that isn't.* New York: Warner.

Taleb, N. (2007). *The black swan: The impact of the highly improbable.* New York: Random House.

Taylor, S. S. (2012). *Leadership craft, leadership art.* New York: Palgrave.

Tepper, B. J., Moss, S. E., & Duffy, M. K. (2011). Predictors of abusive supervision: Supervisor perceptions of deep-level dissimilarity, relationship conflict, and subordinate performance. *Academy of Management Journal, 54*(2), 279–294.

Turkle, S. (2015). *Reclaiming conversation: The power of talk in a digital age.* New York: Penguin.

van Vugt, M., & Ahuja, A. (2011). *Naturally selected: The evolutionary science of leadership.* New York: HarperCollins.

van Vugt, M., & Ronay, R. (2014). The evolutionary psychology of leadership: Theory, review, and roadmap. *Organizational Psychology Review, 4*(1), 74–95.

Von Hippel, W., & Trivers, R. (2011). The evolution and psychology of self-deception. *Behavioral and Brain Sciences, 34*, 1–16.

Watts, A. L., Lilienfeld, S. O, Smith, S. F., Miller, J. D., Campbell, W. K., Waldman, I. D., Rubenzer, S. J., & Faschingbauer, T. J. (2013). The double-edged sword of grandiose narcissism: Implications for successful and unsuccessful leadership among U.S. presidents. *Psychological Science, 24*(12), 2379–2389.

Weisinger, H., & Pawliw-Fry, J. P. (2016). *Performing under pressure: The science of doing your best when it matters*. New York: Crown.

Williams, J. C., & Boushey, H. (2010). *The three faces of work-family conflict*. Berkeley, CA: Center for American Progress.

Zaccaro, S. J. (2014). Leadership memes: From ancient history and literature to twenty-first century theory and research. In D. V. Day (Ed.), *The Oxford Handbook of Leadership and Organizations* (pp. 13–39). New York: Oxford University Press.

Zaccaro, S. J., Kemp, C., & Bader, P. (2004). Leader traits and attributes. In J. Antonakis, A. Cianciolo, & R. Steinberg (Eds.), *The Nature of Leadership* (pp. 101–124). Thousand Oaks, CA: SAGE.

About the Author

Jeffrey A. Kottler, PhD, is one of the most prolific authors in the fields of psychology and education, having written over 90 books about a wide range of subjects related to human experience, learning, advocacy, and professional practice. His textbooks and resources have been translated into over two dozen languages and are used by universities around the world. He has also written a number of books about psychological change, including *The Language of Tears; Divine Madness: Ten Stories of Creative Struggle; On Being a Therapist; Changing People's Lives While Transforming Your Own; Private Moments, Secret Selves: Enriching Our Time Alone*; and the best-selling true crime book *The Last Victim* (also produced as a feature film).

Jeffrey has served as a Fulbright Scholar and Senior Lecturer in Peru (1980) and Iceland (2000), and worked as a Visiting Professor in New Zealand, Australia, Hong Kong, Singapore, and Nepal. Jeffrey is Clinical Professor of Psychiatry at Baylor College of Medicine in Houston and Professor Emeritus of Counseling at California State University, Fullerton. He is also founder of Empower Nepali Girls, an organization that provides educational scholarships for at-risk children in Nepal.

Name Index

Subject Index

Storytelling (*cont.*)
matching story to context and
situation, 243–45
and neurobiological response to
stories, 180–83
reasons for, 241–42
revealing truth in, 249–50
by Franklin Delano Roosevelt, 234–35
and seminal stories of
organizations, 169–73
in speeches and presentations, 238–52
and stories as reality, 176–78
surprising audience in, 250–51
and use of stories, 184–89
wonder and meaning-making
in, 251–52
Strategic tasks, 43, 49
Strategies, letting go of, 147–49
Strengths, identifying, 48–49, 91–92
Stress
chronic, 192–93
for leaders, 192–95, 228–29, 254
and self-talk, 164–66
and turnover, 37
Stretch goals, 156–57
Suicide, 129
Summaries, meeting, 80–81
Superstar model, 37, 68
Support
in group settings, 122
from leader, 124
social, 203
for telecommuters, 56–57
Surprises, in stories, 250–51
Sustainable work practices,
modeling, 263

Tactical errors, 105
Teach for America, 139
Team building, 153–55
Teams, relationships in, 131

Teamwork stories, 172
Technology, 25–26, 191–92
Telecommuting, 56–58, 224–26
Telephones, 191
Temper, bad, 109
Tempered narcissist, 107
"Tend and befriend" behavioral
pattern, 128
10,000-hour rule, 98, 266
"10 Seconds to Take Your Leadership
From Good to Great," ix
Tesla, 178
Testosterone, 95
Therapists, 15, 265–67
This isn't about me mantra, 207
Thoughts, effects on feelings of, 163
360-degree assessment, 47
3M, 240
Tie-eem mantra, 206–7
Time management, 98–100
Time spent at work, 98–100, 216,
217, 266
Titanic, 46
TOMS Shoes, 35–36, 187
Total leadership, 7–8
Toxic leaders, 104, 105, 111
Toxic organizational cultures, 33
Toyota, 31
Toy Story (film), 180
Trafalgar, Battle of, 121
Tragedies, 246
Training, ix, 42, 62, 240
Transactional purpose, 169
Transcendent purpose, 169
Transference, 135
Transparency meetings, 65
Tribal cultures, 34–38
Troubadour school of leadership
studies, 9
Trust, 8, 14–15, 132, 267
Truth, 132, 175–76, 249–50